Praise for
Street Smarts from Proverbs

"STREET SMARTS FROM PROVERBS is a gold mine of truth—the strongest, most challenging, most convicting book on unlocking wisdom you will ever read. I have witnessed firsthand the incredible impact of Mitch's journey from money to wisdom, and he has inspired and motivated multitudes who will never be the same...and neither will you after you take the opportunity to absorb this fantastic book!"

—Gregg Bettis, assistant to the president of
Kanakuk Ministries

"Mitch aligns leadership with biblical principles in a way that people in all vocational walks and callings can relate to. STREET SMARTS FROM PROVERBS brings alive valuable tenets of Scripture within a context of practical principles of discipleship, active followership, and mentorship."

—Dr. Sherilyn R. Emberton, president, Huntington University

"I highly recommend Mitch Kruse's book STREET SMARTS FROM PROVERBS. Mitch's ability to connect life experiences with Scripture is amazing. I know you will enjoy it."

—Ed Placencia, Purple Heart, Bronze Star, and
Silver Star recipient as squad leader sergeant E5,
173rd Airborne Brigade

"If ever there was a need for a succinct and applicable description of Proverbs, it's today! Mitch has a gift of breaking down truth in a way that makes God's word and wisdom come alive. What a welcome challenge in a world of confusion and anxiety!"

—Bay Forrest, codirector of FOCUS Ministries,
evangelist, and former center for the Phoenix Suns

"Life is a journey of discovery, and Mitch takes the reader on a memorable trip revealing practical principles for handling conflict in every aspect of life, personal and professional. Every business owner, corporate executive, and team member should read this book. The timeless truths Mitch shares about wisdom can be applied at all levels of every organization."

—Chuck Surack, founder and president,
Sweetwater Sound, Inc.

"Biblical wisdom is rare in our world today. In STREET SMARTS FROM PROVERBS, Mitch not only takes us to God's Word to point us to the truth—he gives us present-day examples of people whose lives demonstrate that wisdom and embody that truth."

—Kraig Cabe, Indiana state director, Fellowship
of Christian Athletes

"The main reason I love and recommend this book is because I know Mitch has personally experienced what he has now written for you and me. He changed his scorecard and now challenges us to do the same. The focus on Proverbs, principles, and practical steps will guide all of us to wisdom and new insights. Let's throw away that old scorecard and start afresh."

—Larry Lance, CEO, Youth for Christ of
Northern Indiana

"Mitch does an outstanding job helping the reader to understand how biblical wisdom applies to real life today. The complexities of today's world can distract Christians easily, but Mitch shares with us how God's Word is our guide for real Christian living. Great read!"

—Marlin A. Stutzman, former U.S. congressman

"What strikes me most about Mitch Kruse is his humility, his wisdom, and his passion for God's power of restoration. Mitch deeply understands our innate need for Godly wisdom—by virtue of his numerous years of corporate success, overwhelming adversity, and faithful ministry. Mitch has graduated from the 'School of Hard Knocks' with vibrant colors and proven 'Street Smarts.' Devour the wisdom contained within these pages, for they are inspired from the very source of Wisdom that formed the Earth. As these timeless treasures of Proverbs helped sustain me after all five of my family members drowned in a 2003 Kansas flash flood, these stories and treasures will help sustain, restore, and propel you toward your divine destiny."

—Robert Rogers, founder of Mighty in the Land Ministry and author of *Into the Deep, 7 Steps to No Regrets,* and *Rise Above*

"Wisdom is such an important character trait, yet so elusive to so many of us. Building on his life experiences, Mitch Kruse takes us on a journey through the wisdom of the book of Proverbs, applying eternal truths to real life situations today. I highly recommend you read this transformational book."

—John S. Pistole, president of Anderson University, former administrator of the TSA, and former deputy director of the FBI

"One of the wisest and most knowledgeable men I have been blessed to know, Dr. Mitch Kruse is just as captivating with his writing as with his speaking. STREET SMARTS FROM PROVERBS uses Dr. Kruse's classic technique of taking biblical truths and delivers them in a fashion that not only helps you better understand Solomon's timeless book of wisdom, but also gives step-by-step practical ways to live them out in every aspect of your life."

—Alyssa A. Welch, Indiana University School of Medicine

"In STREET SMARTS FROM PROVERBS, Mitch presents wisdom as the principal thing. Weaving in the stories of everyday believers, Mitch shows why we so desperately need God's wisdom in every area of our lives. This is a must read!"

—Shirley Woods, founder of the
Euell A. Wilson Center

"No matter where you are in the 'journey of life,' we all have faced some form of adversity or trials. I believe that STREET SMARTS FROM PROVERBS will connect with and impact you in some way, shape, or form as Mitch Kruse reveals his experiences by applying Solomon's 'twelve words.' Wisdom is a priceless gift that should never be taken for granted. I hope this book impacts the reader's heart."

—Jody Martinez, women's basketball assistant
coach, University of Illinois

"The stories and experiences that Mitch shares while applying Solomon's twelve words to the wise in his new book, STREET SMARTS FROM PROVERBS, will transform your heart forever. They are timeless, practical experiences for your life, family, and relationships. They are the keys to unlocking wisdom."

—Gordon D. Bell, author of *Discover Your Next Best Step: 10 Proven Principles of Servant Leadership Wisdom*

"Mitch Kruse brilliantly articulates why all the street smarts in the world is meaningless if you are a godless fool. He clearly and concisely addresses why a gullible fool is still formable, but the godless fool has no hope unless he/she repents. This is a must-read book for anyone challenged with a personal conflict between choosing a life that is self-centered, or a life that is God-centered."

—Duane DuCharme, Indiana state representative for Celebrate
Recovery, business entrepreneur

"If you are looking for a shrewd understanding of how to survive or succeed in any situation—whether it is a seemingly impossible situation or just everyday life, you need this book! Mitch Kruse has condensed the book of Proverbs to twelve keys that will unlock your world in a way you never dreamed!"

—Dr. Garth W. Coonce, founder and CEO of
TCT Network, author of *A Voice, A Vision, A Victory*

"While educating struggling teens, we utilize the book of Proverbs daily for wisdom and discipline. We are more than excited to utilize STREET SMARTS FROM PROVERBS as one of our key resources in transforming lives through teaching what is right, just, and fair."

—Robert R. Staley, founder and CEO,
Crossing School of Business & Entrepreneurship

"From a professional athletic perspective STREET SMARTS FROM PROVERBS outlines amazing concepts (four chambers) that athletes overlook when striving for success. You must have the drive (will) to succeed, know what you are doing (intellect), and have a peaceful mind (spiritually and emotionally) to be successful. Dr. Mitch Kruse and D. J. Williams artfully show readers how to use these concepts to strike a meaningful balance in their lives as they work hard to achieve success."

—Joe Odhiambo, fourteen-time Guinness World Record holder
and world-renowned basketball freestyler

"It's been said that if you know the man, you'll love the book. Mitch Kruse is a dear friend, *and* I loved his book. He's one of the few people in my circle of friends where every time he speaks, I take mental notes. Mitch is that wise. He has a bit of Solomon in his step, which is one of the reasons this book will resonate with readers: Mitch had it all, lost most of it, and then asked God to recalibrate. STREET SMARTS FROM PROVERBS is multifaceted: it will not only give you a different lens to look at life, but it's also a must-have for the workplace, marriage, and family."

—David Dean, comedian

"As a professional athlete, coach, and business owner, I have experienced firsthand, the priceless value of wisdom from Proverbs taught by Mitch Kruse. In STREET SMARTS FROM PROVERBS, Mitch conveys these timeless truths in a relevant manner that will help anyone wisely manage conflict both on and off the court. These amazing principles have shown to be extremely applicable and successful, in the spiritual development of our elite level athletes at Empowered Sports Club. I look forward to sharing this book with all my professional teammates, business associates, players, and coaches."

—William Robbins, professional athlete, coach,
and CEO of Empowered Sports Club, Volleyball
Academy, and Pro Beach Juniors

"You'll find yourself ready to persevere through any challenge after reading what Mitch Kruse reveals from the words of wisdom found in the book of Proverbs and how those words apply to real-life events. This is a fantastic spiritual guide for not only those that are just now beginning their walk with Christ but also for the lifelong followers that desire to learn even more."

—Cam Tribolet, author of *Dead 13 Times*

"Mitch has an encyclopedic knowledge of the Bible and an incredible ability to relate its messages to the everyday lives of people today. His insight is amazing, and this book will inspire you to draw closer to God."

—Curtis Smith, director of community
outreach, Parkview Health

"Having just re-read Proverbs, I am very excited to see Mitch's real-life applications in his new book. My spiritual journey began with humbling myself before the Lord. Jesus meets us at the bottom—only then can He begin to use us for His Kingdom purpose. I am sure STREET SMARTS FROM PROVERBS will provide a map to continue this life-long journey."

—George Del Canto, founder and
co-owner of Kingdom Racing

STREET SMARTS
from
PROVERBS

STREET SMARTS

from

PROVERBS

How to Navigate through
Conflict to Community

MITCH KRUSE

with D. J. Williams

NEW YORK NASHVILLE

FaithWords
Hachette Book Group
1290 Avenue of the Americas, New York, NY 10104
faithwords.com
twitter.com/faithwords

First Edition: June 2017

FaithWords is a division of Hachette Book Group, Inc. The FaithWords name and logo are trademarks of Hachette Book Group, Inc.

The publisher is not responsible for websites (or their content) that are not owned by the publisher.

The Hachette Speakers Bureau provides a wide range of authors for speaking events. To find out more, go to www.HachetteSpeakersBureau.com or call (866) 376-6591.

LCCN: 2017936231

ISBNs: 978-1-4789-2139-4 (hardcover), 978-1-4789-2138-7 (ebook), 978-1-4789-7560-1 (audio download)

Printed in the United States of America
LSC-C
10 9 8 7 6 5 4 3 2 1

I dedicate this book to Uncle Derald for asking me the question, "Have you ever thought about changing the scorecard of your life from money to wisdom?" Thank you for directing me to God's street smarts in Proverbs.

Contents

Introduction

Conflict is all around us and often is found raging inside us. As history's wisest king, Solomon assembled the book of Proverbs to help emerging leaders, including you and me, to make wise choices. In this book, we will examine the purpose of Proverbs, centering around twelve words—each fleshed out with four practical principles—that will transform your life when you apply them to the external or internal conflict you face. These twelve words are:

1. Righteousness
2. Equity
3. Justice
4. Wise Behavior
5. Understanding
6. Wise Communication
7. Prudence
8. Discretion
9. Wise Counsel
10. Discipline
11. Knowledge
12. Learning

Is there a pressing issue that is causing you stress? Would you like to gain wisdom for that and for all the other conflicts in your life? If so, this book is for you! The God-inspired lessons that Solomon recorded in Proverbs will lead you on a journey of discovery, providing you with a road map to walk in the wisdom of Jesus. I invite you to study and apply each principle discussed in the upcoming chapters so that you can learn to live your life by God's wise principles. As you do, His wisdom will permeate your life, helping you navigate through every conflict toward healthy, full, vibrant community.

A CHALLENGE TO SEEK WISDOM

As a practical consideration, I'd like to invite you to dive into the book of Proverbs as you study these twelve words. To that end, I encourage you to read one chapter of Proverbs every day, reading the chapter that corresponds to the day of the month: Chapter 1 on January 1, Chapter 2 on January 2, etc.

If you choose to follow this simple reading plan, in just a month's time you will have read through all of Solomon's ancient wisdom. To deepen your study and allow God's incredibly practical and useful wisdom to soak into your heart and life, follow this reading plan for two months. Or three. In fact, take on this challenge for the full twelve months and you will read through all thirty-one chapters of Proverbs twelve times during the next year!

As you read each day, pray for wisdom from God and make it your goal to apply one verse to your tasks. This has been my practice for decades because I needed wisdom for the conflict around me. I owned the world's largest collector car auction

company, and every one of my thousands of business transactions each year was surrounded by conflict. The most difficult conflict I encountered was the morning the criminal
investigation division of the IRS raided my business, thinking
we were money launderers. The courts and I can assure you
we were not. That night, I knelt beside my bed and surrendered everything I had been holding back from God, including my business. The following day, my attorney uncle Derald
asked a question that would forever change my life: "Mitchell,
have you ever thought about changing the scorecard of your
life from money to wisdom?" Over the next several months,
my uncle's words seared into my mind, and I began to pursue
street smarts from Proverbs. I read many business books over
that time, but none transformed my company and my family
like the book of Proverbs.

I sincerely believe God used Proverbs to restore my life,
leading to the sale of my business to eBay in order to earn my
master's and doctorate degrees in religious studies, allowing
me to become a carrier of Christ's message of grace and wisdom. He has made me a better father to my four daughters and
husband to my wife, Susan. Because I have read a chapter a day
in Proverbs, praying for wisdom and applying a verse to my
daily calendar for many years, I'm confident that as you begin
to apply this book of practical wisdom to your daily decisions,
God will bless you with a wisdom that comes straight from
Him. You will find yourself blessed with a broader perspective on your daily conflicts, and you will begin to move wisely
through that conflict toward deepened community.

Mitch Kruse
June 2017

STREET SMARTS
from
PROVERBS

Part One

CONFLICT, THE FOOL, AND WISDOM

Part One of this book is designed to outline key terms and ideas behind the book of Proverbs.

The first chapter introduces the idea of the cycle of conflict and discusses the wisdom of moving in a positive direction when conflict comes. Chapters Two and Three are longer than the following chapters in Part Two for a reason. A study of the book of Proverbs is delightful, practical, and useful in and of itself. However, in order to fully appreciate the detail of this immensely wisdom-packed and commonsense book, a deep dive into the terms that form the backbone of Proverbs is warranted: first, examining the definition of the word *fool*; second, taking a look at the multiple nuances of the word *wisdom*.

I've written Part One to prepare you for the more detailed, in-depth study in Part Two. May you be blessed as you spend this time growing in the grace, knowledge, and wisdom of Jesus Christ.

Chapter 1

The Cycle of Conflict

My family and I arrived at a picturesque spot on Lake Tahoe for a short vacation in Reno, Nevada. Susan and I were newlyweds. We had a choice between spending the afternoon on a big boat with the rest of the Kruse entourage or venturing out together on a smaller boat to spend time alone on the lake. Of course, as starry-eyed newlyweds, we decided to take the small boat out for the two of us.

The lady who managed the boats stood on the dock watching us climb into the boat. "Have you ever operated one of these before?" she asked.

"Uh-huh," I replied.

I was nonchalant; however, the situation was about to get complicated. As I rotated the throttle on the small outboard engine, simultaneously steering the motor mounted to the rear of the boat, we lurched toward an obstacle . . . the big boat. For a split second, I feared that if I jammed the gear of the motor from forward to reverse, the transmission would fall out, and I would become the unhappy owner of the boat.

Before I could react to avoid it, my small boat hit the bigger boat! If only I could repeat what the lady on the dock said. She was not happy, to say the least. And I can still picture Susan's face—the girl who had practically grown up on a lake during her summer vacations, herself a master yachtsman—wondering what in the world I was doing.

While we survived the first bump against the bigger boat's hull, neither vessel was safe just yet. I hit the gas again—even harder this time in an attempt to provide more thrust to turn away from the big boat, thereby avoiding another collision. This time, the boat leaped out of the water like a missile that had been fired with full force, right into the big boat. I pictured us fully airborne with no chance to change our direction. I was suddenly jerked back to reality when I again felt the second jolt reverberating through my body. If the first bump was a love tap, this hit was a knockout. *Ka-bam!*

The sound waves echoed from the big boat, and I heard from above, "Blaahh! What's that?" I looked up to see my father peering over the edge of the boat with all seventy-four of its other passengers, including my mom and brother. "It's Mitchell!" Dad yelled in his auctioneer's voice, helpfully identifying me by name to his fellow endangered travelers.

This large audience, people who once presumably considered themselves safe aboard the big boat, now stared down at me, convinced that I was going to sink them all.

If I didn't sink it first, I feared the weight of all the gawkers transferring to one side would cause the bigger boat to tip over on us. Finding reverse, I got us out of there before I could hear my dad announce any further incriminating information about me—or before the dock lady could hook me with the long arm of that metal lifesaver apparatus.

As Susan and I finally made our way safely from the dock, I considered myself a fugitive from maritime law, hiding in plain sight on the glass waters of Lake Tahoe.

I tell this story because it illustrates a critical point as we approach the study of Proverbs: Sometimes we get *caught* in the cycle of conflict, and sometimes we get *taught*.

CAUGHT OR TAUGHT?

In the boating episode I was caught in the cycle of conflict because I lied to the dock lady in my eagerness to prove my machismo to my new wife. That pride caused me to make a foolish choice. And I paid the price. My family has joked about that episode many times over the years.

Left to ourselves, we approach conflict as a zero-sum game. In other words, we imagine that for every winner there must be a loser. I made a foolish choice to believe I could maneuver the small boat out onto the lake even though I had never learned how to properly operate the craft. The result was a face-off with Goliath, and I lost.

As you assess the most pressing conflict situations in your life, are you *caught* or *taught* in the cycle of conflict?

To help you uncover if you're caught or taught, let's examine the key words in the above question. *Caught* implies that you are trapped in your conflict—stuck fast, seemingly without a way out. *Taught* means that you learn from your conflict so that you don't repeat the same cycle of behavior. *Conflict* is literally defined as two objects attempting to occupy the same space at the same time (from the Latin words *con*, meaning "together," and *fligere*, meaning "to strike").

In the case of my boating story, conflict occurred when I attempted to make two boats occupy the same space. The same thing happens when two toddlers want the same toy, two teenagers make simultaneous plans to use the same car, or two coworkers apply for the same promotion.

When conflict arises, are we caught or taught? Do we believe conflict is a zero-sum game? Does someone always have to lose when another wins?

In his attempt to lead the people of Israel three thousand years ago, King Solomon faced the inevitable conflict that came with his position. So when God offered Solomon the opportunity to ask for anything from Him, Solomon requested wisdom (see 1 Kings 3:5–15).

As we examine Solomon's first recorded decision, you'll see that *conflict* is either *positive* or *negative*. Positive conflict includes two good objects attempting to occupy the same space at the same time: Consider such scenarios as lifting weights, studying, or working. When we engage in this kind of conflict, we maneuver to improve our lives and move the ball forward. Negative conflict arises when at least one negative potential outcome is a possibility. Such conflicts, including arguments, fistfights, or cheating, are typically a result of sinful behavior.

In Solomon's first case as king, two prostitutes arrived with their conflict story. They lived together, and each had given birth to a child. During the night, one of these two women tragically smothered her child in her sleep. When she discovered her nightmare, she exchanged her dead baby for her sleeping roommate's live infant. The dawn of the new day brought negative conflict—two women who wanted the same live baby, but only one was his true mother.

King Solomon was presented with a choice, to act wisely or foolishly. After confirming his understanding of the conflict, Solomon called for a sword so that he could cut the live baby in half, giving half to one woman and half to the other.

The woman who was the baby's real mother was filled with compassion for her child. Consequently, she begged the king to give the infant to the other woman. The guilty party, blinded by her own grief, cruelly challenged King Solomon to carry out the execution so that neither would have the child. Solomon's wise choice to give the baby to his real mother revealed one woman's truth and another woman's pretense.

The wisdom of Solomon's first judicial decision rang throughout the kingdom. As word of his legendary wisdom spread, the world flocked to Solomon for his discernment in their conflicts.

A CYCLE OF CONFLICT ASSESSMENT

Are you living in positive or negative conflict? Maybe you have relied on your street smarts alone and doing so has led to foolish choices. Maybe your success and knowledge in the marketplace have convinced others you are bulletproof, yet inwardly you are still questioning what life is really all about. Maybe the conflict in your life has created a deafening noise that stops you from hearing the wise words found in Proverbs.

In this life we will live in two worlds of conflict—positive and negative. What would happen if you chose to trade your knowledge, your street smarts, and your selfish desires for the freedom found in the wisdom offered by the Creator? Today is the day for you to make a life-altering decision to follow God's wisdom instead of your own.

Let's try an experiment as we start down this road to finding wisdom and building community. Take a pen and paper, and try to define the conflict that is at the forefront of your life. Is it positive or negative? Write down what two objects in your life are figuratively attempting to occupy the same space at the same time.

Conflict presents us with a *choice* for our next move that will be either *wise* or *foolish* (see 1 Kings 3:23–25). King Solomon's decision to cut the baby in two revealed the motives of the hearts of the two women. His wisdom in forcing the women to respond to his judgment resolved the issue.

As you write, examine whether the conflict in your life has been caused or perpetuated by a foolish choice. If so, complete the following sentence, and write it on the same note card: "I fostered this conflict when I made the choice to _____."

If your choices regarding the conflict have been wise, then thank God for the wisdom that He is teaching you through the struggle, and write your note of thanks on the same card.

Choice brings *change* that reveals either *truth* or *pretense* (see 1 Kings 3:26). We see this in the story of the two women and the baby. Solomon's wise judgment caused each woman to react honestly, and Solomon was able to reveal the truth.

When our hearts are hard, we make foolish choices that we then have to pretend to defend. My eldest daughter, Megan, was sixteen when this practice began to surface frequently in her life, much like it used to do in mine. After making a foolish choice, she would persistently pretend in order to defend her slippery position. One day during a conflict, I finally said—as only a dad could—"Megan, please stop! I know what you're doing, because you get this tendency to stick to your guns, no matter how misdirected your actions or decisions are. Whatever you do, please don't continue to pretend in order to defend your foolish choice."

Megan found, as I had many times before, that foolish choices lead us to be caught instead of taught; however, wise choices lead to God's truth and provide us with wisdom that we can use when we face future conflict. As we continue to make wise choices, we learn wisdom that will transform our pattern of making foolish choices into a pattern of making wise ones.

As you look at the conflict scenario that you just wrote down, reflect on whether your choices regarding your conflict brought change that revealed truth or pretense in your life. Write down the result by completing the following sentence: "My choices regarding the conflict have revealed _____ in the relationship with my counterpart." Notice the correlation between wise choices and revealed truth as opposed to foolish choices and revealed pretense.

Change affects *community* that is either *deepened* or *lessened* (see 1 Kings 3:27–28). Solomon gave the baby to the mother who had pleaded for his life because her self-sacrificial heart revealed that she was his true mother. Solomon's wise choice revealed the truth about the conflict, and when the country heard of it, all Israel held the king in awe for his God-given wisdom. Solomon's wise choices led to deepened community on a national scale.

Too often we respond to conflict with foolish choices that lead to pretense, and as we continue to hide the truth, our relationships suffer. The end result is weakened community. Anyone who has had a disagreement with a family member can tell you how community can be affected by an unwise response to conflict. But when we choose to follow God's way, our wise choice becomes the hinge point that moves us through conflict toward deepened community.

In order to envision your eventual success in your choices, picture the wisest person you know and consider these questions:

1. Is that person rich?
2. Does he or she have a PhD?
3. Is he or she characterized by good relationships?

I'm guessing that your answer to my first two questions was no. However, your answer to my third question was most likely yes. The lesson to be learned here is that, more often than not, the people we find to be the wisest are not the richest people nor the most well educated; rather, the wisest people in our lives are those who are characterized by sound, quality relationships. Choosing wisely on a consistent basis builds this kind of reputation.

Follow these steps the next time you assess your behavior in a conflict situation:

- *Pray*, asking God to reveal to you the potential for deepened or lessened community within the relationship in conflict.
- *Define* the conflict. What two objects are attempting to occupy the same space at the same time?
- *Examine* whether your choices in this instance are wise or foolish.
- *Reflect* on the change that your choices bring to the relationship. Do they reveal truth or pretense?
- *Determine* the effect your choice has on your community. Is it deepened or lessened?

Conflict presents a choice. Choice brings change. Change affects community. Community creates conflict.

Solomon left us a legacy of nearly one thousand wise sayings for dealing with conflict. The book of Proverbs holds amazing treasures of commonsense wisdom that has been true for thousands of years. Since three millennia have not changed humanity's fallen nature, God's wisdom is still relevant to us today. Through the study of Proverbs, we can be *taught* to move from the foolish side of conflict's equation to the wise one, from the *crisis* of "either–or" in *conflict* to the "both–and" of *community* discovered through wisdom. Through the study of these proverbs, we will attain both God's righteousness and street smarts—an acute awareness of how to apply God's heart's desire to all our circumstances.

The beautiful irony is that God's solution to two objects attempting to occupy the same space at the same time is represented in the cross, where two objects actually do occupy the same space at the same time: the vertical (God's righteousness) intersecting with the horizontal (street smarts). This sweet spot is where we transition from being "caught crosswise" to being "taught cross-wise" from God's cross of wisdom.

Proverbs personifies Wisdom as a woman who cries out to the foolish young man, pleading with him to follow the way of the wise and to steer clear of foolish choices. This personification of wisdom was first embodied in Christ, who was present at creation. Jesus, as God's Wisdom, existed before the Lord gave any order to creation's story. Christ's action in creation parallels the role of the incarnate and resurrected Christ as described by the apostle Paul: "The Son is the image of the invisible God, the firstborn over all creation. For in him all things were created: things in heaven and on earth, visible and invisible, whether thrones or powers or rulers or authorities; all things have been created through him and for him" (Col. 1:15–16).

Jesus was fully God and fully human, the perfect embodiment of the vertical (God's wisdom) intersecting with the horizontal (street smarts). He was and is "the power of God and the wisdom of God" (1 Cor. 1:24). Jesus lived a perfect life, died at the center of a cross, and was raised again on the third day so that we could live in the center of His wisdom.

Chapter 2

A Fool Defined
From Gullible to Godless

A few years ago, Susan and I took our four daughters to vacation in Southern California, where we visited the Walk of Fame outside of Grauman's Chinese Theater. This is where many famous actors and actresses have over the years placed their handprints in wet cement that eventually hardened and cured, leaving impressions that people can see and feel. While studying the handprints of one of my favorite actors, I looked around to see what the girls were doing. I noticed that all six of us had assumed the same posture: We had bent down and placed our hands in the concrete impressions of our favorite celebrity icons.

What an image for us to consider as we move forward in our study of Proverbs. Like those handprints in the sidewalk, our hearts start out like wet cement, and each one carries an impression: either our own handprints or the handprints of God. The former is foolish; the latter is wise. Which set of handprints do you have embedded on your heart? As we experience conflict, the end result of whether we are caught or taught begins in our hearts. That's where God begins his work, because He is an inside-out kind of God. Solomon communicated it this way: "Before his downfall a man's heart is proud, but humility comes before honor" (Prov. 18:12).

Left unchecked, our hardness of heart will travel through five progressive stages of playing the fool. Through this chapter, we'll examine each of those stages in turn. As we do, examine your own heart to find out whose handprints are there.

The cement in the earlier example provides us with a good analogy to illustrate this teaching. When it's initially poured, cement is wet and formable, but soon afterward it begins a hardening process that culminates as cured concrete. No longer malleable, the hardened chunk of concrete requires heavy equipment to roll in and pick it up before it can be moved. So also the gullible fool is still formable, but the godless fool has no hope unless they repent.

Have you ever played the fool? As people who pursue God's will and way, we want to avoid playing the role of the fool at all costs. A study of Proverbs gives us five stages of foolishness from the Hebrew language. Each of these stages represents a progression of increasing hardness of heart, from gullible to godless. Let's examine them:

1. THE SIMPLE FOOL

The *simple fool* is gullible. "A simple man believes anything, but a prudent man gives thought to his steps" (Prov. 14:15).

However, the consequences that the simple fool experiences still leave hope for him to develop a heart of wisdom. If we are ever going to play the fool, we want to do it only in this first stage so that we learn from and respond to consequences from our foolishness with repentance and wisdom. Many parents advise their children to fail in the small things now so that they learn wisdom when facing big things later in life. That same principle applies here.

An excellent example of a simple fool responding to consequences with repentance and wisdom is King Solomon's father, King David. The books of 1 and 2 Samuel record the life of David, one of the Old Testament's central figures. The writer paints David's journey as traveling straight up a path of blessings until 2 Samuel 11, which records his encounter and adultery with Bathsheba—an extramarital affair that left her pregnant with David's child and led to the contrived murder of her husband, Uriah the Hittite, one of David's own "mighty men" (2 Sam. 23:39). David's foolish choice represented a turning point in his life that caused him to spiral downward as he foolishly covered his terrible decision with pretense that turned deadly.

When confronted through a parable by the prophet Nathan, David pronounced a fourfold curse on the parable's antagonist, only to learn that he was in fact the man Nathan's story addressed. Consequently, the writer of 2 Samuel suggests that David actually pronounced the fourfold set of curses on himself. These four curses brought on the relational damage and lessened community that we see evidenced in David's later relationships. First, David and Bathsheba lost their son (see 2 Sam. 12:22–23). Second, David's son Amnon raped his half sister Tamar (see 2 Sam. 13:1–22). Third, David's son Absalom (the full brother of Tamar) killed his half brother Amnon to avenge the rape of his sister (see 2 Sam. 13:23–38). Fourth, Absalom, who had fled Jerusalem, returning only to experience a strained relationship with his father, was killed when he rebelled against David and tried to usurp his throne (see 2 Sam. 14–19).

David's foolishness with Bathsheba might have seemed simple, but it carried devastating consequences. When rebuked, King David responded with repentance and wisdom. He immediately acknowledged that he had sinned against God (see 2 Sam. 12:13). He quickly humbled his heart in contrition toward the Lord. David recognized something that each of us must understand regarding our hearts: We detach our hearts from the heart of God before we commit gullible behavior, and in doing so, we bring significant, sometimes devastating, consequences on ourselves.

I can be gullible, especially when someone says something I want to hear. On the same California vacation that I mentioned earlier, my family visited Universal Studios. While we were standing in line to purchase our tickets, I noticed a sign advertising a special pass that allows its holder to move to the front of every line in the park. Reading it, my mind raced at the possibilities: We could be first in line on every single ride! We could maximize our time in the park, not having to spend the majority of our day waiting in long lines under the hot sun with a thousand other sweaty riders.

When we finally arrived at the admission ticket booth, I blurted out the pressing question at the front of my mind, "How much is it?"

"Two hundred and fifty dollars," the attendant behind the glass answered.

"Sign me up!" I said emphatically. I had waited in line long enough already—I wouldn't have to wait in another line all day!

I paid for the tickets, received the golden passes, and walked through the turnstile. Within seconds we were inside. I was dying to see how much time the gold passes would save us, so I literally skipped ahead of the girls to read the board that recorded the updated waiting time for each ride. As I squinted to keep the glaring sun out of my eyes, I scanned the entire list of times. When I saw what it said, I imagine I must have been making the face of Dirty Harry before he goes off on someone.

The longest line was . . . five minutes. I might have felt better if it had been measured in seconds. We didn't need those gold passes—the ones that cost me an extra two hundred fifty. I had thought that I was going to be significant, privileged, that my money would buy me special status within the park. I had been so proud of my decision, right up until I saw the sign that read, "Five minutes."

At the end of the day, any of us can be gullible. I certainly am, especially to words of comfort and encouragement that give me a sense of security and significance. These kinds of words compel me to pay double the price of amusement park admission in order to become number one. Although the natural consequences of my naïve behavior usually get my attention and lead me to repentance and wisdom, I realize that chasing after my desires apart from God always precedes my gullibility.

This kind of gullibility is present in teenagers, big-time. When I taught a relationship class to a group of teenage guys and girls, I found that the girls' gullibility showed their vulnerability to the attentions of a guy. At one point in the class, I picked the most outgoing young woman, whom I had coached and knew well, to read aloud a phrase from Genesis that explained the reality behind the phenomenon in which the ugly guy catches the pretty girl. She cringed as she read the following: "To the woman he said, 'I will greatly increase your pains in childbearing; with pain you will give birth to children. Your desire will be for your husband, and he will rule over you'" (Gen. 3:16).

I asked the girls in the class, "Do you want to nurture that pursuit of a guy now, or in college, or do you want to wait to open yourself up to a relationship with a guy until you're settled in your career?" I did not have a particular answer in mind; I merely wanted them to consider their vulnerability as well as how, when, where, why, and by whom they wanted to be pursued.

I continued, "After the fall, God instilled in Eve a desire for her husband. Likewise, there are desires resident in each of us that make us vulnerable. So we have to ask ourselves, 'How am I going to actually satisfy these desires?' The answer is in Christ. Only He can truly satisfy all of our desires, and He empowers us to pay that forward to our marriage partners."

To illustrate the frail nature of someone other than God satisfying our desires, I motioned for a handsome guy to stand up who I knew was in a relationship with a girl in the group. I put my arm around him and asked the young women in the class,

"Girls, are you going to continue to put all that pressure on someone like poor old Carson here? Are you going to expect someone like Carson alone to satisfy all your desires?" Poor Carson. His face was beet red.

Being gullible to the satisfaction of your desires apart from the wisdom of God is the first heart-hardening stage of playing the fool. Naïve, self-centered gullibility leads to significant consequences that can provide us with a gracious opportunity to respond with wisdom and repentance.

Give thought to your steps. Are you gullible to any foolish behavior? Open your calendar and examine your appointments for the week. Ask God to show you any naïve movements in your life. If He does, confess the pride underneath the foolishness, humbly surrender it to Him, and ask His Spirit to lead you to wisdom.

2. THE STUPID FOOL

The second stage in the progression toward a hardened heart is the *stupid fool*. He *repeats* his gullible behavior. "As a dog returns to its vomit, so a fool repeats his folly" (Prov. 26:11). This fool repeats anger, strained family relationships, wickedness, deceit, slander, and shame. Unlike the gullible fool who learns from his mistakes and doesn't make them again, this fool's repetitive folly carries deeper consequences.

- *The stupid fool is dangerous with money.* Solomon revealed: "Of what use is money in the hand of a fool, since he has no desire to get wisdom?" (Prov. 17:16). He went on to say that the stupid fool chases fantasies with his eyes, choosing to make the same mistake over and over again until he exhausts all of his resources—his time, talent, and treasure. He is complacent in his foolish behavior.

- *The stupid fool trusts in his own heart.* Proverbs records: "He who trusts in himself is a fool, but he who walks in wisdom is kept safe" (Prov. 28:26). This self-trust and self-reliance pushes aside wise counsel and leads to talking rather than listening. "A fool finds no pleasure in understanding but delights in airing his own opinions" (Prov. 18:2). The stupid, self-reliant fool is hotheaded and reckless and hates knowledge and correction.

About nine months after our trip to California, we headed to Orlando, where we visited another Universal Studios theme park. I promised myself I was not going to make the same mistake I made in California, but the lines in the park on this day looked really long. I estimated the size of the crowd and decided I had to do it. It was simply a wise decision; after all, when would we be back here? We had only one day, and I didn't want to stand in lines all day. I knew the drill. I got up to the ticket booth where I quickly said, "Sign me up for six editions of the 'A Pass.'" I paid double the standard admission rate to move my family to the front of every line, every time.

This time around, my perspective on the lines and the crowd had changed. Since I had invested the extra money, I wanted to feel shrewd. Therefore, I wanted the lines to be *huge.* And guess what? The lines were long. I was feeling really smart when we were escorted to the front of the mean, green roller coaster called the Incredible Hulk. What a ride that was! After we finished, I shouted to the girls, "C'mon, let's go again!" We sprinted around the ride to its entrance, boldly holding up our A Passes to the park staffer guarding the gate, when we heard the most sobering words an A Pass holder can hear: "I'm sorry, sir, but your passes are good for only one use per ride."

I started to search for hidden cameras and a television personality to deliver a punch line, but there were none. I had repeated my gullible behavior. Now I was the stupid fool.

The same heart issue—pride—that had led me to my original gullible behavior caused me to repeat that same mistake, propelling me to become a stage-two fool. I had hardened my heart at the next level—stupidity. Just as I had in California, in Florida I shelled out the extra cash for passes without finding out sufficient information to make a wise decision. Instead, I chased my fantasy to be privileged, to be special, to be number one. In my process of decision-making, I had been quick to speak and slow to listen. That's my personality. I typically want to quickly understand the parameters of the game so I can get to the front of the line every time. My entire life can be summed up in this statement: "Just tell me what it takes to get the A Pass, and I will earn it."

Many of us who call ourselves Christians have summed up our beliefs in the same fashion. We have perpetuated a religion and called it Christianity. We believe that our rewards with God are predicated on our own righteous efforts, something that we will discuss later in the Righteousness section. We believe that people who are moral are "in" with God and people who are immoral are "out."

Jesus taught from a different perspective: He taught about *relationship.* Jesus' teaching on the kingdom turned the world's values upside down. He told his followers that people who are humble are in and people who are proud are out. Therefore, our very finest efforts to do good and be like Jesus will fail miserably if we do them with the expectation that with these good deeds we will manipulate God. Such actions, rather than crediting some celestial account, are actually indicative of stupidity. Consequently, the term *stupid fool* does not apply only to the loose, licentious types who appear out of control; it's for the hard-hearted religious group as well.

When we come to understand our own unworthiness, we make a paradigm shift from our foolish religious perspective to Jesus' relational view. As the heart of Christ softens our own hearts, His humility that leads to true wisdom radically transforms our lives. Our tasks and relationships begin to demonstrate a much clearer kingdom purpose as they become acts of worship. When we begin to live life this way, we are finally able to see every encounter as an opportunity to discover and reveal the wisdom of Christ.

Are you ready to make all of this very real, very quickly for yourself? Ask your spouse or a close friend the following questions regarding your areas of potential stupidity:

- Is folly evident in my life?
- Do I repeat the same gullible behavior—like a dog returning to its vomit?
- By biblical standards, are my time, talent, and treasures managed foolishly or wisely?

- Am I chasing fantasies?
- In my relationships, do I talk more than I listen?

If the answer to any of these questions is yes, examine your life to see whether you are trusting in yourself rather than in God.

3. THE STUBBORN FOOL

The third stage is the *stubborn fool*. The word translated as "stubborn" here is the same Hebrew word, *ewil*, which is translated in English as "evil."

- *The stubborn fool is right in his own eyes.* "The way of a fool seems right to him, but a wise man listens to advice" (Prov. 12:15). He is so sure of himself that he declines sound advice in nearly every aspect of life. Financial, spiritual, relational—whatever the topic, the stubborn fool accepts advice from no one.
- *The stubborn fool despises wisdom and discipline.* In his heart, he hardens his thoughts, choices, and feelings against connecting his life with God. He closes the door on learning how to be transformed by God.
- *The stubborn fool is full of folly.* He repeats his stupidity at such a level that he is utterly filled with foolishness, which often displays itself in outbursts of anger. His pattern of folly in terms of anger management can be remembered as "quick to pick and stick." He is *quick* to

quarrel. Solomon taught: "A fool shows his annoyance at once, but a prudent man overlooks an insult" (Prov. 12:16). He will *pick* a fight: "Stone is heavy and sand a burden, but provocation by a fool is heavier than both" (Prov. 27:3). He will *stick* the blame on someone else, rather than reconcile: "Fools mock at making amends for sin, but goodwill is found among the upright" (Prov. 14:9). This unwise, self-centered pattern of communication destroys relationships.

Israel's first king, King Saul, hardened his heart to the point that he became a stubborn fool. Saul even built a monument to himself. When we become stubborn fools, we build monuments in our own honor. That is, convinced of our own rightness, we will fight to protect our position (our "monument to self"), regardless of how foolish it is. As a recovering perfectionist, I am no exception to this rule. When my heart is hardened, I become set in my ways during conflict. I build an immovable monument in honor of my perfectionist perspective, and I defend it at all costs. I become quick to pick and stick.

One example of my stubborn fool behavior occurred several years ago when I was an assistant coach to my daughter's high school basketball team. I saw coaching as an opportunity to pass on the knowledge gained from my high school basketball career at DeKalb, where I had been blessed to be a member of what was arguably one of the best basketball teams in our school's history. This was back when basketball was one class in Indiana—just as God intended it to be. Each of our home games was sold out: Forty-two hundred fans filled every seat in our enormous gym. We played our final game in front of the largest crowd to ever watch a basketball game at the Allen County War Memorial Coliseum—10,250 screaming fans, breaking the record set by an NBA game played decades earlier when the Zollner Pistons (forerunner of the Detroit Pistons) hailed from Fort Wayne. In Indiana, it just doesn't get any better than that. I hoped I could inspire the girls to have the same love for the game that I developed during that time.

During our team's practice, I was becoming increasingly frustrated as the girls repeated the same mistakes. My high school basketball environment had been intense. Coach yelled a great deal. Occasionally, he yelled like the angry dock lady from Lake Tahoe. Now that I was a coach, I realized this intense, angry, stubborn perfectionist from twenty years prior was once again awakened inside me. I watched as the girls passed the ball at least five times without hitting the undefended, wide-open player underneath the basket. My hard heart intended to build a basketball monument to itself, causing my blood pressure to rise to a level that nearly made it erupt into a geyser.

As a girl made an errant pass off the foot of an unsuspecting teammate, the ball bounced over to the baseline where I was standing. I picked up the basketball and heaved it eighty-four feet, where it crashed off the backboard at the other end of the court. I screamed, "I'm so tired of our team making the same mistake over and over again! At least five times, we missed the wide-open post player in the lane!"

Just then, I heard snickering from the other two assistant coaches who flanked my left and right. I looked at the head coach, who had previously had some vocal outbursts of his own. He looked at me and said, "I told the girls that in order to improve their ball movement, they were required to make five passes before they could shoot."

Just like the stubborn fool, I jumped to a conclusion based on my own experience and what *I* wanted to see happen and hadn't paid attention to the coach's instruction. There I was, playing the same perfectionistic, stubborn fool that I had back in my days as a high school player. I had only one response to this news: I burst out laughing, and the girls' demeanor quickly changed from horror to humor. Right then and there, I gave them a memory they would remind me of for a lifetime.

I wish that was the only time I had been quick to pick and stick; unfortunately, it was not. I have been stubbornly right in my own eyes with my wife, my children, and my business associates. I have despised wisdom and discipline from friends, acquaintances, and fellow believers. I have even been stubborn in church. Much of this behavior comes from a fixed mind-set, one that is closed to anything that differs from my perfectionist perspective. Basically, my stubborn behavior flows from a hardened and prideful heart.

That is why I need the kind of wisdom from God that comes only to a humble heart. When we ask for it, we receive it, but the only way to receive it is to humble our hearts to God, the author of wisdom. God's desire is that we would humble our hearts to others as well so that they can see God's wisdom in our lives and discover for themselves the sweet spot where the vertical intersects with the horizontal. If we are going to help others find wisdom, then we must come alongside those with whom we come in contact and avoid statements like, "I think you are a stubborn fool." Such a statement may, in fact, perpetuate more foolish behavior.

Once again, Jesus offered a different way. He was wise in how He interacted with people. He understood His audience and connected with each person's heart. He opened their perspective by asking penetrating questions that seemed to soften their hearts, thereby exposing their desires. When Jesus said that the two greatest things we can do are to love God and love others (see Matt. 22:37–40), He modeled both in word and in deed while He was here on earth. Influenced by the Spirit of Jesus, the apostle Paul reflected: "To the weak I became weak, to win the weak. I have become all things to all men so that by all possible means I might save some" (1 Cor. 9:22). Jesus met people where they were; He searched for common ground in order to connect others with wisdom. God desires that we do the same, even with the stubborn fool.

Take the Proverbs stubborn fool test:

- Do you always have to be right?
- Do you resist advice?
- Do you despise wisdom and discipline?
- Are you full of folly—repeating stupid behavior, including outbursts of anger?
- Is your heart so hard that you show your annoyance at once, refusing to overlook an insult?
- Is your quickness to quarrel evidenced in your provocation of more negative conflict?
- Do you scoff at the thought of making amends?

If the answer to any of these questions is yes, then it is time for a heart change.

4. THE SCORNING FOOL

The fourth stage is the *scorning fool*. The scorner's pride (hardness of heart) is so great that typically his arrogance rules him. This person is often referred to in Proverbs as a "mocker." "The proud and arrogant man—'Mocker' is his name; he behaves with overweening pride" (Prov. 21:24). He has moved from being teachable and having low-level but redeemable foolishness, past stubborn pride, on to mocking.

- *The scorning fool is averse to wisdom.* It does not flow in his life. "The mocker seeks wisdom and finds none, but knowledge comes easily to the discerning" (Prov. 14:6). *Discerning* means "separating." A mocker or scorner struggles to separate wise choices from foolish ones.
- *The scorning fool causes dissension in organizations.* This is due to the fact that he ignores rebuke and refuses to learn from past mistakes. Thus, he must be removed from an organization in order for it to thrive: "Drive out the mocker, and out goes strife; quarrels and insults are ended" (Prov. 22:10). Relationships can flourish when the scorner leaves.
- *The scorning fool is opposed by God.* He is known as a scoffer who picks a fight with the Almighty, mocking at reconciliation and justice. However, God has a pattern in His response to this level of hard-heartedness: "He mocks

proud mockers but gives grace to the humble" (Prov. 3:34). God takes a position of direct opposition to the scorner in an effort to bring him back to wisdom.

King Nebuchadnezzar was a scorning fool who eventually responded in humility to God's opposition (see Dan. 4). Iraq's late leader Saddam Hussein idolized Nebuchadnezzar at least in part because he conquered Jerusalem in 586 BC. Nebuchadnezzar leveled the city, including Solomon's Temple. In doing so, this king demonstrated an internal condition that scorned wisdom. In fact, little wisdom literature has been discovered in Babylonian remains (southern Iraq). Envisioning himself as the new Nebuchadnezzar, Hussein built a replica of that king's war chariot; he also beamed his likeness along with Nebuchadnezzar's into Baghdad's evening sky; and he rebuilt Babylon, Nebuchadnezzar's capital city (Eric H. Cline, "Saddam Hussein and History 101," *BY GEORGE! Online.* March 2003). Scorning fools like Nebuchadnezzar and Hussein are mocking and arrogant. Averse to wisdom, they cause dissension in organizations and eventually experience opposition from God. After regaining his sanity (see Dan. 4), Nebuchadnezzar finally responded in humility. Barring an unreported last-minute confession at his execution, Saddam Hussein did not.

The personality of a scorning fool is not limited to foreign despots with large kingdoms. As a teaching pastor, I encountered a man—a Midwestern, church-attending person—whose heart had become so hard that he wanted to leave his spouse, causing dissension in his marriage and family. As is typical of the scorning fool, this person was averse to wisdom. Imagine how difficult it is to have a rational discussion with someone who wants a divorce, especially when that person is physically or romantically involved with someone else. That's what I experienced with this man.

When engaging with him, I asked if he remembered the Bible teaches that God disciplines those He loves. He did. I asked if he had felt resistance in his life from his desire to leave his wife and family. He nodded affirmatively. I asked him if he thought it possible that God had mercifully instituted natural consequences against his hard heart because of His great love for him. He nodded. I explained that, much like the way we parent our kids, God desired to return him to wisdom, to stay married and be a father to his children. My acquaintance's response was revealing: "I've been told that sort of thing before, but the way you said it is much more palatable." Not exactly what I was going for, but at least he was listening.

An unfaithful and exiting spouse, like the one described, is usually in scorning mode. One week, I asked two different persons filled with this level of foolish pride the same three questions that I derived from Romans 1:32: "Do you know that in God's eyes what you are doing is wrong? Do you understand the potential consequences for you, your career, your spouse, your family, and your future relationships? Do you want to go through with it anyway?" Both of these people answered yes to all three questions. While I could not possibly know everything that had occurred in their marriages, it was evident that their hearts had become hardened to what was right. These two people had attained (or dropped to) the level of a scorning fool.

How would you answer these same three questions regarding your foolish actions? My hope is that, if you are caught in foolish, scorning behavior that has sparked God's merciful consequences designed to bring you back to wisdom, what I am saying is "palatable" to you.

- Is it a challenge for you to separate wise choices from foolish ones?
- Would anyone at work, home, or play say that you are the cause of organizational dissension?
- Do you feel like you are "kick[ing] against the goads" (Acts 26:14) with God?

If your answer is yes to any of these questions, you are behaving like a scorner, and it's time for a change.

5. THE GODLESS FOOL

The fifth stage is the *secular,* or *godless, fool. The secular fool exalts himself rather than God.* "If you have played the fool and exalted yourself, or if you have planned evil, clap your hand over your mouth" (Prov. 30:32). The godless fool manipulates those who invest in him. Proverbs communicates that the godless fool is unsatisfied by spiritual things. He brings no joy to his father. This secular fool has hardened his heart with the image of his own handprint impressed solidly in his inner being.

Nabal, the husband of Abigail (who later became David's wife), was a godless fool (see 1 Sam. 25:25), which didn't work out so well for him. His rigid heart literally failed him, and he became as hard as stone. Then God struck him dead. While God's response appears harsh, it is important for us to notice the text reveals this godless-fool poster child had known what he was doing when he snubbed David and his men after they had protected Nabal's flocks. David sought only the payment that would have been typically given at shearing time, so Nabal's rejection was considered a major offense in that culture.

A thousand years later, God acted similarly with Herod Agrippa I, the grandson of Herod the Great. His heart was as hard as cured concrete. As many leaders had both before and after his reign, he considered himself a god. When Herod was dressed in his royal robes, sitting on his throne, delivering a stirring public address to his people who had depended on him for their food supply, they praised him as a god. He willingly received the label of deity, thereby rejecting God, so the angel of the Lord struck him dead (see Acts 12:21–23).

I have to admit there was one time in my life when my own heart came close to being that hard. I had worked hard, scorned rebuke, ignored God, and advanced my earthly kingdom at the expense of God's. I may have been one step away from hell when my heart was softened and I turned toward heaven. Unfortunately, many Christians who function as gods in their own lives may similarly think they're one step from heaven, but are actually headed for hell. Some people act this way in an attempt to control God by their religious acts. In the end, whether we are licentious or legalistic, we all risk being a god in our own lives. However, on this side of eternity, we are · never beyond the reach of the God who is ready, willing, and able to soften our hearts back toward Himself and then transform those hearts to pursue His wisdom.

The next verse in the aforementioned passage in Acts 12 reads: "But the word of God continued to increase and spread" (Acts 12:24). Looking back, I realized that my rejection of God did not detract from His deity, nor did my acceptance of Him somehow make Him more the Lord of the universe. He already is. The wisdom of God will continue to increase and spread whether we are godless fools or not. So the damage we do is more self-inflicted than anything else. When we turn from God, we hurt only ourselves. In light of this truth, the question for each of us is: "What am I going to do with the hard spots in my heart?" Will we allow God's wisdom to increase and spread in our own hardened hearts? The answer will be yes only if we soften our hearts to the handprints of the one true God of all wisdom.

Carefully consider your own heart:

- Is there any area in which you have exalted yourself above God?
- Is there any area in which you refuse to seek God's heart by way of a thought, choice, feeling, or prayer?
- Are you living your life on autopilot apart from God?
- Do you need more and more of your "fix" of choice to advance your own earthly kingdom at the expense of Christ's because you perceive your desires are not truly satisfied in Him?

If your answer to these questions is yes, you may be coming dangerously close to playing the secular fool.

★   ★   ★

It's easy to read through these lists describing the progressive hardening of the heart and think of someone else who fits each stage. However, the list is for our own self-examination. Each of us must ask: "Is there any area of my life where I have hardened my heart to the Spirit of God?" If we consider our answer prayerfully and ask for God's guidance, the answer will be yes more often than we think. After identifying the foolish behavior, we must confess our pride to God, humbly surrender it to Him, and ask His Spirit to lead us to wisdom.

Chapter 3

The Key to Unlocking Wisdom

How do *you* plan to unlock wisdom's gate? Wisdom represents the idea of God's heart of righteousness combined with street smarts. Wisdom makes our relationship with God "sticky," or consistently applicable, to our tasks and earthly relationships. Thus, it is the sweet spot where the vertical intersects with the horizontal.

Whenever a vertical line intersects with a horizontal line, four quadrants appear. This is the case with the human heart (*leb* or *lebab* in Hebrew, meaning "one's entire inner being"). Just as the physical heart is comprised of four chambers, so the spiritual heart is comprised of four chambers. We can remember them with the acronym WISE:

- Will
- Intellect
- Spirit
- Emotions

In order to experience wisdom in our lives, we must humble all four chambers of our spiritual hearts to God. *Humility*, or *anavah* in Hebrew, means "to make lower than" or "to bend the knee." A person who pursues wisdom with a humble heart toward God surrenders their all to Him, the author and provider of wisdom. Humility is the key that unlocks the gate to wisdom: God gives wisdom to those who are ready to ask for and receive it.

Jesus Christ said that He was humble in heart. He surrendered His all to the Father. Jesus personified wisdom from God in all of His interactions with people. His life offers clear evidence that humility toward the Father precedes wisdom. Selecting the Jews' ultimate word to describe God, Paul referred to Christ as the wisdom of God. Even Proverbs describes the preincarnate Christ as Wisdom.

Pride infiltrates the human heart, leading to foolishness. It is the antithesis of wisdom because it breaks apart the vertical from the horizontal, moving a relationship with God away from the practical, everyday process of seeking divine guidance. This problem manifests itself in two ways: (1) seeking God at the expense of seeking men or (2) seeking men at the expense of seeking God.

When we find ourselves focusing on seeking God and forsaking all others, we fall into religion rather than relationship— *legalism* rather than love. Someone might refer to such a person with the old adage: "He is so heavenly minded that he is of no earthly good." This is often the risk of those inside a church body. They can have hearts as hard and rigid as stone.

When we find ourselves focusing on seeking men and forsaking God, we fall into *license*—a life directed by self, not by God. An observer might look at such a person and say: "He is so earthly minded that he is of no heavenly good." This is often the risk of those outside a church body. They can have hearts like sand: loose and easily scattered.

Ironically, the solution to conflict, defined as two objects attempting to occupy the same space at the same time, is wisdom. This wisdom is not merely a principle; rather, it is a person: Jesus Christ, the One who was and is fully God and fully human, the One who reconciled mankind with God. And if we allow His wisdom to permeate our lives, He can reconcile humans with one another.

But to gain access to wisdom, we must welcome humility. A good metaphor for a humble heart is clay. Whereas stone requires a hard tool in order to be shaped and sand requires a storm in order to be formed, clay is malleable in the hands of its potter. All three substances come from the ground, but a person who possesses a malleable heart of clay allows space for the impression of God's handprint upon it, to be shaped and formed by His will and His way. He understands that he has no true value unless shaped by the potter.

When we humble all four chambers of our spiritual hearts to God, we begin to act humbly and wisely in our relationships with others.

THE FOUR CHAMBERS OF THE HEART: W.I.S.E.

Will

The *will* is the chamber of our *choices*. Nearly every action is preceded by a choice. In order to experience wisdom in our lives, we must surrender our will—that is, our choices—to God. Humbling our will to God in order to experience wisdom is a clear choice. In essence, it is the flip of a switch. Humility says to God, "I can't. You can." "I can't pay for the penalty of pride and foolishness in my life. In Christ, You can. I can't free myself from the power of pride and foolishness in my life. In Christ, You can."

Jesus surrendered His will to the Father. Just before His arrest and subsequent crucifixion, Jesus said, "Father, if you are willing, take this cup from me; yet not my will, but yours be done". (Luke 22:42). Surrendering His will to the Father gave Jesus the wisdom to interact with Judas, the chief priests, Pilate, Herod, Peter, John, Mary, and the Roman soldiers, among many others, in order to accomplish the will of the Father. This led to the glorification of Christ and the ability for us to be saved. In other words, Jesus' surrendered will changed the course of history. Now that's saying something about the value of submission!

When I volunteered as a teaching pastor at Blackhawk Ministries, God brought many addicts to our Wednesday evening church services. I believe all of them surrendered their lives to Christ as Savior and Lord because they truly understood surrender. Before Christ, they were great at surrendering but were surrendering to the wrong objects. They needed to flip a switch and surrender their wills to the loving God who created them.

God is inviting us to flip the switch, to say to Him, "I can't, but You can. Not my will, but Yours be done." Great power flows from a person with a humbled will who makes the wise decision to allow God to influence their choices.

Intellect

The *intellect* is the chamber of our *thoughts*, including all the information, images, and ideas in both our conscious and subconscious. The humbled intellect is open to the wisdom of God, the divine light that illuminates our hearts. King Solomon preached: "The fear of the LORD teaches a man wisdom, and humility comes before honor" (Prov. 15:33). "The fear of the LORD" is humility toward God. Solomon said that if we accept God's wisdom, store it up, listen to it, apply our hearts to it, call out for it, even cry aloud for it, then we will understand "the fear of the LORD" because it is the Lord who gives wisdom (Prov. 2:1–6).

Jesus is the Word, the expression of the mind of God (see John 1:1). When walking this earth, Jesus surrendered His thoughts to the Father (see Matt. 22:37). Paul said that when we imitate Jesus and seek after the mind of God, "We demolish arguments and every pretension that sets itself up against the knowledge of God, and we take captive every thought to make it obedient to Christ" (2 Cor. 10:5). When we humble our intellects to God, we have the mind of Christ (see 1 Cor. 2:16). This moves us from pretense to authenticity.

Below is a priceless approach to studying wisdom that I follow. Over the years, it has filled my mind with the wisdom of Christ:

- **Study Wisdom 101:** Read one chapter in Proverbs each day that corresponds with the date of the month. Proverbs has thirty-one chapters, so you will read through the book once each month during the course of the year. For

months that have thirty days or less, you can either read
the remaining chapters or begin anew with Proverbs 1 at
the beginning of the following month.

- **Study Wisdom 201:** Follow Study Wisdom 101, plus read
  a chapter from the New Testament each day. This allows
  you to read the entire New Testament in less than a calendar year.

- **Study Wisdom 301:** Follow Study Wisdom 201, plus read
  three chapters each day in the Old Testament so that you
  read through the entire Bible in a year.

- **Study Wisdom 401:** Follow Study Wisdom 301, plus
  memorize one verse each week that you can apply to
  your daily life.

These four disciplines have proven to be so valuable to me
that I continue to pursue them each day. I encourage you to
select one or more of these disciplines today!

As you read from the Bible, apply what you learn from the
wisdom of God—either from His Word, His people, or His
Spirit—to the appointments on your calendar. This means
that you will approach every encounter and task with wisdom
from God.

Something changes in our lives as we pursue wisdom
and as God exchanges our sand and stone intellect for a
mind of clay that is malleable to His direction. Softening
our thoughts to God's wisdom illuminates His vision for our
lives. In our sand and stone intellect, we tend to see nearly
every encounter as an interruption to our own agenda. Then
as we allow God to transform our thoughts with wisdom, we

begin to see every encounter as a divine appointment. This one shift in perspective can make an enormous impact on our lives.

Spirit

The *spirit* is the chamber of our *prayers*. The Bible refers to the spirit as the lamp of God. He uses it to search our innermost being. When we pray, we connect our hearts with God's. In essence, when we pray, we are online with the Creator. Paul said that he prayed with his mind and with his spirit, indicating that prayer is not limited to just one quadrant of the heart. However, the spirit is the lead chamber of prayer. In order to humbly surrender our spirits to the Father, we must *pray* for wisdom.

James, the half brother of Jesus, is believed to have had calloused knees from the amount of time he spent humbling his body as well as his heart in prayer. He penned: "If any of you lacks wisdom, he should ask God, who gives generously to all without finding fault, and it will be given to him" (James 1:5). Solomon said: "The LORD is far from the wicked, but he hears the prayers of the righteous" (Prov. 15:29).

When we humble all four chambers of our hearts to God, we receive His righteousness. This gives us a clear connection to the heart of God.

Jesus surrendered His spirit to the Father. Each of the Gospel writers recorded Jesus praying alone daily with the Father and living 24-7 with Him. Luke captured Jesus' last words, complete with the inflection that only an eyewitness would have known: "Jesus called out with a loud voice, 'Father, into your hands I commit my spirit'" (Luke 23:46).

I created the acronym PRAYS from the Lord's Prayer, where Jesus taught His disciples how to pray (Matt. 6:9–15). This five-fold pattern—Praise, Renew, Ask, Yield, Surrender—has transformed my prayer life:

Praise—Jesus prayed: "Our Father in heaven, hallowed be your name" (Matt. 6:9). *Heaven* has many different meanings: the location of the throne of God, where we go when we die if we believe in Jesus, the stars (as in "heavens") in the sky, and the air around us. *Hallowed* means "holy." When I pray, I praise our heavenly Father for who He is (holy) and for being as close as the air is around me.

Renew—Jesus prayed: "Your kingdom come, your will be done, on earth as it is in heaven" (Matt. 6:10). Jesus understood that after God's kingdom came, His will would be done on earth as in heaven. Jesus ushered in God's kingdom. As a result, this part of Jesus' prayer calls for a renewing of our minds in order to experience God's kingdom and will in our lives. This is a 180-degree turn from our world's standards. Jesus prayed for His Father's will to be done. When we pray, He renews our minds to be about His kingdom.

Ask—Jesus prayed: "Give us today our daily bread" (Matt. 6:11). This referenced God's miraculous provision of manna in the desert for the Israelites. It is an illustration of total dependence on God to bring Him glory and advance His kingdom through His people. When I pray, I ask God for what I need to advance His kingdom, whether it be knowledge, new ideas, relationships, clarity, or guidance.

Yield—Jesus prayed: "Forgive us our debts, as we also have forgiven our debtors" (Matt. 6:12). C. S. Lewis said that *as* is the most sobering two-letter word in all of Scripture because the prayer is for God to forgive us in the same exact manner in which we have forgiven others. For some of us, this is a scary prayer. We have to yield all unsettled accounts to God, radically issuing to others the forgiveness that we have received from Him. If we do not, then we really have not received God's forgiveness. When I pray, I yield all of my unsettled relational accounts to God.

Surrender—to be Spirit-led. Jesus prayed: "And lead us not into temptation, but deliver us from the evil one" (Matt. 6:13). The Aramaic sentence structure might indicate "Let us not sin when tempted," rather than "Let us not be tempted." This is supported by the fact that James 1:13 tells us that God does not tempt anyone. When I pray, I surrender my heart to be Spirit-led in order to become a rapid Holy Spirit responder.

Become a person who PRAYS. Ask God to lead you to the intersection of His heart with street smarts. Pray for this before, during, and after your Scripture reading as well as when you are making a significant decision or encountering another person during a divine appointment. You'll become a rapid Holy Spirit responder when you begin to pray this way.

Emotions

Our *emotions* represent the chamber of our *feelings*. These are the multiple reflectors, or mirrors, of the light in us. The exhaustive list of emotions is a difficult one to complete. But my uncle Derald, a man I admired greatly for the wisdom he exemplified through his life both personally and professionally as a lawyer, simply categorized them as follows: mad, sad, glad, or afraid. In order to fully surrender our heart to the Father, we must feel like doing so. We must desire to bend our knees to his will. This is a desire that includes an emotive component.

Solomon not only challenged young leaders to choose wisdom, but he also went on to say that they should desire it above all else: "For wisdom is more precious than rubies, and nothing you desire can compare with her" (Prov. 8:11).

Many of us need to make a shift in what we desire. Too often we enter a conflict emotionally, seeking victory that is measured in time, talent, or treasure, wishing for falsely promised significance, contentment, control, or security. Consequently, we become mad, sad, glad, or afraid over whether or not we will win when we pursue our own satisfaction. But the irony is that apart from God we will never be fully satisfied because only He can truly satisfy our desires.

Jesus surrendered His emotions to the Father. When being crucified with criminals as Roman soldiers divided up His clothes by casting lots, Jesus prayed: "Father, forgive them, for they do not know what they are doing" (Luke 23:34). Peter, who witnessed this scene, said: "When they hurled their insults at him, he did not retaliate; when he suffered, he made no threats. Instead, he entrusted himself to him who judges justly" (1 Pet. 2:23).

When my daughter Kelsey was about twelve years old, I was trying to teach her about emotions and how they reflect our hearts to others. One day I said, "Kelsey, I want you to vacuum the cars, all three of them."

Kelsey is our perfectionist who almost always attempts to do what is right, but out of character, she argued with me. I was amazed at how I had to return to her over the course of an hour in order to motivate her to accomplish the task.

Finally, she vacuumed the cars. I checked in as she made her way through the floors of the vehicles. She was a little sad and a little mad—totally out of character for Kelsey. I checked in one last time, only to be amazed by the sight of the vacuum hose and attachments lying on the garage floor, where she knew they should never be. So I walked upstairs for an overdue appointment with Kelsey in her room.

In my pocket were three denominations of bills: a five, a twenty, and a hundred. I walked into Kelsey's room and placed the pictures of Abe, Andrew, and Benjamin on her bed.

"Kelsey, when I asked you the first time to vacuum the cars, I knew these were in my pocket. I thought I'd give you the twenty. There was even something inside of me that said, *She's been supporting a girl through Compassion International; she needs money to buy Christmas presents; maybe I'll just go for it and give her a hundred.*" Kelsey's big blue eyes got even bigger as she stared down at Benjamin Franklin.

"Kelsey," I continued, "look at these three denominations and tell me what you think you earned based on what kind of job you did."

"Maybe the five," she said.

"That's right, and that's what I'm giving you. I just want you to know that your emotions cost you something today. What do you think they cost you?"

"Probably dinged my relationship with God," Kelsey said spiritually.

"What else?"

Kelsey's eyes scanned the three bills. "Somewhere between fifteen and ninety-five dollars," she said.

"Kelsey, your emotions dinged your relationship with God and with me because you didn't reflect His heart during the process." Then I drove the message home: "You know what? That's the same thing that's happening all over our world today. Ministries and businesses are failing because their leaders and employees are reflecting negative emotions to those they encounter, and it is dinging the advancement of the kingdom of God!"

When I finished, I walked away. But a few minutes later I decided to return to my perfectionist daughter to give her the twenty and a lesson on grace, along with another speech.

Humble your emotions to God and desire wisdom. In every encounter, desire it. Feel it. Want it. Joyfully embrace it. Just as changing your diet from junk food to healthy food will create a desire for different tastes, so desiring wisdom will lead to a different appetite for life.

Applying God's wisdom to my collector car auction career restored my relationships and my capacity to lead. After a few very tough years of struggling to meet our financial obligations, we paid our creditors in full, created the first auction that was broadcast live on the Internet, produced a celebrity car auction broadcast to a record Labor Day audience on ESPN2, pioneered corporate sponsorships for auctions, and completed the best year in our business's history when we became a coveted entity to many suitors who recognized that the hottest buzzword on the Internet was *auctions*. After a record-setting run on Wall Street, a young start-up company named eBay merged with Kruse International. That move afforded me the opportunity to become a carrier of the message of restoration through wisdom in leadership. I enrolled in seminary and earned my master's and doctorate degrees, volunteered as a teaching pastor at a local church, and now I communicate with marketplace and ministry leaders like you in order to connect our culture with Christ.

Remember that pride is the lock on the human heart that keeps us from pursuing the wisdom of God. Humility is the key that unlocks the gate to wisdom, and that wisdom is a person: the person of God in Jesus Christ.

When we humble all four chambers of our hearts to God, we receive Christ, who is the wisdom of God as He dwells in us through His Holy Spirit. Jesus Christ is the intersection of the vertical with the horizontal. He is fully God and fully man. He is God's heart combined with street smarts. He has reconciled mankind with God and people with one another. Paul referred to Christ in us as "the hope of glory" (Col. 1:27). *Hope* is confident assurance—not wishful thinking, as we tend to characterize it. *Glory* is the revelation of Christ's character and presence. When we humbly surrender all four chambers of our hearts to God, we can be confident that God's wisdom in Christ will be manifested in and through us.

The book of Proverbs reveals twelve steps toward wisdom

that represent twelve characteristics of Christ. By His Spirit, these distinctively divine traits help us to navigate through conflict toward community. Let's look at those twelve words in the second part of this book, remembering our organizing principles. Each of these twelve words is a pearl that represents the pursuit of wisdom.

Part Two

TWELVE WORDS

Proverbs is the Old Testament's book of wisdom. While it appears to be a list of nearly one thousand pithy sayings in random order, Proverbs is actually one of the Old Testament's most tightly outlined books. It is designed to equip young leaders with wisdom to navigate through life's conflict toward community. In its introduction, Solomon reveals twelve words to the wise—twelve pearls of wisdom—that serve as the foundational teachings of this literary gem. Pursue these in order to discover a life filled with wisdom!

The following chapters are a result of my years of pursuing these twelve words: righteousness, equity, justice, wise behavior, understanding, wise communication, prudence, discretion, wise counsel, discipline, knowledge, learning. Applying these twelve timeless truths will significantly transform your life, allowing you to navigate through conflict to community.

Let's begin.

Chapter 4

Righteousness

RIGHTEOUS DECISIONS

I coached a young lady on one of my basketball teams who is an incredibly talented human being. She was the state champion in horse jumping, a multiple award-winning pianist, at the top of her class academically, and an amazing athlete who earned a scholarship at a Christian college to play basketball. Born in Sierra Leone, where her parents served as medical missionaries, she ran incredibly fast and could jump higher than any other player on her team. She lived a life of extreme accomplishment, all directed by her own personal discipline and diligence. She'd been raised right, and so when she did what was right in her own eyes, it looked a lot like what God would have her do.

When she moved away to college, her successes continued; while there, she added an NCCAA National Championship to her list of accomplishments. However, her new friends were not like the friends she had in high school; they encouraged her to drink alcohol, flying under the radar of campus rules that prohibited the practice. At first, she resisted the temptation to be accepted socially by this group, recognizing how it went against her upbringing. But through the added pressure of a boyfriend, she finally caved in.

Once she started, she moved quickly toward taking her drinking to an extreme. After all, she had been the best horse jumper, the best piano player, the best student, and the best athlete, so now she would be the best partyer. Even though she and her teammates hid their partying well for some time, it didn't take long for someone to talk, and soon their careless behavior was exposed. Needless to say, the coach was very unhappy.

I learned about the problem when she returned home for a weekend and asked me to rebound for her. While passing her the ball after several made shots and examining her shooting form, I asked a couple general questions that led to her sharing the entire experience with me. Her coach suspended all the girls on the team who had been caught drinking. Their season was done. He would reinstate them the following season, but only if they signed a contract—including the promise not to drink. If they were caught violating this commitment, they would be permanently dismissed from the team. She mentioned how most of the players who had been caught drinking were planning to quit rather than face the suspension.

Her parents, unaware of their daughter's violation and suspension, were traveling across the planet to celebrate their twenty-fifth wedding anniversary. Soon they would return, and all would be revealed. I was her one remaining source for navigating the conflict with her teammates, her coach, and her parents.

As we talked that day, this young woman and I reflected on her situation—how this was a precious period in her life for her to play collegiate basketball; what would happen if she were to follow her teammates' lead to give up their careers; and what might be the benefits if she agreed to sign the coach's contract, endure the punishing daily practices, and play the long grueling seasons.

Finally, we developed a plan for her to make a right decision in the midst of these new challenges. We discussed how she could bring honest, hopeful, and helpful speech to her conversations with her coach and her teammates. She needed to experience righteous strength that could come only from God, one that would provide her with resilience, would deepen her relationship with Him, and give her the resolve to endure her suspension for the remainder of the season. We discussed how the righteousness of Christ would give her the power to guard her heart from the onslaught of pressure to drink that she would experience; we also talked about how that same righteousness would give her the abundant life she was truly seeking.

Now, many years later, this young woman would tell you that her decision to accept the punishment, sign the contract, and miss out on a second NCCAA National Championship during her suspension was painful, but coming back was worth all the pain she experienced. When she rejoined the team under the terms of the contract, she played a significant role when they went on to compete in the NAIA National Tournament over the next two years. She found a new boyfriend, who later proposed. I officiated at their wedding, with her college basketball coach in attendance.

She is now completing medical school and plans to continue

to use her talent, expertise, and education to bring healing to sick children in third world countries. She recently shared, "When I moved from doing what was right in my sight to doing what was right in God's sight, I felt free of the unrealistic expectations I had been placing on myself. In high school, I was disciplined and determined, but I felt I could never measure up. That changed in college, and I now know that I need the righteousness of Christ and His wisdom for every part of my life."

When it comes to conflict, we want to make the right decisions, say the right words, garner the right power, and do the right thing so that we can get the right result. The only problem is that since the first sin, people throughout history have determined for themselves what is right and wrong—including you and me. Our perspective of right and wrong is clouded, as if we're peering through a foggy window. Consequently, we need to seek God's wisdom in order to discover His crystal-clear perspective on what is truly right.

Righteousness is translated in the New International Version as "doing what is right" (Prov. 1:3) in God's sight. It comes from God rather than the good works of any individual. Righteousness is often juxtaposed in Proverbs with wickedness—doing what is wrong in God's sight. Left to our own pride and foolishness, we will too often choose what God calls sin over what He sees as right action. Solomon clarified God's perspective on this: "To do what is right and just is more acceptable to the LORD than sacrifice" (Prov. 21:3). As I examined the uses of righteousness in Proverbs, I uncovered four contextual patterns: *righteous decisions, righteous talk, righteous strength,* and *righteous walk.*

Our major decisions surface in many areas, but we're going to look at just three: career, community, and challenges. Proverbs equips us for righteous decisions in all three areas. Solomon penned: "The plans of the righteous are just, but the advice of the wicked is deceitful" (Prov. 12:5). Wisdom offers us a righteous grid to process our decisions before we make them.

Career

Righteous decisions enrich our careers, and more frequently *in the midst of* our work than in our choice of the right profession. Though the latter carries long-term consequences, Proverbs does not neglect the weight of the former: "The wicked man earns deceptive wages, but he who sows righteousness reaps a sure reward" (Prov. 11:18). Life flows inside out from the heart. Who we are to *be* determines what we are to *do*, which determines where we are to *go*. Too often we get it backward. We believe that if we go somewhere, we will do something in order to be somebody. Consequently, it is important for us to work wholeheartedly, right where we are, sowing righteousness in order to reap a sure reward. When thinking about a career, we must remember that God cares much more about *who we are* than *what we do*.

The righteous are delivered from evil desires that stem from an unfaithful heart—one that is duplicitous and divides its loyalty. Frequently this is fleshed out as the employee leverages his or her present employer against a potential future one. Solomon warned of the consequences of this alluring sin versus the reward of doing what is right in God's sight: "Misfortune pursues the sinner, but prosperity is the reward of the righteous" (Prov. 13:21). Proverbs alludes to the fact that those who are righteous generally have employment while those who are wicked often go hungry. It's generally true, most of the time, that righteous decisions regarding how we function in our careers lead to a financial cushion, whereas the income of the wicked is spelled *t-r-o-u-b-l-e.*

In my early days of deal making, I envisioned that my auctioning days would be numbered. I was always looking ahead to something better. Consequently, I overlooked the present, deeming it less important than the future. The end result was that I was never fully present in my relationships, and I never achieved the blessings that God had in store for our customers, our employees, our vendors, or for myself. When I realized who I was designed to be determined what I was designed to do, which determined where I was designed to go, I surrendered to experiencing what was right in God's sight. By making the switch toward deepening my community and living fully in the present, I began to experience deeper relationships as I pursued wisdom in all the decisions in my career. Incredibly, this actually led to more deals and a more successful business—both relationally and monetarily.

My friend, former senior pastor, and now leadership development expert, Kelly Byrd, taught me about righteousness in career decisions when he shared a story from the early days of his career. He was a janitor; part of his job involved cleaning toilets, a job he disdained. He was frustrated that his NIT Basketball Champion six-foot-seven-inch frame was being wasted cleaning the remnants of other people's waste. A minister once noticed Kelly's negative demeanor, displayed during the course of his "sanitation engineering" duties. This wise pastor put his arm around Kelly and uttered four words that Kelly would never forget: "Bloom where you're planted."

This is a potent idea to mull over in your mind. Are you struggling with the validity of your career? Are you earning deceptive wages by not fully applying yourself? Do you think that your identity consists of what you do, and you don't like what you do? Are you searching for another job on your employer's dime, disseminating your résumé on the computer they have provided? Maybe it's time to refocus and work wholeheartedly, right where you are. I share this story with many young people who are in the early stages of their careers. I emphasize that they will realize their full potential only if they choose to discover the blessings God intends to offer through them in their current position.

Community

Righteous decisions enhance relationships in *community* with others; wicked ones hurt them. Similarly, righteous decisions improve our relationship with God, whereas wicked decisions damage our relationship with Him. Solomon wrote: "The LORD's curse is on the house of the wicked, but he blesses the home of the righteous" (Prov. 3:33), and "When the righteous prosper, the city rejoices; when the wicked perish, there are shouts of joy" (Prov. 11:10).

Remember, the wisest people are not always rich, nor are they always formally educated, but they are very relational. Wise people enjoy life-giving relationships because they pursue God's view of relationships in their circle of influence and community, regardless of where they reside on the socioeconomic ladder.

Challenges

Righteous decisions *guide* us through life's challenges. Wicked decisions *hide* us. Typically, we follow our wicked decisions with pretense in an effort to hide the source of those decisions—an unrighteous or unfaithful heart. Solomon described the guiding versus the hiding when he wrote: "The righteous man is rescued from trouble, and it comes on the wicked instead" (Prov. 11:8); that is, the wicked get punished, but the righteous go free. When referencing the challenges of life, Solomon equated the benefit of righteous decisions to freedom and the consequences of wicked ones to a trap. How many of us haven't felt the truth of that comparison in our own lives?

Turn up the pace or the seriousness of the challenges in life, and you turn up the need for right decision-making amid conflict. As we age and move from stage to stage in life, the seriousness of our conflict typically gets only more complex. If we marry, we have to adapt to another person's influence. When babies come, our patience and faith are tested. Once the kids are in school, their relationship problems and academic challenges appear. When they finally get through high school, we have to manage college expenses and help guide our adult children to owning their faith. Once the grandkids come, we may have our own health issues to deal with. I have watched many people who made the right decisions to guide them through life's challenges. I have also witnessed many people who made the wrong decision to hide through life's challenges. The benefits of the former are obvious; the deficits of the latter can be serious.

Let's take a closer look at this. A car collector who had purchased several hundred beautiful rolling sculptures from our auctions over the previous two decades called me one day and asked me to fly to his home and look at his collection; he was considering selling it at auction. I was on the next plane to Colorado, where this client picked me up. As we made the drive to his warehouse, I asked him to tell me about his business. I learned that he had once worked for a firm that, after enjoying decades of his leadership and faithful service, decided to fire him. The reason for the firing seemed unjust to my friend. As he pondered his challenge, he decided that the right decision was to continue the investment of his time, talent, and treasure in the industry he knew so well. As a result, he began to see his former employer's action as a gift. He seized the opportunity to start his own business, since he had never signed a noncompete agreement. The rest was history. Later in life he bought his own *mountain* where he built his home and the buildings that housed his two hundred collector cars.

I have met many others who fell into depression over the loss of a job, paralyzing them from taking the next step in their journey toward career restoration. Some languished for an extended period of time because they failed to see the event as an opportunity. I remember pleading with one person to see his job loss as a temporary setback; however, he wanted to hide through life's challenges and remain miserable in what he saw as a final, tragic event in his career. Like my friend in

Colorado, I had hoped he would allow right decisions to guide him through life's challenges, pick himself up, and prayerfully find out what God had planned for his future. But he refused.

What decisions are you facing that require righteousness? Are you in the midst of making decisions in your career, in your community, or in your other challenges? Has your pattern been paraphrased as, "If I just *go* somewhere, then I will *do* something in order to *be* somebody"? Let who you are designed to *be* determine what you are to *do* and where you are to *go*. Read through the book of Proverbs, and seek out God's wisdom and his righteousness before you make your next major decision.

RIGHTEOUS TALK

Solomon said: "The tongue of the righteous is choice silver, but the heart of the wicked is of little value" (Prov. 10:20). Righteous *talk* is paramount if we want to live out God's wisdom for the conflict in our lives. Proverbs offers three wise traits for righteousness in our speech: honest, hopeful, and helpful.

Honest

Righteous talk is *honest*: "The mouth of the righteous is a fountain of life, but violence overwhelms the mouth of the wicked" (Prov. 10:11). A fountain of the type that Solomon describes is pure, clear, consistent, and life-giving. Contrastingly, the words of the wicked are dishonest. They are impure, confusing, unpredictable, and life-taking. Not for nothing has the adage "Honesty is the best policy" been passed down from generation to generation. It's absolutely true.

Hopeful

Righteous talk is *hopeful*. Amid life's storms, the righteous are hopeful with their words, but the wicked are full of despair. Solomon described the aftereffects of a stormy conflict, the kind where our words can often get us into trouble: "When the storm has swept by, the wicked are gone, but the righteous stand firm forever" (Prov. 10:25). After their heated exchanges, the wicked often flee the scene. Solomon went on to describe this hopelessness of the wicked: "The prospect of the righteous is joy, but the hopes of the wicked come to nothing" (Prov. 10:28). Positivity characterizes a person whose hope is in the Lord; they trust in God's wisdom and guidance. One who understands the free gift of God's grace and has accepted it cannot help but utter hopeful speech. Conversely, hope will not come from wicked words.

Helpful

Righteous talk is *helpful*. First, because righteous words are nourishing: "The lips of the righteous nourish many, but fools die for lack of judgment" (Prov. 10:21). Second, they are helpful because they are wise: "The mouth of the righteous brings forth wisdom, but a perverse tongue will be cut out" (Prov. 10:31). Third, they are helpful because they are fitting: "The lips of the righteous know what is fitting, but the mouth of the wicked only what is perverse" (Prov. 10:32). "Fitting" is translated from the Hebrew word *ratson*, translated as "accept-able," which means "bringing favor, or goodwill." When our talk is righteous and helpful, we bring favor and goodwill to our conversations.

Each of these three traits of righteous speech is a characteristic of Christ. He is honest; namely, He is the truth of God (see John 14:6). He is hopeful; specifically, He is the hope of God for all who will believe (see 1 Tim. 1:1). He is helpful; certainly, He is the help of God for those who put their trust in him (see Heb. 13:6). In order for our talk to be honest, hopeful, and helpful, we must surrender our hearts to Christ. Then His wisdom and righteousness will flow through our words.

I believe that righteous talk is the most challenging as we engage with those who are closest to us. For example, I find I am the harshest relationally with my immediate family. My high expectations oftentimes become unscalable walls for my wife and four daughters. When my words are dishonest (impure, confusing, unpredictable, and life-taking) and hurt-ful, I tear down those around me and our family community suffers. When my words are honest (pure, clear, consistent, and life-giving), hopeful, and helpful, I build up those around me and our family community flourishes. My wife, Susan, once told me that my choice of words either infuse her with anger or defuse her tension in conflict. That left a significant impression on me; consequently, I began to examine my speech. I realized that if I was going to stop dishonest, hurtful, and negative talk, I was first going to have to stop thinking dishonest, hurtful, and negative things.

This realization was the catalyst to an exercise I try to remember to this day. When I experience negative thoughts on the inside, I surrender them to God, seeking His restoration (before the words are ever even uttered). When I give up my frustration, I find that I am more realistically inclined to come into an encounter seeking a good solution. When I do this, my words are more encouraging to those I come across, including (and most importantly) my wife. I have learned that I find what I seek. When I seek evil, I find it; when I seek good, I actually find goodwill.

Do you find the same to be true in your own life? What part of your speech needs to change in order for your words to be righteous? Is your talk honest, hopeful, and helpful? Ask a close friend the answer to these questions, and begin a step-by-step process of planning to exchange your wicked words that tear down others for righteous ones that build them up. Step one is realizing that your words have either a positive or negative effect; step two is making a mental note of checking yourself when you're in conflict to understand what your approach is and how it impacts your community; step three is to surrender your inner conflict to God, and ask Him to help you build relationships with your words rather than tearing them down.

RIGHTEOUS STRENGTH

Often in life we try to get ahead more quickly by taking short-cuts that twist something that's wrong to make it appear right. Solomon warned of the consequences of such foolishness when he said: "A man cannot be established through wickedness, but

the righteous cannot be uprooted" (Prov. 12:3). True, endur-
ing strength and success is found in the pursuit of righteousness, which provides both a foundation and framework that
will endure: "Wicked men are overthrown and are no more,
but the house of the righteous stands firm" (Prov. 12:7).

This righteousness is not a righteousness that comes from
our own abilities, or even our own desire to do good; rather, it
is a righteousness that comes from God. Solomon wrote that
nothing is stronger than the righteous identity of God: "The
name of the Lord is a strong tower; the righteous run to it and
are safe" (Prov. 18:10). This righteousness is available to those
who humble themselves and turn to the Lord when faced with
a difficult situation. Righteousness strengthens us with resilience, relationship, and resolve.

Resilience

Righteousness strengthens us with resilience—the ability to
endure or withstand conflict: "For though a righteous man
falls seven times, he rises again, but the wicked are brought
down by calamity" (Prov. 24:16). The righteous, who look
to God for direction and pursue His will for their lives, tend
to experience more success and longevity in their endeavors,
whereas the wicked are more likely to encounter failure: "The
righteous will never be uprooted, but the wicked will not
remain in the land" (Prov. 10:30). Paul challenged believers to
resilience when he said: "And as for you, brothers, never tire of
doing what is right" (2 Thess. 3:13). *Never.*

We should never tire of doing what is right in God's sight.
As we dive deeper into pursuing wisdom, God will grow His

resilience in us. He will use us to do the same with others. The more we endure, the more we *can* endure.

Relationship

Righteousness strengthens our relationship with God. Solomon observed: "He whose walk is upright fears the LORD, but he whose ways are devious despises him" (Prov. 14:2). Our bond with the divine is enhanced through prayer—the connection of our hearts with His: "The LORD is far from the wicked, but he hears the prayer of the righteous" (Prov. 15:29).

When I owned my auction business, I pondered the verses about building a strong relationship with God through His righteousness. As an indicator of the strength of my relationship with God, I examined my business relationships. That's when the Holy Spirit convicted me that *perhaps I didn't have any relationships.* Unfortunately, I had initiated business-related *encounters* with people merely to have them do something for me—I had built a one-way street with the arrow pointing in my direction. This analysis revealed a similar aspect in my relationship with God.

I wondered what would happen if I started to see my business relationships as a two-way street. I envisioned my one-way encounters becoming two-way relationships. As a result, I started calling customers for the express purpose of building our relationships, rather than talking about business deals or seeking ways to make money. I asked them about their day, their children, their likes and dislikes, their travel plans, and their businesses. I began to subtly communicate about God as well. In doing so, I discovered that listening was paramount to building strong relationships and that my success in business was indeed a by-product of those true relationships.

And I did something else: I began to pray for my customers, vendors, employees, and even my competitors. When I did, God permeated my relationships with His righteousness. I firmly believe this radically influenced the transformation of my company from merely a business to a ministry.

Resolve

Righteousness strengthens us with *resolve*—the motivation to manage, work out, or settle conflict. "Righteousness exalts a nation, but sin is a disgrace to any people" (Prov. 14:34). A nation is exalted when righteous resolve flows from righteous leaders. This kind of resolve provides courage to properly manage and resolve conflict because the righteous have nothing to hide. King Hezekiah's men copied Solomon's wise saying regarding this matter: "The wicked man flees though no one pursues, but the righteous are as bold as a lion" (Prov. 28:1).

Unfortunately, I mishandled a lot of the conflict that I came up against and left much of it unresolved. When I decided to face conflict head-on and make it a priority to resolve it, my business relationships were more honest and forthright. When my vendors and others in my organization discovered that I was serious about looking for the win-win in each conflict situation, I found that my relationships deepened and my customers were more open to new business possibilities. I also discovered that a satisfied customer becomes a carrier of your company's message, therefore producing more satisfied customers.

When I held my business interests too tightly, I lost business. When I opened myself up to the righteous pursuit of wisdom in regard to conflict and prioritized relationships over the bottom line, my business increased, as did my satisfaction with the work that I was doing. I encourage you to examine this in your own life. Do you leave conflict unresolved and find that it only produces more conflict? Learn from me what I had to learn the hard way: Make it a priority to pursue a righteous approach to resolving conflict.

What weaknesses of yours can be transformed into strengths through your renewed pursuit of righteousness? Would you like to experience more resilience and greater strength in the face of conflict? Are you willing to pray in order to strengthen your relationship with God? Are you in need of resolve to work out your conflict? Schedule five minutes each day on your calendar to pray that the Spirit will lead you into righteousness. Ask God for strength that is evidenced in resilience, relationship, and resolve.

RIGHTEOUS WALK

The Bible's authors use the term *walk* as a metaphor for life. The path where our feet take us comprises our life. Every single day, in a thousand different ways, we choose either a pathway toward righteousness or one that takes us toward wickedness. God's desire for us is to follow the wise pathway of righteousness. Characterizing wisdom's connection with righteousness, Solomon wrote: "Thus you will walk in the ways of good men and keep to the paths of the righteous" (Prov. 2:20; cf. 8:20).

The righteous path is free of blame; it is one that, through personal example, can be passed on to further generations: "The righteous man leads a blameless life; blessed are his children after him" (Prov. 20:7). Jesus summed it up this way: "Wisdom is proved right by her actions" (Matt. 11:19)—heart-guarded, abundant, and eternal.

Heart Guarded

A righteous walk is heart-guarded. Solomon wrote one of the most foundational bits of wisdom for humans when he penned: "Above all else, guard your heart, for it is the wellspring of life" (Prov. 4:23). Paul said that when we fully surrender our hearts to Christ, we receive not only His righteousness, but also His prayer-inspired peace that guards our hearts like a military fortress. Solomon described this same kind of divine protection when he wrote: "Righteousness guards the man of integrity, but wickedness overthrows the sinner" (Prov. 13:6). *Integrity* indicates a state of being whole, of being undivided. The person who pursues integrity in all his dealings works out of a context of complete surrender to the Lord, accomplished by praying for it daily.

This is a great lesson to learn as adults; it is also an important principle to emphasize with kids—especially teenagers. When our eldest daughter Megan turned thirteen, we gave her a purity ring to symbolize her commitment to remain sexually pure until she is married. In the card we gave with the ring I wrote a note and ended it with the verse from Proverbs 4:23. As Megan finished reading her card, I explained to her that, when relationships are managed appropriately and with

God at the center, a physical connection is always preceded by an emotional one. Therefore, as a young woman, it was paramount that she thoughtfully consider why, where, when, how, and by whom she wanted to be pursued. I wanted her to enter into the world of relationships with boys with her eyes wide open, to consider the quality of the boy before any emotional connection ever materialized. I went on to share my interpretation of Genesis 3:16, that because of the fall, girls desire to be pursued by guys, and they nurture that pursuit as a fundamental instinct that God put within them. Something inside a female's heart says that she will be satisfied by a male, at times even at the expense of her relationship with God.

Sharing these thoughts with Megan at a young age, in advance of any serious male pursuit, proved to help her understand the importance of guarding her heart. I remember a few weeks later we were attending a school function when my dad radar went up: The boys were watching her.

As are all four of my daughters, Megan is beautiful on the outside as well as the inside. So I decided to test how well she had listened to my heart-guarding advice. I asked her about a couple of the boys by name. Were any of these boys ones she might be interested in? "No way!" Megan said.

Then something funny happened: One of those boys pursued her. After two weeks of receiving his texts, emails, and school hallway conversations, Megan's guarded heart began to crack. I came to the rescue with the best words I could muster: "Wait a minute, sister! Remember what you said a couple of weeks ago?"

"Yes," she whispered reluctantly.

"You're the one who decides why, where, when, how, and by

whom you want to be pursued. Initially, this guy did not make your cut as a wise choice. Now because you have been pursued, your heart is reconsidering." I reiterated my Genesis 3:16 principle, noting that in her life as a beautiful young woman this was going to be the norm for her. She really needed to pray for and pursue God's wisdom for her life. I suggested that she ask Him to guard her heart, rather than trying to do so by herself. This advice sunk in a little deeper and has served her well in her decision-making about relationships with the opposite sex.

Abundant

A righteous walk is abundant. Solomon observed: "The light of the righteous shines brightly, but the lamp of the wicked is snuffed out" (Prov. 13:9). A light that shines brightly illuminates abundantly, providing all of the light we will ever need. Jesus' wisdom is that light—a light so strong and persistent we will never need another. Solomon proclaimed: "The path of the righteous is like the first gleam of dawn, shining ever brighter till the full light of day" (Prov. 4:18). Solomon wrote: "Better a little with righteousness than much gain with injustice" (Prov. 16:8). He concluded that a righteous walk satisfies with the hallmarks of an abundant life: "He who pursues righteousness and love finds life, prosperity and honor" (Prov. 21:21).

Eternal

A righteous walk is eternal. According to Solomon, this kind of a walk brings life that never ends: "In the way of righteousness there is life; along that path is immortality" (Prov. 12:28). Eternity includes judgment, one that each of us will face with God. When we do, no amount of earthly success, either in money gained or good works done, will pay for our unrighteousness. Only the righteousness of another can pay for our sin. Solomon reflected: "Wealth is worthless in the day of wrath, but righteousness delivers from death" (Prov. 11:4). If we reject the righteousness of Christ, we will experience death—eternal separation from God. Solomon summarized: "The truly righteous man attains life, but he who pursues evil goes to his death" (Prov. 11:19). He added: "When calamity comes, the wicked are brought down, but even in death the righteous have a refuge" (Prov. 14:32). Jesus Christ is indeed the refuge of those who accept His righteousness as their own and live in the pursuit of His wisdom.

The idea of an abundant and eternal life surfaced for me in the refuge of our annual fishing trip in Canada. Dad, Grandpa Russell, my brother Stuart, and I traveled by seaplane each year to Watson's Pine Portage Lodge on Kabinakagami Lake in Northern Ontario, far from civilization and the chaos of our 24-7 business. One peaceful, sunny day as our boat drifted along on the glassy lake, my dad looked at our guide, who was fishing from the back of our vessel, and reflected, "Guys like us beat our brains out working just to come up here and fish once a year. Our guide does it every day. It makes you think about your perspective on life."

Right then and there I began to reflect on Dad's comments and examine my steps. In my mind, I pictured the interior of my office where I spent most of my time when I was not traveling to auctions across the country. Sitting at my desk, I was surrounded by several original bronze sculptures I had purchased from artists I had known, acquired as a symbol of my success. It dawned on me how the automotive- and Western-related art in my office represented a counterfeit version of an abundant life. Those purchases had put me in a spiral, leading me to want ever-more expensive acquisitions so I could feel more of a rush. What I thought would fulfill my desires actually proved to be only a temporary fix that left my searching heart dissatisfied. Contrasted with the relationships that really made life abundant, such as the one I was enjoying with my dad at the moment, and the brief time I had on this side compared to eternity, I thought, *What good would those bronzes be to me right now in this boat?* I concluded that they would act only as a good anchor.

Are material possessions weighing you down and keeping you from an abundant and eternal life? Have you recognized the false expectations that you place on their acquisition? The problem is not you owning things; rather, it is that things can own you. Thus, the core of the problem lies in an unguarded heart, one that allows other priorities to take the place of Jesus in your life. It's easy to want the biggest and best and to feel like we deserve the newest and shiniest possessions. But Jesus calls us to walk the narrow path that places our desire for material possessions in perspective. Again, if you've been blessed by God and are able to enjoy many good things in this life while still responsibly supporting kingdom work, that's wonderful. But the guarded heart holds temporal possessions loosely and is guided by the wisdom of God in Christ.

What part of your *walk* needs to change in order to pursue righteousness? Where do your feet take you? That's your life.

Do your steps lead you to a click, a smoke, a toke, a binge, a pop, a fix, a fling, or even a self-righteous act? Those acts that come from a selfish heart lead to your death. Are you willing to walk toward the heart-guarded, abundant, eternally righteous refuge of Christ? Your life led to His death; His death leads to your eternal life.

In His Strength Alone

Jesus called us to seek first God's kingdom and His righteousness. No one can meet that standard by their own efforts. The only righteousness that surpasses that of the Pharisees and the teachers of the law is the righteousness of Christ Himself because He alone is the Righteous One. We must humble our hearts to Him in order to receive His righteousness. Then He brings His wisdom, His righteousness, into our *decisions*, our *talk*, our *strength*, and our *walk*.

Chapter 5

Equity

STRAIGHT PATHS

One of the first phrases we learn to utter is, "That's not fair!" A slick five-year-old, street-smart beyond his years, devises a way to commandeer another boy's favorite toy during kindergarten playtime, and the victim shouts, "That's not fair!"

At fifth-grade school play tryouts, the teacher's pet connives the lead role away from the girl who has diligently practiced her lines and was obviously better prepared. She goes home to her parents and cries, "That's not fair!"

High school homecoming arrives. The ridiculously advantaged girl wins yet another coveted crown, and the other girls on the court say, "That's not fair!"

Entering college, a young man's name is somehow misplaced by the admissions office, resulting in an austere assignment to the dorm with no air-conditioning. If that's not bad enough, he also gets the nonaccommodating class schedule with the 8:00 a.m. World History assignment. "That's not fair!" he cries.

A loyal employee of twenty years loses her position to a ladder-climbing former college intern who has the ear of the vice president and gets promoted, even though he has little experience. Colleagues whisper in the hallway, "That's not fair!"

On we go through career, marriage, home buying, parenting, and all other manner of relationships. Faced with the myriad inequities in life, we all at different points in our experience cry out, "That's not fair!"

Too often, well-intended Christians interpret fairness in terms of some sort of divine socialism, crying "Foul!" when God doesn't disperse the opportunities and the resources of life evenly among all people. While such people agree that each person is unique and has a particular calling on his or her life, they still desire that every individual have the same amount of stuff, the same number of years on this earth, the same set of circumstances, the same opportunities, the same answered prayers—basically, the same lot in life.

What if God's perspective of *fair* is not equal to being the *same*?

Praying to Trust in God's Will

My good friend Shirley Woods grew up attending church every Sunday, in Norfolk, Virginia. In 1970, after graduating from high school, she moved to Indiana. There she married, had two children, and later divorced. Though she knew about God, she wasn't really living for Him. Meanwhile, Shirley's son Euell became one of the best football players in the nation, selected as a *Parade* All-American and touted as one of the top fifty-six players in the United States. Euell committed to Indiana University, whose coaches suggested he attend Triton College in Illinois his freshman year in order to improve his SAT scores.

In November of his first semester at Triton, tragedy struck. Shirley received a knock on her door by the local police who gave her the heartbreaking news that Euell had died in his sleep. Shirley later learned that the diagnosis was Sudden Adult Death Syndrome.

Immediately upon hearing of Euell's death, the word *safe* repeatedly came to Shirley's mind. It stayed with her all during her son's funeral. Then later in the service her friend sang the song "Safely in His Arms." After the funeral, Shirley kept asking God for confirmation that her son was with Him.

A few days later, Shirley received the poem "Safely Home" in the mail. While reading the words of the poem, she began to sense God's confirmation of her prayer. A couple of days after that, Shirley received the very same poem from another friend. Neither knew Shirley's prayer or that the other had sent the poem to her.

Shirley knew she had to surrender her motives to keep her son on this side to God. Rather than selfishly hold on to Euell, she decided to stop worrying and selflessly release him to heaven. She had work to do, and she did not need to keep crying.

Shirley returned to her Christian roots and began to praise God, trusting that He was who He claimed to be in His Word as she entrusted her heart and resources to Him.

Almost three months after her son's funeral, Shirley went to lunch with her employer. There, her boss asked if he could help

Shirley do something in Euell's memory. Shirley took the offer to heart and began thinking about what she might do.

It didn't take long for her to find her cause. Her neighborhood was filled with gang activity, and gunfire was a common sound each evening. She knew she had to help those kids. With financial help from her employer, Shirley asked her high school–aged daughter to invite her friends to their backyard. Fifteen teens came. They ate a meal Shirley prepared for them and heard the Bible read and applied in a relevant way.

At the next gathering, thirty-nine teens attended. That number soon nearly doubled, and Shirley began to use local sports facilities to minister to the more than seventy-five students who were seeking safety and acceptance in the midst of their troubled neighborhood.

Due to the rapid increase of young people who wanted to attend her after-school programs, Shirley began to pray, asking God to provide a permanent facility focused solely on her ministry. God prompted her to drive through her neighborhood to look for a building. Shirley saw a beaten-down structure with potential and mentioned to her employer's wife, "I like looking at broken things and envisioning how they can be revived."

The owner was willing to allow Shirley to use the building if her ministry team would clean it up. Nine years later, Shirley's nonprofit organization raised the funds to purchase the partially renovated structure. The new facility was named the Euell A. Wilson Center, a place that allowed neighborhood kids to eat a meal, do their homework, and receive free tutoring. While there, they were taught from a Bible-based character-building curriculum titled "Jewel" for the girls, "Onyx" for the boys. Shirley's kids were also trained in the arts and worked their craft in the center's recording studio. Finally, Shirley saw the need to minister to the parents of the students, so she started programs to serve them as well, even offering a monthly opportunity for them to meet with a Christian attorney who provided legal advice at no charge.

Each week, the Euell A. Wilson Center opens its doors from 3:00 p.m. to 7:00 p.m., Monday through Friday, and hosts up to ninety students, ages five to eighteen. "The greatest need in a child today is to be loved, accepted, and understood, while also being given direction toward their life's purpose," Shirley told me.

Shirley has grown in her intimacy with God as He has walked with her through her most trying moments in life. She's had to confess her shortcomings and ask Him to complete her, giving her the integrity and vision she needed to found and build a ministry to reach students in need. Shirley often reflects on how her restorer has used the untimely death of her son to help others. "I've learned so much about the character of God that I wouldn't have learned without the loss. It wasn't the mountaintop experiences that allowed me to see God. It was the valley, and through the valley, I made it to the mountaintop."

Shirley treasures a particular life-giving verse from the Scriptures: "You will keep in perfect peace, him whose mind is steadfast, because he trusts you" (Isa. 26:3). When she revisited the poem "Safely Home" seventeen years later, she discovered the phrase "Pray to trust our Father's will," a line from the poem she'd never noticed before. Trusting in God's will and following His direction gave Shirley the peace she was seeking.

To anyone experiencing a tragedy that has left the lingering thought that God is not fair, Shirley would say, "I understand your pain, and I know the reality of it. The Creator brought me through it. He did not create any of us so that He could leave us. He has promised to be with us in good and bad times. If you trust in Him, only He can walk you through your tragedy. Give Him a chance. Just trust Him. He will walk you through it."

If anyone could accuse God of not being fair, it would be Shirley Woods. Instead, she sought to walk straight paths, prayerfully examined her motives to make sure they were pure, deepened her intimacy with God, and lived with integrity to lead a ministry that is still transforming lives today.

What is fair? We often ask this question in dating, marriage, parenting, education, sports, friendships, business partnerships, ministry collaborations, and national alliances. The wisdom literature in Proverbs offers us the answer in a key word embedded in the twelve signs of wisdom. That word is *equity* (*meyshar* in Hebrew). The New International Version translates *equity* as "doing what is . . . fair" (Prov. 1:3). In a world where some say, "God isn't fair," the Bible speaks to the contrary: "God is fair" (Heb. 6:10; cf. Ps. 145:17 GW).

Proverbs provides insight into how we apply not only *what* is fair, but also *who* is fair to those occurrences in our lives when we experience conflict. A study of Solomon's uses of the Hebrew word for *equity* in his book of wisdom reveals four contextual patterns to help us wisely navigate through conflict toward community. "What is fair" includes *straight paths, blameless motives, intimacy with God,* and *integrity.*

First, we see that what is fair includes straight paths. Solomon passed along his father's advice, saying: "I guide you in the way of wisdom and lead you along straight paths" (Prov. 4:11).

Straight is interpreted from the same root as *equity*, or what is fair. That root can be interpreted as "smooth" or "evenly applied," a reference to the fashioning of metal. Paths represent our track, or course, of life. Typically, when we experience interpersonal conflict in our lives, we do not evenly apply the principles of risk and return between the other person involved and ourselves.

Risk is the potential for loss. *Return* is the profit, gain, or reward. When relational tension arises, we tend to pile up risk on the other party while we attempt to retain all the return. Consequently, our paths become crooked or uneven. Wisdom's tool for evening our paths is equity that begins by placing all the risk in the exchange on God. Solomon encouraged: "Trust in the LORD with all your heart and lean not on your own understanding; in all your ways acknowledge him, and he will make your paths straight" (Prov. 3:5–6).

When we surrender to God, we place all the risk on Him for our heart's choices, thoughts, prayers, and feelings. When we trust in Him for all our ways—our time, talent, and treasures—God responds by making our paths straight, or fair. The antithesis of equity is trusting in our own imperfect understanding. This minimizes our vulnerability in an attempt to maximize our self-centered return.

Let's take a look at a well-known example of this principle. After David's sin with Bathsheba and his subsequent plot to kill her husband, Uriah, the prophet Nathan explained to the king through a parable that he had been unfair (see 2 Sam. 12:1–9). The reason for the inequity was that David had taken all the return while Uriah had unknowingly assumed all of the risk. The same risk-to-return relationship is also evidenced in the balance of responsibility (risk) with authority (return). In this situation, David's responsibility was not commensurate with his authority.

In his incarnation, life, and death, Jesus offered a dramatically different example of this principle that provides insight into the heart of God. When He was treated unfairly, the One with ultimate authority equally exercised His responsibility and risked everything with His Father, trusting in God to judge what is fair (see 1 Pet. 2:23). By sending to earth His Son, Jesus Christ, God took all of the risk to provide those who believe in Him with all of the return (see 1 Pet. 2:24).

When I auctioned collector cars, I noticed astute automobile aficionados who would stand at one end of a car and look down the side to make sure that the metal was evenly applied and free of cheap fillers. A straight line is also valued by race car drivers, who want to maintain the straightest line possible in order to achieve the highest speeds around the track.

I was sitting in a Pontiac Bonneville at the start-finish line of the Daytona International Speedway with its president behind the wheel. He took off toward turn one's steep embankment, cruising at eighty-four miles per hour as he nonchalantly instructed me about the intricate design of the course. My face must have matched my white knuckles as we raced for the wall when he mentioned, "This track is designed with an embankment that guarantees the driver never need turn the wheel at eighty-four miles per hour."

In a similar way, God constructs the course of our lives so that we can faithfully serve Him. When we place all our trust in God, we may get dinged by others in the race, but we know He'll keep us from hitting the wall.

Are your paths uneven? When relational conflict occurs, do

you risk little in an effort to gain much? Do you create in your finite perspective your own limited scale of what is fair? If so, you are leaning on your own understanding rather than trusting in God. Trust in the Lord with all your heart and let Him shoulder the risk. With all your time, talent, and treasure, seek after the One who is fair. He will straighten your paths by bringing equity to your conflict.

BLAMELESS MOTIVES

Solomon wrote: "The righteousness of the blameless makes a straight way for them, but the wicked are brought down by their own wickedness" (Prov. 11:5). *Blameless* refers to our motives, which can be defined as our desires, intentions, drives, or purposes. These represent the spiritual heartbeat that connects the heart with the three resources of life: time, talent, and treasure. God's perspective of equity includes peering into our hearts and weighing our motives (see Prov. 21:2).

Blameless motives make us concerned for the things God characterizes as fair. When our motives are selfless and in line with God's concerns, then they can be characterized as blameless. But too often in interpersonal conflict, we are selfish.

The apostle Paul wrote: "Do nothing out of selfish ambition or vain conceit, but in humility consider others better than yourselves. Each of you should look not only to your own interests, but also to the interests of others" (Phil. 2:3–4). When we find ourselves in the midst of conflict, we need to look to our own *selfless* interests, not selfish ones. This is how we know that our motives are true and blameless.

As we have seen previously, doing what is fair begins with risking our heart and resources for God's glory. Our motives, or our desires, link our hearts with our resources. Paul said that *blameless motives* are a by-product of our hearts being united with Christ and having fellowship with the Holy Spirit (see Phil. 2:1).

What is fair includes what God allocates to each of us: the combination of our distinctively designed hearts with our subsequent desires (motives) and our resources. Our hearts are unique (see Ps. 139). Our desires are unique (see Ps. 37:4). Our gifts, or our resources, are unique (see 1 Cor. 12:4–6). God specifically orchestrates these so that we will serve the interests of others in an effort to reveal His grace and give Him glory (see 1 Pet. 4:10). He holds us accountable to blamelessly steward our unique gifting (see Matt. 25:15). This exclusive talent is the one-of-a-kind expression of His story in us.

We are not to selfishly compare or contrast our circumstances with others, spending our time searching for and calling out inequities (see Gal. 6:4). After Jesus alluded to the tragic death that Peter would endure for his faith, He balked when His rocky disciple asked comparatively about what would happen to John. In essence, Peter was asking if Jesus would be fair. Jesus said: "If I want him to remain alive until I return, what is that to you? You must follow me" (John 21:22). Jesus was saying that the Creator determines what is fair and always considers the unique expression of His story in Peter, in John, and in each one of us. Individually, we are called to trust in the One who sees all things and is building His kingdom through us in fairness and equity.

At the same time, God is not giving us a one-for-one

punishment for our sin (see Ps. 103:10). Nor is He divvying out tragedies onto people who are "worse sinners." He merely desires that we individually repent with all of our hearts, all of our desires, and all of our resources (see Luke 13:1–5) and surrender these to Him. In doing so, we are free to have blameless motives in interpersonal conflict.

Our internal motives, our innate self-interests, are oftentimes much closer than they at first appear—much like that message printed on your vehicle's rearview mirror. Unfortunately, those motives are not always obvious because our perspective is skewed by selfishly comparing our circumstances with others. When we spend too much time searching for inequities, our motives cannot be called blameless.

After I had discerned God's prompting for me to move from the auction business to becoming a pastor, I earned my master's and doctorate degrees in seminary. At the conclusion of my formal education, I sought wise counsel from a friend to help me decide whether I should start a church or accept a full-time voluntary teaching pastor position at an existing church led by another friend. After spending a day of asking me questions and diagramming on a flip chart, my friend sat down with my wife and me in our kitchen. As we talked about the future of our family, tension began to build. Earlier in the day Susan and I had disagreed on a few issues, and now we had another heated exchange. At that moment, my friend asked one of the most poignant questions we had ever pondered in our married life: "Why are you talking to each other as though you are miles away when you are only inches apart?" His question caused us to recognize what we had been doing and realize that we did share the same interests and motives, though our words had not been reflecting it.

Inventory Your Motives

Are your motives blameless? Does interpersonal conflict cause you to first look toward your selfish interests, or do you approach conflict selflessly in the interest of others involved? During the next week, ask the Holy Spirit to help you inventory your motives whenever you find yourself in conflict. When two objects attempt to occupy the same space at the same time, let the Holy Spirit examine the selfishness or selflessness of your motives. When you uncover ignoble motives, humbly surrender them to God and ask His Spirit to move you from *selfish* to *selfless* (see Phil. 2:3). Then pursue the interests of the other parties involved in the conflict before your own, being careful to manage the conflict at hand toward solutions that are truly equitable.

INTIMACY WITH GOD

Third, "what is fair" includes *intimacy with God*—the connection of our innermost being with His. Solomon said: "For the devious are an abomination to the LORD; But He is intimate with the upright" (Prov. 3:32 NASB). *Upright* refers to those who are fair. The New International Version translates this intimacy with God as being taken "into his confidence" (Prov. 3:32). The King James Version says: "His secret is with the righteous" (Prov. 3:32). The Amplified Bible Classic Edition references intimacy with God as "His confidential communion *and* secret counsel" (Prov. 3:32).

The more intimate we are with God, the more we will work toward fairness in conflict. The more we work toward fairness in conflict, the more intimate we will be with God. This cycle changes how we measure the success of conflict management in our lives as we move from horizontal, competitive victory to knowing God more deeply and keeping His selfless perspectives in mind.

Through interpersonal conflict we can grow in our intimacy with God by doing all things through Christ who gives us strength (see Phil. 4:13). As we draw near to God, He draws near to us (see James 4:8). He never leaves or forsakes us (see Heb. 13:5). He is our helper, freeing us from the fear of man (see Heb. 13:6). In Christ, He understands our temptation to be unfair (see Heb. 4:15). He allows us to endure only what temptation we can bear, always providing a way out (see 1 Cor. 10:13). He comforts us (see 2 Cor. 1:5). He matures us (see James 1:4). He gives us wisdom (see James 1:5). He develops our perseverance (see Rom. 5:3). That perseverance produces character that gives us hope because we have intimacy with God through the indwelling of His Holy Spirit (see Rom. 5:4–5). He works in all conflict for our "good" (Rom. 8:28); *good* here is defined as His work to shape us to be like Christ. Then He uses our intimacy with Himself to, through us, introduce Christ to others who are encountering similar trials.

At least three avenues exist for us to increase our intimacy with God: the Word of God, the people of God, and the Spirit of God. I experienced this in my life when I was asked by a friend to be his "accountability partner." The title made me cringe. It felt like the makings of a guilt group. Instead I asked him if we could call it a "mutual walk relationship," one in which we were safe to share everything in our lives. We decided to meet weekly. We read the Bible, confessed our sins, and prayed together. That relationship taught me the power of the Word of God, the Spirit of God, and the people of God. The Word of God provided me with the benchmark of wisdom that I could apply to my life 24-7. Using a car analogy, it was and continues to be my owner's manual. The Spirit of God led me on the fly in every step of my life's path, making my connection with God relational rather than religious. However, through this mutual walk relationship I learned even more about horizontal confession.

I experienced the freedom that comes when sin is confessed, when the dark places of my life were exposed, and my motives were laid bare. I learned that talking about these things with a trusted friend, another one of God's imperfect people, made me more honest with myself about who I was and what I thought and felt. Over time, I learned that confessing a particular sin usually led to the death of that sin. Confessing a temptation led to me being delivered from desiring that object outside of God's design. I also learned that closer intimacy with God led me to being more sensitive to the prompting of the Holy Spirit and that sharing with another person the Holy Spirit's prompting to act on a vision led to experiencing God's provision. Consequently, my intimacy with God became deeper. I began to learn what it meant to abide, or remain, with God (see John 15:4) on a minute-by-minute basis.

Get Intimate with God

How well do you know God? Are you familiar with His will, His mind, His emotions, and His Spirit? If you've decided to follow one of the reading plans outlined in the introduction of this book, single out one verse in Proverbs each morning, and meditate on it with God, applying those wise words to all of your tasks and appointments throughout the day. Pray for God's specific leading through the verse. If you're not following a reading plan, that's okay, but please do take the step of opening your Bible to the book of Proverbs and writing down one verse to think about throughout your day. Carry that verse with you and read it often. At the end of the day, take a few moments to reflect on what you learned about the heart of God through that verse. Do this for the next thirty days as you learn to search for fairness and equity in interpersonal conflict.

INTEGRITY

What is fair includes *integrity*, the sense of being of one mind, complete and undivided. Solomon observed: "The integrity of the upright guides them, but the unfaithful are destroyed by their duplicity" (Prov. 11:3). Once again, the "upright" are those whose paths are straight. When we are fair with others, we are guided by integrity. God calls us to be completely fair in all that we do, all of the time.

Too often we become "weary in doing good" (2 Thess. 3:13) after we have endured being fair for what we thought was a sufficient period of time. Weary from our efforts to look after the interests of other people, we finally see an opportunity where looking out for our own interests might provide immediate gain.

Often, we look at the other party involved in our conflict and see them as unfair, which helps us justify our own self-centeredness in return. In these cases, we become divided, or duplicitous, in our attempt at equity and our integrity suffers.

In order to have the mind of Christ and work toward being completely fair in all our dealings, we must pursue wisdom with all our heart. Referencing the benefits of an all-out pursuit of wisdom, Solomon said: "Then you will understand what is right and just and fair—every good path" (Prov. 2:9). God uses that pursuit in the midst of our conflict to complete us (see James 1:4). His wisdom prompts us to selflessly perceive what is fair (see Prov. 8:6).

A story of this kind of God-centered integrity was carried on the national news a few years ago. It unfolded through a young boy whose dad I know through a mutual friend. This boy was walking down a sidewalk in New York City when he stumbled on Yankees tickets that were right at his feet. These were not your normal Yankees tickets. Rather, these were a bundle of tickets to the American League playoffs at Yankee Stadium where the Bronx Bombers were playing their archrival Boston Red Sox, whom they were pummeling in their best-of-seven series, 3–0. The tickets the boy held in his hands were worth more than $20,000. Now think of what converting the tickets to cash might have represented to that boy: a game console with every game imaginable, a tricked-out Harley, a gently used Corvette, even a year of college tuition.

But this boy had integrity. After thinking about his conflict and weighing his options, he selflessly decided to take the tickets to the police, acting with the kind of integrity that comes only from the equity of wisdom.

On a bus ride home after a victory by the high school girls' basketball team I helped coach, the girls were chatty. Their conversation quickly moved to the topic of their cell phone usage. Listening in, I learned that many had the same experience I had with my eldest daughter, Megan: They had exceeded their program's limits on either minutes or text messages (this, of course, was in the days when teenagers actually *talked* on their phones and when text messaging was limited). One girl told of how her mom handled it: She shut down her daughter's cell phone and made her pay the overage fee before her phone could be turned on again. I loved it! She was teaching her daughter restraint, responsibility, and integrity, helping her to learn how to be complete and fair.

When it comes to being fair, having integrity means that our authority will equal our responsibility. In other words, what we are in charge of must be equal to how we are held accountable. If we have a cell phone, we need to pay the bill.

Too often our children do not understand this concept. Contrast the above-mentioned mother's actions with many other parents who simply cover their child's mistake. When I called our cell phone carrier to understand why my daughter's portion of the bill was so large, the telephone company's representative burst out laughing and then said, "Excuse me, sir. Please pardon my outburst, but I've never seen this many text messages in one month." Guess who was about to get a lesson on authority equaling responsibility? If she was going to have the freedom of using a cell phone, she was going to be responsible for keeping the usage within the limits of our plan.

Allow me to give an example from the sporting world of NASCAR where authority did not equal responsibility. Following Carl Edwards's victory at the Las Vegas Motor Speedway in

March 2008, NASCAR officials examined the victorious driver's machine only to discover that a lid for the oil encasement
was missing. NASCAR officials penalized the driver and the
car's owner one hundred points. Crew chief Bob Osborne was
fined $100,000 and suspended six races for Edwards's car not
having all the parts.

Those NASCAR officials held Carl Edwards's team accountable for attempting to gain an unfair advantage by not including all the parts required by NASCAR. Edwards's machine was
lighter than those driven by his competitors, making it faster
while using less fuel. In other words, in this case they enforced
the inequitable balance of authority and responsibility. They
came down hard on Edwards's entire team as a lesson to others
who might try to do the same.

Integrity means that we make sure to have all the parts.

Our negotiations and conflicts always present us with an
opportunity to be fair, to have integrity, to give "full disclo-
sure." Regardless of the interaction we're faced with, we will
be tempted to be like that NASCAR crew chief and leave out
some of the required parts. If we are tempted to not pursue
integrity, we must confess our divided nature to God and
admit our wrongdoing.

Why is confession so important? I learned the hard way. For
years, I held in my unconfessed sins, and consequently, I was
held captive by the guilt of my transgressions. It wasn't until
I confessed my sins to a trusted and godly person that I discovered the freedom that only confession and forgiveness can
bring. The act of agreeing with the Almighty's perspective on
my sins of inequity by sharing them with another believer put
flesh on God and freed me from my guilt-forged prison.

Confess and Complete

We are called to love deeply, but differently. Equity means treating people fairly, but not the same. What about you? Are you completely fair to both sides whenever you experience conflict? Is there any conflict with a spouse, a child, a friend, a relative, a coworker, a customer, a vendor, a competitor, or even a fellow church member in which you have cut equity short? If so, confess and complete. Confess your shortfall to God, who will complete His work in you to be like Christ. Christ's work in you through the Holy Spirit will assist your attempts to find equity in your interpersonal conflicts.

Chapter 6

Justice

LISTENING TO OTHERS

In our study of Proverbs, we find that Solomon has uncovered four weights inside justice's measurement bag that we will study in sections throughout this chapter: *listening to others, equal opportunity, impartiality,* and *resolving conflict.* If we add to or subtract from one or more of these four weights, we elude justice in our relationships.

My good friend William Robbins is a professional indoor and beach volleyball player who owns the club where my daughters train. He stands six foot five inches with the muscular composition of an NFL player. Will experienced a unique pathway to justice in his personal life.

Will's parents divorced when he was two. Consequently, Will spent every other weekend with his dad, who taught him how to work with his hands. Together with his dad, Will learned about the construction trade, as his dad was an electrician at a large automotive supplier. The two of them also worked together to rebuild old International Scouts, off-road vehicles.

One day, when Will was about nine, he noticed several hundred-dollar bills in his dad's wallet after his dad had cashed his paycheck. Angry that his dad had made him shovel snow, Will decided to steal one thousand dollars from his father's billfold. Always the talker and the life of the party among his friends, he spent the money playing video games with his buddies at the local laundromat's arcade and buying them all the candy they could eat. When his dad discovered the missing cash, Will confessed. He was embarrassed when he had to tell his dad what he had done, and the consequences of disappointing his father were enough to stop him from ever doing it again. Will's dad showed him that in stealing the cash, Will was looking for significance and status in the eyes of his friends. Like all of us, he had a desire to tip the scales of justice and equity in his favor, regardless of the potential consequences.

Despite being a three-sport athlete during his junior year of high school, Will continued to prioritize his social acceptance. He drank heavily, partying hard to gain popularity with his peers. Further deafening himself to God, Will chose not to listen to his mother's warnings. He acted out of pure self-interest, listening only to those who would benefit him personally. In doing so, Will caused a lot of relational division and left a trail of unresolved conflict in his wake. Frustrated with his selfish actions, Will's mother had him live with his dad for the summer, knowing it would mean working hard manual labor. The quality time he shared with his dad during that summer led to Will living with him during his final year of high school.

Will joined club volleyball in Fort Wayne during his senior

year of high school, which garnered him a scholarship to play at Indiana University–Purdue University Fort Wayne for legendary coach Arnie Ball. During his freshman year at IPFW, Will started drinking every night at the local clubs and smoking pot, but he was still able to carry a 3.0 GPA. Will's sophomore year was different. Still continuing his hard-partying ways, he let the morning hangover win and skipped classes, which eventually made him academically ineligible to play.

Since he now had more time on his hands, Will discovered that he could finance his partying lifestyle by dealing drugs. What began as taking short trips to supply his using friends eventually led to Will running a major drug operation. With local authorities watching him as a suspected dealer, Will moved to another city where he decided to lie low and play volleyball until he could crack in to the increased economic opportunity offered by selling drugs to students at a larger college campus. He made a couple of connections and multiplied the dollar volume of drugs he had sold in Fort Wayne.

To stay ahead of local police, Will moved to a third city and started selling to students at an even larger university. But the pressure of living a different lifestyle than his mother had taught him weighed heavily on Will. He remembers, "I had to constantly stay drunk or high to avoid the regret that ate at my soul."

Finally, Will moved to Indianapolis, where he supplied high-profile businessmen with cocaine, crack, acid, and every other drug that was popular at the time. Although he would earn $1,000 to $5,000 per run, Will continued to struggle with remorse. But that didn't stop him from building and leading a theft ring that focused on stealing motorcycles and automobiles. To further fly under the radar and not have to face his own conscience, Will cut off all communication with his family. About seven years into this lifestyle of injustice, Will started thinking more and more about the big score: robbing a bank.

In November 2001, when a desperate high school friend and former college football star reconnected with Will, the big score grew inevitably closer. This man had been recently cut off from his family due to his drug abuse, his new car was about to be repossessed, and he was close to being evicted from his apartment. He asked Will if he was serious about robbing a bank. Will told him that he was all in.

After devising a foolproof plan and targeting a particular bank, Will and his friend fitted themselves with ski masks, camouflage, netting, zipped-up pullovers, and gloves. They drove to the bank and waited for the bank manager to open the doors. When the man arrived, Will grabbed the unsuspecting soul, dragged him inside the bank, and stole all of the cash on hand. Will and his partner forced a bank teller, who had unfortunately reported to work during the heist, to drive them outside the city where they had another vehicle hidden in the woods. They sped to a hotel and divided the cash—in total $200,600. They had finally made the big score and got away with it. Later that day they found out that their disguises had worked: the police were looking for a six-foot-two-inch black male, rather than someone fitting Will's physical description.

Ironically, Will had selfishly prayed before the bank robbery, as he grabbed the gold pendant fashioned like the head of Jesus that was hanging on his necklace, "God, if you let me get away with this, I will stop all this illegal activity, and I will be yours." With only his partner aware of the crime, Will's mind was at ease. He traveled to Costa Rica to relax and reflect. Now alone with his thoughts, Will tried listening to God. He recalls, "Lying on my hammock, for the first time I called out to God. I confessed that what I had been doing was wrong. I asked Him to show me His purpose for my life."

Will returned home to Indianapolis, where he later learned that he and his friends were under surveillance. While driving across town, Will noticed two unmarked cars following him. Unsure of who was tailing him, Will stopped at a gas station a few blocks from his friend's house where he had been heading to complete a drug transaction. As he peered down the street, Will noticed several police cars outside his planned destination. He turned his vehicle around and drove to the highway, watching in his mirrors as the unmarked cars followed him. He recalls, "Even if I slowed my car down to forty-five miles per hour, they still followed me."

For reasons that he still doesn't know, Will was not arrested that night. While parked near his house, he looked outside his Lincoln Navigator's sunroof and saw what he now recalls as a vision from God: It included a house with a beautiful front yard and a gorgeous wife, two things that because of his chosen lifestyle he never imagined he would have. That night, Will began to see the other side of his story. About five months later, Will's mom surrendered her life to Christ, and the two of them talked about it. Intrigued by the peace that she had found, Will started attending church with his mom. There he started to listen to the Holy Spirit's whispers.

Meanwhile, motivated by how flawlessly the first bank robbery had gone, Will's partner planned to rob another bank.

When he approached his former partner, Will told him about his oath to God to stop his life of injustice after the first heist. However, Will chose to be involved in the planning of the second robbery. Rather than being a two-man job, this plan led to more people being involved—people who talked. One of those worked at a club Will had frequented. This man told the FBI about Will's involvement in illegal activities. He was a six-foot-two-inch African American fitting the description of the suspect from the first robbery. Even though Will had been sensing God's still, small voice, he and his partner discussed killing the "snitch" and framing him with that crime. With a near-perfect plan in hand, Will struggled with whether he should conceal the truth, condemn this innocent man, and condone the actions of him and his partner.

Will was arrested about two weeks after the tailing incident. He sat in a jail cell for thirty days, where he decided to read the Bible, beginning with Genesis. He no longer wanted to be deaf to what God wanted in his life. Federal investigators released him for two weeks, during which time the Holy Spirit spoke strongly to Will. He was tormented over his choice—would he select Plan A and confess his crimes or Plan B where he would kill a man, framing him with the first bank robbery? After cursory conversations with his family, he chose Plan A. The FBI gathered enough evidence to arrest Will along with thirty-two of his associates. Will faced the stiffest potential penalties: twenty-seven years to life for his federal charges.

While Will was in jail on Easter Sunday, a last-minute substitute chaplain, Dr. Robert Cosby, arrived to give a sermon. Will and his bank-robbing partner decided to attend that service. After hearing the gospel message, Will and his partner wept, as they surrendered their lives to Christ. Will was now all in with God.

Dr. Cosby returned to the prison and discipled these two new converts each week. After his trial, Will was convicted of dealing drugs and committing armed robbery. He was sentenced to serve seven years in federal prison. There he continued to study the Word, lead Bible studies with fellow inmates, and work out. While in prison, he studied to become a certified fitness trainer.

After serving his sentence, Will was released, but he could not land a job as a convicted felon. Sensing the Holy Spirit's prompting, Will called Rev. Ron Gaston, who had advertised his Temple Total Fitness "building the temple from the inside out" in the local newspaper. Reverend Gaston had been a football player who'd been offered a full-ride scholarship to play for Michigan State University. However, he never made it to MSU—he lost his scholarship his senior year of high school from making poor personal choices. Now in his forties, Reverend Gaston wanted others to share the gift of grace that he had received. A full-time electrician and part-time pastor, Gaston had started an after-school program, Working Out with the Rev, where he invested physically and spiritually in the lives of his students. Will was a perfect fit to volunteer with the program.

Within a week and a half of being released from prison, Will received a second chance. Reverend Gaston gave Will the key to his two-thousand-square-foot gym, empowering him to help him with the students. He also entrusted Will to train his wife and her friends. Encouraged by Reverend Gaston's trust in him, Will thrived in his newfound career. Today, Will wears a different symbol around his neck: It's a sterling-silver copy of that key. It's a symbol of trust stemming from faith in the Savior who transformed Reverend Gaston's life and who would do the same for Will.

In a story that only God could design, Will met and married a girl like the one he had seen in his vision that night. Together they have a beautiful home and a ministry to thousands through their sixty-thousand-square-foot volleyball, tennis, and fitness facility. In Christ, a convicted felon now listens more than he talks, gives equal opportunity to both sides of every story, acts impartially, and resolves conflict. "God brought justice to my life, so I could bring His reconciliation to those I encounter. I have been transformed from a life of strife to one of reconciled relationships, as far as it depends on me."

How do you apply justice to your relationships when conflict has occurred? Our next pearl of wisdom is justice (see Prov. 1:3). Whereas the pearl of righteousness precedes the adjustments made in conflict, and the pearl of equity is often applied during adjustments in conflict, the pearl of justice is most predominant after adjustments in conflict. The word *justice* comes from the Latin root word that means "lawful." The concept of justice applies to God's moral law, to our civil laws, to our organizational rules, and to our relational boundaries. The repentant thief on the cross referred to *justice* as "getting what our deeds deserve" (Luke 23:41). When justice is served, the truth is revealed. The wicked get punished. The innocent go free.

The concept of justice is often represented using the image of scales. Solomon referenced how these scales affect those in the marketplace: "Honest scales and balances are from the LORD; all the weights in the bag are of his making" (Prov. 16:11). Similar to today, three thousand years ago merchants used scales to determine the weight and correlating market value of goods exchanged. The goods for sale were placed on one side of the scale while the merchant placed weights—often stones—in a bag on the other side to determine the value of the commodity. It didn't take long for a merchant to learn how to circumvent justice. When buying goods, the owner of the scales would secretly add to the weights in the measurement bag, thus receiving more product for less money. When selling goods, he would secretly subtract from the weights in the measurement bag, thus delivering less product for more money (see Lev. 19:35–36). Meanwhile the unsuspecting purchaser trusted that the measurement bag weighed what the seller had indicated.

Distressingly often, we are like that dishonest merchant. In applying the scales of justice to our interpersonal conflict, we are tempted to either secretly add to or subtract from the truth inside our weighing process in an effort to tip the scales in our favor. Our problem is fourfold: We speak more than we listen; we act on one side of the story; we are partial to the people who benefit us; and we promote division. The result is injustice, a situation in which the truth is concealed, the wicked go free, and the innocent are punished. However, the God who is just requires that we measure justly. Jesus reinforced this idea when He said: "With the measure you use, it will be measured to you" (Matt. 7:2).

Unjust measurement catches us in the most unsuspecting places. I remember one day when I was a young kid, my dad took me to the grocery store with him. I remember it because this was a rare occasion. Mom usually did all the shopping, because whenever Dad went to the grocery store, the total bill was astronomical. My dad is a self-diagnosed food addict, so everything that looked good to him in the store found its way into our cart.

Standing in front of the meat counter, I was about to learn a valuable lesson. After ordering steaks that cost about five dollars per pound, Dad watched as the manager carefully unrolled the paper and placed it on the scales before weighing the filets. Then in his auctioneer's voice he proclaimed, "Look! They're selling that paper for five dollars a pound!"

With all due respect to the Auburn meat man, too many of us are slipping our paper-thin, concealed, selfish adjustment into our interpersonal conflict management. In other words, we're weighing the factors in our favor and are unjustly selling them to unsuspecting parties. More often than not, this kind of injustice is simply a factor of us not listening well.

Let's look at one example. After selling his business, a successful entrepreneur went on an extravagant spending spree. One of the items he purchased was a beautiful Hawker jet. The aircraft was incredible: The interior was plush, the seats were oversized, and the bathroom offered plenty of room to move around.

However, after flying it to several cities, a funny thing happened. With his Hawker parked at a fixed-base operator in the southern United States, this business mogul was introduced to an even bigger jet: a Challenger, one of the largest, fastest, most luxurious private aircraft available. While one of the world's best jet marketers described the details of this flying masterpiece to our impulsive entrepreneur, including its dimensions, the impatient owner of the Hawker interrupted him with an abrupt, "I'll take it." Easiest sale ever made; the jet dealer must have been overjoyed.

After working out the deal points and trading in his Hawker, this businessman climbed into his new multimillion-dollar purchase. The trip home to his local airport seemed to last only seconds as the owner of the Challenger became acquainted with his new airship. Shortly after the wheels touched down, the happy purchaser skipped off the plane, made a pit stop, and glanced back to a perplexing picture: His new plane was too big to fit in his hangar, which was the largest available at his home airport. Two objects could not occupy the same space at the same time. Unfortunately, this entrepreneur had never been one for details.

Knowing this story, if you were to drive by the airport where this crown jewel of an aircraft sits outside, susceptible to the winter elements, you would think, *Listening actually has dollar value.*

When it comes to listening with equal opportunity, we rarely give it. Too often we are willing to listen only to the people who can benefit our position. I remember having this conversation with a few of our basketball players in the weight room one day. They agreed that if a friend tells us something, we believe it; but if someone who's not a friend tells us the same thing, we fail to receive it as truth. Left to ourselves, we fail to listen to others and instead promote division in our relationships. Consequently, we function with a load of unresolved conflict. When we assume instead of listen, when we make snap judgments before getting the full story, we unwittingly promote injustice.

But God tells us that justice is of paramount value for our relationships: "To do what is right and just is more acceptable to the LORD than sacrifice" (Prov. 21:3). "More acceptable" implies using a weighting system in our interactions that begins with God: No amount of outward activity can outweigh what is truly right and just. Jesus taught that justice is one of the weightier components of the law, a component that leads to and is inseparable from sacrificial giving.

As with wisdom, justice begins when we humbly pursue God—we don't insert any paper-thin, concealed, selfish adjustments: "Evil men do not understand justice, but those who seek the LORD understand it fully" (Prov. 28:5). Justice begins with the Lord because He is just. Consequently, the indwelling of His Spirit requires that we as believers act justly in our relationships. David said that when we humble our hearts to the Lord, He leads us in dealing with justice. A man after God's own heart, King David administered justice and righteousness for all his people. David's son Solomon humbly asked God to give him wisdom so that he could institute justice into his conflict management, and God granted his wise request.

The first weight in the measurement bag of justice is the one we've been examining in this section: listening. Solomon wrote: "He who answers before listening—that is his folly and his shame" (Prov. 18:13). In order to act justly, we must listen beyond the surface meaning of the words spoken and look to the underlying interests in the heart of each person involved in our conflict.

Too often in our interpersonal conflict, we are so quick to speak that we miss out on the weightier component of communication: listening. When we speak too hastily, we act on less than all the information that we need to make a decision, including the core interests that are resident in the other person's heart. When we fail to listen, our counterparts recognize this. Consequently, they discount our words, often hardening their hearts to justice as well. Someone who doesn't feel heard or understood is going to be less likely to listen to another person's part of the story. That's when communication breaks down, and community is decreased.

Listening is vital to bringing justice to our relationships because God listens to us. God hears our prayers for justice. It is imperative that we listen to God in return. Therefore, those of us who act with true justice in mind not only listen horizontally to what others are saying in conflict; we also listen vertically to what the Holy Spirit is saying to us. Jesus lived such a life—one of bidirectional listening. Listening is one of the primary acts of *love* that Jesus defined as the greatest vertical and horizontal commandment of the Law. In Christ, we can wisely listen both vertically to God the Father and horizontally to others, resisting the desire to add to or subtract from justice.

To picture this idea, think about earbuds and iPhones. We can't listen to a playlist if we don't put the earbuds in our ears. The same is true for interpersonal conflict management. If we refuse to be intentional about listening, then we become deaf to the desires of others, including God. All the depth of understanding that exists on the "iPhone" of the other person's heart is useless to our conversation unless we intentionally plug in and are quiet long enough to listen.

This kind of deafness often occurs in marital conflict. Usually husbands are out to fix a situation quickly so that the conflict can be resolved, whereas wives usually want their husbands to listen to and feel with them. Wise is the husband who learns to hold his words, who listens by recognizing his wife's nonverbal cues, holds her hand, and restates in his own words what she is feeling so that she can confirm what's going on in her own experience. In marriage and in every other inter-personal exchange, listening is paramount to wise conflict management.

In addition, when we listen, we receive credibility for the time when we finally speak. My pastor of twenty-two years was an astute listener. Listening was a characteristic of his personality, his heart, and his psychological acumen. I went to him on two separate occasions to help me discern wisdom for the choices I had in two conflict situations. Both times, I talked for almost an hour as he listened intently to every word I shared. He never once interrupted. His eyes were focused on me, but he did not stare. His body posture confirmed to me that he was paying attention. His facial expression and verbal-izations communicated that he understood what I was saying. His hand gestures revealed his interest. Only after he heard everything I had to say did he offer his advice—which I was eager to hear because I knew he had listened. He had earned my trust by putting in the hard work of listening carefully before speaking.

Too often we answer before listening, seeking to be under-stood before we fully understand. When we do, our counter-part discounts our advice because we have not heard the entire set of facts. To put it succinctly, *people listen to people who listen.* Tommy Franks, retired United States Army general, revealed one of the secrets to his successful leadership as follows: "I lis-ten more than I speak."

Our horizontal listening improves when we develop our vertical listening. Since I first decided to apply what I learned in the Bible to my conflict, I have read through the entire Bible every year. Every day, when I put my Bible down, I ask God, "How does this apply to my life today?" Pondering this question and allowing the Spirit of God to lead me has become the most impactful few minutes of my day. As I pray for help, I begin to see my tasks through the lens of a particular verse and have found that it even becomes part of my vocabulary on that day.

When I began this discipline and experienced the blessing that it brought, I eagerly anticipated the wisdom that this practice would reveal in my business, in my family, and in my social interactions. Consequently, I sought to become a rapid Holy Spirit responder, tuned in to His promptings. This began a pattern of bidirectional listening that brought justice to the conflict in my relationships. To this day even though I'm out of the business, I'm convinced that this Spirit-inspired skill was instrumental in resolving many after-auction conflict situations that saved the company countless dollars in legal fees. I can tell you from personal experience, listening adds real value to conflict management.

Listen to Others

When facing a conflict, your goal should be to *listen to others at least as much, if not more than, you speak.* If you are typically quick to speak, build a new habit of jotting down your thoughts while the other person is speaking, rather than interrupting because you fear that you'll lose your train of thought. In order to accomplish true bidirectional listening, summarize what you're hearing and ask questions that reveal motives, interests, or desires while you maintain vertical sensitivity to the Holy Spirit. Maintain eye contact as well as heart contact, and use body language, facial expressions, and gestures that communicate understanding. While active horizontal listening repeats their words in yours, active vertical listening reveals His Word in yours.

EQUAL OPPORTUNITY

The second weight in the measurement bag of justice is equal opportunity. One of the biggest mistakes we make in not bringing justice to our interpersonal conflict is acting on only one side of the story. This behavior further hardens our spiritual hearts: our emotions flare, our thoughts wander, our judgments rush, and our prayers miss the mark. In doing so, we internally add to or subtract from the measurement bag of justice in order to tip the scales in our favor. This leads to concealing the truth, condemning the innocent, and condoning the guilty.

Wisdom calls us to a more complete standard: "The first to present his case seems right till another comes forward and questions him" (Prov. 18:17). When we're seeking justice, we're wise to get both sides of the story. Justice allows equal opportunity for each party in a conflict to share their side of the story before making any judgment.

In our pursuit of the other side of the story, wisdom warrants that we do not betray confidence, we do not condemn, and we do not cut anyone short. Equal opportunity flows from the heart of God in Christ.

Back to our iPhone illustration, let's look at the pause button. It has two vertical lines, but if we turn that pause symbol ninety degrees, then it becomes an equal sign. When it comes to equal opportunity within conflict, we need to pause, turn, and listen to the other side of the story before we make any choices or judgments.

Additionally, we must be positively inclined to hear both parts when exploring opposing positions on an issue; this applies even to people who are on our side of the issue! President Ronald Reagan quipped, "The Eleventh Commandment is 'Speak no evil about a person from your own political party.'" Too often, we speak ill even about fellow believers, community members, coworkers, teammates, or our own family. This stifles equal opportunity.

I'll admit I've done this in the past, but I work hard to try to assume the positive when I encounter opposing positions. For example, a high school student shared derogatory information with me about a teacher that seemed to be misguided. "I know that teacher," I said, "and what you described does not reflect his heart. There has to be some explanation. I encourage you to get the other side of the story."

Reacting to only one side of the story is dangerous, but doing so often flows from our own selfish interests. My dad told a story about how one day he was sitting in an attorney's office with his client. The client shared a fact about the opposing side in a real estate closing. The attorney, with a shocked look on his face, flung his wheeled desk chair back into the wall and shouted, "You're kidding me!" in a show of support for his client's position. My dad's eyes turned to the wall behind the attorney's desk chair where he noticed many dings, scuffs, and gouges in the plaster. This wasn't the first time this lawyer reacted in this fashion. His common practice was to continually react to one side of the story in order to keep his clients paying fees.

My uncle Derald practiced law a different way. He counseled his clients to consider equal opportunity when they encountered conflict, knowing that the justice system would operate in a similar way. I know this from personal experience, because in every conflict I consulted him on, whether relational or legal, he encouraged me to see the other side of the story.

At Uncle Derald's funeral, a banker shared with me that his financial institution had been owed a large sum of money from a customer who had filed bankruptcy. Uncle Derald was the borrower's attorney in the proceedings. The banker's words reverberated in my spirit: "It was the only bankruptcy where we, as a creditor, were made whole. We were paid the entire outstanding balance because your uncle understood the justice system." Uncle Derald sought equal opportunity in conflict to garner both sides of the story. His law practice, as a result, had a reputation for honesty and integrity. God's wisdom shone through in his life and work.

Get Both Sides of the Story

Keep your thoughts, choices, feelings, and prayers surrendered to the Holy Spirit. Wisely gather the rest of the story from all parties involved in the conflict. In doing so, do not betray confidence, do not condemn, and do not cut anyone short.

IMPARTIALITY

The third weight in the measurement bag of justice is impartiality. "It is not good to be partial to the wicked or to deprive the innocent of justice" (Prov. 18:5; cf. 24:23). In our frailty, we are tempted to be partial or one-sided—that is, incomplete with justice. We favor one side of a conflict over another because we have something to gain or lose in the process. At risk might be our time, talent, or treasure—things that may potentially satisfy our primary desires for significance, contentment, security, and control.

Desiring the gain or fearing the loss that results in partiality flows from a heart of pride. By contrast, a heart of humility seeks the impartiality of justice that hears both sides of the conflict. God said that partiality perverts justice—it deceitfully adds to or subtracts from justice's measurement bag.

Partiality often results from some kind of bribe—some benefit promised by a person on one side of a conflict to one judging, in an effort to influence the outcome. The Bible says that a bribe toward partiality "blinds the eyes of the wise and twists the words of the righteous" (Deut. 16:19). Whereas justice is blind and impartial to the conflicting parties, injustice is blind toward true wisdom and true justice. Partiality leads to twisted words that pervert justice. Solomon said: "A wicked man accepts a bribe in secret to pervert the course of justice" (Prov. 17:23).

Wisdom allows us to practice interpersonal conflict management that is impartial and just. Solomon wrote that one of those practices is to be cautious of a corrupt witness: "A corrupt witness mocks at justice, and the mouth of the wicked gulps down evil" (Prov. 19:28). The New American Standard Bible refers to this witness as "rascally." Literally, such a witness adds no value to justice because he or she is partial.

God is impartial. God's heart desires that justice reach even the poor who cannot afford a defense—the powerless who engender and are themselves the victims of favoritism. Solomon's "Thirty Sayings of the Wise" teaches: "Do not exploit the poor because they are poor and do not crush the needy in court, for the Lord will take up their case and will plunder those who plunder them" (Prov. 22:22–23). At the same time, true justice does not show favoritism toward the poor in a lawsuit. Neither does it side with the crowd, displaying favoritism to the majority by doing what is merely popular apart from justice. Because God is impartial, justice is impartial. And in Christ, God's impartiality is available to all who will trust the Savior for their salvation (see Acts 10:34).

Now, let's refer back to our iPhone illustration. Impartiality is incomplete apart from justice. Will our iPhones work if they are incomplete? If we start removing parts from the iPhone, it will stop playing music or videos; it will refuse to display photos or give us access to our contacts. The same holds true with justice in our relationships: When we are partial to one side or the other, our understanding of the issues is incomplete, and true justice cannot be served.

Impartiality is the underlying foundation of our nation's justice system. My uncle David, another wise attorney like my uncle Derald, told me once that one of his Indiana University law professors said, "We are a land of partiality toward ideas, not toward people." In the United States' justice system, justice is to be evenly applied to all parties without any display of favoritism.

What would our personal interactions look like if we did the same? An impartial attitude can transform our relationships. When we are careful to listen and reflect impartiality, our very demeanor can motivate others to be impartial as well. God's idea is that we apply justice mercifully. Whereas mercy without justice slides into license, justice without mercy escalates into condemnation. I watched as a wise person delivered both justice and mercy to a high school student after he made a foolish decision. The administrator said words to this young man that I will never forget: "It's not necessarily these consequences or the rebuilding tools we are offering that will bring restoration to your life. Rather, it will be *your attitude toward them* that will make a difference."

Be Impartial

When it comes to interpersonal conflict, do you tend to be one-sided? Do you favor a particular kind of person or behavior over another? Do you find yourself either giving or receiving relational bribes? Have you ever allowed a corrupt witness to sway your judgment without carefully weighing both sides of the issue? If so, you are adding to or subtracting from justice's measurement bag in order to receive more for less or to deliver less for more. Each day during the next month, read Solomon's Psalm of Justice—Psalm 72. Let the words sink into your soul, allowing them to assimilate into your life. This will help you to be impartial in your interpersonal conflicts, as the presence of Christ in you brings justice to your relationships.

CONFLICT RESOLUTION

The fourth weight in the measurement bag of justice is conflict resolution. Too often, we are quick to condemn another party when we are wronged. This creates division rather than resolving the conflict. Jesus warned of the adverse effects on one who harbors condemnation.

"There is deceit in the hearts of those who plot evil, but joy for those who promote peace" (Prov. 12:20). Justice, or true conflict resolution, promotes peace. "By justice a king gives a country stability, but one who is greedy for bribes tears it down" (Prov. 29:4). Justice upholds peace through conflict resolution that brings joy for the righteous, but terror for the wicked (see Prov. 21:15). While we are not guaranteed peace in all of our relationships, conflict resolution must be our goal. The apostle Paul said: "If it is possible, as far as it depends on you, live at peace with everyone" (Rom. 12:18). Complete and lasting peace might not be possible because it takes two to agree on that kind of peace, but as far as it depends on us, we must seek peace in our attempts to resolve conflict. A favorite saying of Uncle Derald's that was distributed at his funeral read, "I can only control fifty percent of a relationship."

As we've seen in previous chapters, justice resolves conflict in part by objectively gathering all necessary information. Solomon counseled: "The heart of the discerning acquires knowledge; the ears of the wise seek it out" (Prov. 18:15). That information might shed light on more than one possible resolution to the conflict. Three thousand years ago, when a judge decided that all possible outcomes to a conflict were equal, a lot was cast: "Casting the lot settles disputes and keeps strong opponents apart" (Prov. 18:18). In the end, righteous conflict resolution was the goal.

Such conflict resolution brings God into the interpersonal conflict. "Many seek an audience with a ruler, but it is from the LORD that man gets justice" (Prov. 29:26). Gideon concluded: "The LORD is Peace" (Judg. 6:24), and we know that Christ is the ultimate embodiment of God's peace. It is Christ in us who empowers us to justly resolve conflict, bringing peace to our relationships.

Uncle Derald was known as one who brought peace to his relationships through conflict resolution. After his death, the Indiana State Bar Association honored him with a memorial service in a DeKalb County courtroom where the judges and his peers gathered. Just before the ceremony commenced, my attorney cousin leaned over to me and said, "Derald didn't see the inside of this place very often. He always found a way to resolve conflict."

Resolve Conflict

Are you known as a person who leaves conflict unresolved? Do you have strife in your life because unresolved conflict is lingering in any of your relationships? Is there a friend or a sibling who you haven't spoken to for years because of this? Pray for the Holy Spirit's guidance; read the aforementioned verses relating to resolving conflict; seek wise counsel; and then, if possible, as far as it depends on you, wisely resolve the conflict to restore the relationship.

Chapter 7

Wise Behavior

CONVINCING

In this chapter we'll examine the benefits of wise behavior that, when applied consistently, affect every area of our lives.

Larry Lance grew up in Centreville, Michigan. Both of his parents were alcoholics, so consequently, in his early years, Larry endured a lot of physical and verbal abuse. To counter the abuse, Larry chose sports as his outlet. He golfed, played football, and excelled in basketball. In his senior year, his basketball team went 21–3, losing in the state quarterfinals to a Detroit team who went on to win the state championship.

After that loss, Larry's father met him at the front door of their home with two suitcases and said, "You're eighteen. You're a man now, and from here on out, you're on your own." With high school classes still to finish, Larry called a friend to pick him up. He got in the car with all his belongings and told his buddy what had just happened. At the first stop sign, Larry broke down crying. The thought that kept running through his mind was that he had never once heard the words *I love you* from either of his parents.

Larry graduated from high school but turned down scholarships to play sports in college. Instead, he tended bar and took a job in a factory. Desperate for attention, acceptance, affection, and approval, Larry cared only about making as much money as possible. During that time, he took his first drink and also experimented with marijuana, hashish, acid, and narcotics, eventually becoming his small town's drug dealer. One of Larry's customers was his younger brother, who began using at age fifteen. This young man dropped out of high school, was arrested, and spent a third of his life in and out of prison. People in Larry's small town discovered the damage he was doing. His foolish behavior killed any credibility he had with his neighbors and the larger community.

To fill the void in his life, Larry became a runner and participated in three adult softball leagues while he continued to work, party, and deal drugs. One night at 3:00 a.m. after Larry closed down the bar, his former assistant high school football coach, Coach Hartong, was waiting for him. He invited Larry and his friends to participate in a softball tournament the following weekend. A little dazed at seeing his coach at 3:00 a.m., Larry accepted.

Larry and his friends played in the tournament and had a great time at the cookout afterward. Later a man pulled out a guitar and played for the three hundred people in attendance. Then Coach Hartong, a part-time preacher, offered a five-minute sermon that was directed at Larry and his friends about their need for Christ.

Larry broke down, as did his friends. At the prompting of his coach, Larry closed his eyes. Coach Hartong prayed for them. When Larry opened his eyes, the three hundred participants were, amazingly, gone. Now alone with the three young men, Coach Hartong pointed his finger at Larry and said, "Larry, what you are doing to the kids of this community has to stop. You need Jesus Christ as your personal Savior, and you need Him now."

Larry responded with the two words that would change his life: "Yes, sir!" The three men surrendered their lives to Christ and listened to their coach's instructions for the next hour. Unbeknownst to them, the church had targeted Larry and his friends; in faith they had planned this worship and evangelism event for an entire year, including a plan to provide a trailer where the three men would stay the night before being baptized the next morning. As Coach Hartong led his three new converts up a hill, Larry saw the three hundred church people standing on the other side, waiting for the young men to return. The large crowd took turns hugging the young men, celebrating the decision they had just made.

Grace Weaver, an elderly lady whose son had grown up with Larry, hugged him and said words he heard for the first time in his twenty-one years: "*I love you* in the name of Jesus." As Larry fell to the ground sobbing, Grace knelt down next to him and told him why this day was such a blessing for her. "When you were in kindergarten, I asked your teacher for a list of the students in your class. Larry, I've been praying for you for seventeen and a half years." Then she repeated those powerful words, "I love you in the name of Jesus." Grace pulled out a hymnal and said, "The Lord told me that when this day came, we were going to sing all four verses of hymn number 206: 'He

Lives.'" On the side of a hill, with three hundred new friends, Larry and his newly saved buddies sang all four verses of their very first hymn.

Larry and his friends spent the night in the trailer and were baptized the next day. Coach Hartong then asked Larry to go with him on the speaking circuit, where he would share his testimony in many different locations, including five thousand people one afternoon at the county fairgrounds.

Coach and others discipled Larry and his friends. Six months later, they sent Larry to Huntington University, a Christian liberal arts school. At the end of one particular semester, Larry walked into the bursar's office to pay his $9,000 tuition bill. When the clerk brought up Larry's account, she said, "Some people back home love you very much. Your bill is paid in full." Larry never had to pay for any of his tuition.

After graduating from Huntington University, where he had become involved with Youth for Christ, Larry joined the evangelistic organization full-time, raising his own support and building the Fort Wayne chapter of YFC into one of the largest in the world. He has served in that community for decades, reaching thousands of teens for Christ each year.

Larry eventually led both his brother and his father to Christ.

As a result of the convincing, commonsense, courageous, and credible efforts of Coach Hartong and the leaders in his community, Larry has spent almost his entire adult life memorizing Bible verses and using them to draw teenage kids to Christ. Larry has applied the Word of God to all his circumstances, inspiring countless young people with common sense. He has courageously shared his experience of the world and of the Word with innumerable parents of teens and supporters of Youth for Christ. Through it all, Larry has given all the credit to God, making him one of the most credible leaders in youth ministry today. Christ has multiplied Coach Hartong's wise behavior—the behavior that reached Larry as a twenty-one-year-old has now been passed on to thousands of other people, many of whom are paying it forward today.

In conflict management, is your behavior wise or foolish? A key indicator of the answer to this question lies in how we utilize the Bible's teachings when two objects attempt to occupy the same space at the same time in our lives. Proverbs demonstrates a direct correlation between wise behavior in conflict management and how we assimilate the Word of God into our lives.

One of the main purposes of Proverbs is to give the reader instruction in wise behavior (see Prov. 1:3 NASB). Wise behavior takes effective communication and allows it to become powerfully persuasive. It delves into the unseen, bringing wisdom into the hearts of others.

In the book of Proverbs, Solomon pleaded: "My son, do not forget my teaching, but keep my commands in your heart, for they will prolong your life many years and bring you prosperity. Let love and faithfulness never leave you; bind them around your neck, write them on the tablet of your heart. Then you will win favor and a good name in the sight of God and man" (Prov. 3:1–4). "A good name" is translated from the same root as the Hebrew word for "wise behavior" (*sakal*). When we learn wisdom, it sinks deep into our hearts and becomes evident in our actions. This leads to wise behavior that is demonstrated both vertically and horizontally.

Whereas someone who practices foolish behavior trusts in their own words, which tend to be unconvincing, nonsensical, fearful, and lacking credibility, someone who practices wise behavior acts in the opposite manner by trusting in and following the Word of God.

Proverbs tells us that wise behavior has four characteristics: *convincing*, *common sense*, *courageous*, and *credible*. First, wise behavior is convincing. This persuasiveness comes from our speech. To be convincing with our words, we must first have wisdom in our hearts. Solomon taught: "The heart of the wise instructs his mouth, and adds persuasiveness to his lips" (Prov. 16:23 NASB). Proverbs precedes this verse with: "He who gives attention to the word will find good, and blessed is he who trusts in the LORD" (Prov. 16:20 NASB). The word translated as "attention" is derived from the same Hebrew word as *wise behavior*. When we give attention to wise instruction, we begin to become convincing in our speech. Our most powerful source of wise instruction is, of course, the Word of God. The more we get into it, the more it gets into us.

Solomon said that the path of life for wise behavior leads upward (see Prov. 15:24). This journey upward also transforms us inwardly. When God renovates our hearts, He revolutionizes our words and they become convincing. Solomon illustrated the value of the right word spoken at the right time when he wrote: "A word aptly spoken is like apples of gold in settings of silver" (Prov. 25:11; cf. 15:23).

My uncle Derald was the wisest person I knew. As a result, I feared confessing my foolish behavior to him. But instead of condemning my behavior, Uncle Derald chose to use it as an opportunity to teach me about grace. Grace does not necessarily remove a natural consequence, nor does it always offer tough love to rough up a sinner. Rather, grace acknowledges the offense but then provides tools for success.

Uncle Derald taught me that my most powerful tool for success was the Word of God, that it was my sword to fight off temptation (see Eph. 6:17). Accompanied by a clear understanding of the natural consequences for ignoring the Word with foolish behavior, Uncle Derald graciously equipped me to study the Bible for myself. The words he chose convinced me: "Mitchell, the one thing that will dramatically transform any man's life is studying the Bible for himself. What about you? What are you going to do?" This wise perspective taught me to integrate the Bible into my speech and in turn become more convincing.

When I called one of my first auctions in 1983, Grandpa Russell taught me one of life's most valuable lessons about becoming convincing. It came at the expense of a curio cabinet he asked me to sell while we stood on the front porch of a small Hoosier town home.

I had watched Dad and Grandpa auctioneer more times than I could count, so I knew that I needed to move the auction quickly in order to sell the final items at a decent hour—time management, inventory management, and knowledge of market values are marks of a seasoned auctioneer.

Russell had placed me right in the center of the action in this little town. My sense was that, with all my years of watching my family work their magic, I could do this. These people were about to witness a master class in auctioneering! I stepped up to the invisible podium, and my voice cut through the public address system, echoing into the air, "One hundred dollars. Now one fifty."

I paused and awaited the crowd's reaction. Nothing. "Anybody else want to bid?" I called.

More silence. I was not sure how to respond, so I rushed to close the sale. That's when Russell abruptly stopped me. I didn't know it at the time, but this was all part of the show. Two hundred bidders watched as he shouted, "Wait, Mitchell! Is there anything else you can say about this curio that might enhance the bid?"

I stood there stunned; I never suspected that Russell would step in.

"It has beautiful woodwork," I replied.

I waited for a response. Nothing happened. So I continued.

"It would probably cost thousands of dollars to build today?" I said sheepishly. Russell leaned forward and loudly instructed, "Don't tell me. Tell them."

In that instant, it was as if a switch turned on inside, a light so bright that it illuminated my soul. It resembled the flash of lightning that struck overhead one year at the Indy 500. My voice grew stronger. Much like a preacher, I became the curio cabinet evangelist.

"This curio cabinet has beautiful woodwork! It would cost thousands of dollars to handcraft today!"

As the seconds passed and I saw the crowd responding to me, my confidence level jumped. "One fifty, now two hundred! Two hundred, now two fifty!"

My words shot out in rapid succession. The crowd's response made my adrenaline flow. I had arrived! Or so I thought.

Before I wrapped up the sale, Russell interrupted me for the second time.

"Mitchell, wait! Is there anything else you can say about this cabinet that might encourage them to bid higher?"

In that split second, he sent my mojo crashing. My moment of glory was gone, and a tight knot in my stomach replaced my confidence. What else was I supposed to say? Russell leaned in closely and crooned, "If I can get you convinced, I can get them convinced." He stepped back and waited patiently.

"The beveled glass is quite incredible," I replied. "Really, I have not seen anything like it." With Russell's nod of approval, I knew I was back in the game. I stepped closer to the crowd and boldly proclaimed, "The beveled glass is incredible! I've never seen anything like it!"

The crowd came alive again as hands were raised. "Two fifty, now three hundred! Three hundred, now three fifty!"

Numbers fired from my lips. In a matter of minutes, Russell had made me believe I could be the world's greatest auctioneer! Okay, maybe in retrospect not the greatest, seeing as we were only selling a single cabinet. Regardless, I was ready to bring down the hammer with such force that the crowd would erupt in celebration; I could already picture myself on the front page of my local newspaper, *The Evening Star.* I gripped the gavel in anticipation, eyes ablaze, waiting for just the right moment.

I glanced toward Russell and watched him raise his hand for the third time. "Mitchell, wait, wait! Isn't there something else you can say to increase the bid?"

I was frustrated, angry, and bewildered. I was seconds away from victory, yet now I had grown to hate the curio cabinet. This cursed cabinet was the one thing that stood between failure and my future as an auctioneer. Russell was not making it any easier. Why was he doing this? I wondered.

I pulled myself together, stepped back, and this time caught him by surprise. "Wow, look at the feet. I never noticed them before. They're hand carved. No one does that today; it's too expensive."

This time I did not wait for his response. I waved my hand high above my head and cried, "Four fifty, five hundred, now five fifty. I have five fifty, now six hundred! Six hundred, thank you! Who'll give me seven?"

Then I went in for the altar call: "Eight hundred, eight fifty, now nine hundred, nine fifty! Who'll give a thousand dollars?" A man standing near the front of the crowd raised his hand.

I pretended not to see Russell, waited a few seconds, and finally turned to him and asked over the public address system, "Can I sell it now?"

"Yes!" he shouted, satisfied that the infamous curio cabinet was about to trade hands for one thousand dollars.

"Sold!" I declared, as I completed my first step toward becoming a seasoned auctioneer.

Now, let's review that important line that forever changed my life: "If I can get you convinced, I can get them convinced." Too many of us are selling out our lives for two hundred or three hundred when God's intent is for us to learn our true worth and push for that thousand. Regarding our passion to convincingly communicate God to other people, I really think He's saying to each of us, "If I can get you convinced, I can get them convinced." Our pursuit of God's Word is a potent tool that empowers us to move from unconvincing to convincing.

My study of the Bible so radically convinced me of God's

relevance to my life that I chose to sell my company to continue to delve into the Word in order to use it to connect others with Christ. However, before I made that decision, I considered whether it was a misuse of my gifts. You see, I was brought up to think big, to conquer the world. So I shared my intentions with Uncle Derald. "I'm thinking of giving the rest of my life to the study of the Bible," I confessed.

"What would be wrong with that?" he confirmed.

What about you? Are you convinced of the power of the Word of God? It is available to you and me today. It is relevant to every aspect of our lives, and it will make our words convincing. If I can get you convinced, I can get them convinced.

Be Convincing

Take a journey upward in order to change inwardly. Memorize a verse or passage from Proverbs. Allow wise behavior to sink into your heart through the power of the Word.

COMMON SENSE

Second, wise behavior includes common sense. The word *wise* stems from the same Hebrew word that is translated as "wise behavior." Solomon said that the fool lacks this commodity (see Eccles. 10:3). To have common sense, we must apply Scripture to our lives. To "apply" carries the sense of "to make sticky." Wise behavior makes the Word "sticky" to our lives. The result of that kind of stickiness is common sense.

Wise behavior applies the Word of God to our work. Solomon wrote: "He who gathers crops in summer is a wise son, but he who sleeps during harvest is a disgraceful son" (Prov. 10:5). When I was steeped in foolish behavior, my business life was void of common sense. One expression of this occurred when I had allowed our cashiers to pay a seller before receiving confirmed funds from a buyer. This created a cash flow problem for my company. You might ask why I would do such a thing. The reason in this instance was fear. I was afraid that sellers would stop consigning vehicles to our auctions if they did not receive quick payment. At the same time, I was afraid that buyers would stop bidding if I demanded clear funds on sale day. Essentially, I had made my business into a banking enterprise, paying out funds to sellers and covering for my buyers. My company was not set up to manage that kind of cash flow.

As I meditated on the priceless pearls of wisdom from Proverbs, I discovered that my behavior lacked common sense. So I applied the Word to my work life and stopped this foolish activity. When I was honest with my sellers and buyers about the transactions, I was amazed at the level of understanding my sellers had when I asked them to wait for payment until we received good funds for their vehicles. I was also amazed at how buyers made arrangements to pay for their purchases before they took delivery on their newly acquired cars and titles. Common sense actually helped our business—not merely because it virtually eliminated these kinds of cash flow problems, but also because it forced us to take greater responsibility in communicating clear expectations to buyers and sellers. I discovered firsthand that working smart was good common sense, as it put less stress on my employees and on me as a business owner.

Wise behavior applies the Word of God to our communication.
Solomon said: "When words are many, sin is not absent, but
he who holds his tongue is wise" (Prov. 10:19). Using restraint
is common sense. This practice of holding my tongue not only
changed my business, it changed me. I began to treat people
differently. Rather than seeing every unscheduled encounter
with another person as an interruption, I began to see each
one as a divine appointment, and chose my words more wisely
when conflict occurred. I realized that if I were going to communicate in ways that built up my staff, I would have to think
in ways that encouraged them. As God began to root out the
foolish negative choices, thoughts, feelings, and prayers from
my heart, He also rooted out the foolish words from my lips. I
found that holding my tongue was common sense.

Wise behavior applies the Word of God to our choice of an audience.
Solomon said: "Do not speak to a fool, for he will scorn the wisdom of your words" (Prov. 23:9). Another benefit of making the
wisdom of the Bible sticky to my life was that it allowed me to
avoid conversations with people who acted foolishly. I worked on
establishing boundaries with these kinds of people. When they
used coarse language, I asked them to stop. If their visit was unpro-
ductive and constituted a poor use of my time, I politely but firmly
cut the meeting short. If they baited me toward a heated exchange
where my words might be used against me or others, I didn't bite.
I learned that anticipating these conversations by preparing for
them and avoiding them when I could was simply common sense.

Wise behavior applies the Word of God to our perspective. Following this line of thinking, Solomon taught: "A man's wisdom
gives him patience; it is to his glory to overlook an offense"
(Prov. 19:11). Overlooking an offense is common sense.

As I've already confessed earlier in this book, I have a perfectionistic streak. In my business, my perfectionism carried with it a lack of patience. Pursuing wise behavior meant that I needed to apply what the Bible said about patience. Confessing my hard-hearted condition meant moving away from perfectionism and toward excellence. A perfectionist attempts to be flawless, but one who works with excellence does the best they can with what they have. In my business I needed to move toward excellence, striving toward positive outcomes and allowing myself grace in the process when my best efforts fell short.

Excellence features two components: authenticity and wisdom. While high expectations are definitely a part of striving for excellence, the perfectionist has a blind spot to the fact that everyone and everything in this life will fall short—except God. Whereas perfectionism implies flawlessness, excellence is authentic in that it recognizes the truth about one's strengths and shortcomings and uses wisdom, which is the intersection of God's righteousness with street smarts, to shrewdly do the best with what one has. Jesus encouraged his followers to strive for excellence rather than perfectionism.

I learned that *perfect* in the Scriptures means "complete" in the sense that Christ completes us. He fills our gaps and makes us whole. In exchanging my perfectionistic tendencies for a striving toward excellence, I started to overlook the minor offenses committed by my staff. As a result, one of the people who meant the most to me in my business, my assistant of many years, began to see the difference. She felt heard, understood, and valued. One day out of the blue she said, "You have really changed!" Again, by deciding to overlook minor offenses, most of which were the result of her not being able to read my mind, I was exhibiting common sense.

Wise behavior applies the Word of God to our pursuit of intimate relationships. Solomon observed: "Houses and wealth are inherited from parents, but a prudent wife is from the LORD" (Prov. 19:14). "Prudent" is translated from the same Hebrew word that means "wise behavior." Listening to a wife whose behavior is wise is common sense. As I began to see the practical benefits of pursuing this common sense, I wisely changed my listening habits with my wife. I had previously viewed her as someone who was disconnected from my business. I thought she had very little value to add to it. Consequently, since I saw no value in integrating her into the thing that I spent most of my waking moments working on, we experienced a wide gap in our relationship. When I came across this verse, I rethought my foolish approach. I learned that my wife, indeed, offered intrinsic value and insight into my daily work life because she was blessed with an immense amount of common sense. And I got to benefit from her wisdom firsthand.

Be Filled with Common Sense

When I applied the Bible's common sense to my everyday life, God transformed my relationship with Him, my relationships with others, and consequently, my resources.

Look at your calendar with your memorized words of wisdom in mind. Ask God how you can apply this wise behavior to your everyday life. Inspire the people you work and live with by approaching every interpersonal interaction with God's common sense.

COURAGEOUS

Third, wise behavior is courageous. When imprisoned, Paul applauded the wisdom of his fellow believers "to speak the word of God more courageously and fearlessly" (Phil. 1:14). To be courageous, we must be willing to share our experience of the Word with another person. Solomon taught: "When a mocker is punished, the simple gain wisdom; when a wise man is instructed, he gets knowledge" (Prov. 21:11).

Wise behavior includes courage to bring consequences to a mocker who scoffs at God. This fosters wise behavior in the simple fool who is watching and who is willing to change his behavior. Conversely, when we are courageous enough to teach a wise person from our experience of applying the Word, he or she will grow in intimacy with God—the source of our courage.

God exercises wise behavior to courageously root out the wicked. Solomon continued: "The Righteous One takes note of the house of the wicked and brings the wicked to ruin" (Prov. 21:12). The term *takes note* is translated from the same root for the words translated as "wise behavior." The indwelling Spirit of God empowers us with courage to implement the same wise behavior in discerning when to remove a wicked person from an organization.

I began to share what I had learned in my experiences with God one-on-one with people who asked about my change. In doing so, I learned how beneficial these discussions were to my own spiritual life. I mustered the courage to ask questions about their lives and learned from their experiences. Next, realizing that my pursuit of wise behavior could help others,

I gained more courage in communicating the Word that was getting into me. Consequently, I was invited to speak to groups about my transformation. I didn't realize it right away, but God had put me on a path toward teaching and preaching.

Along the way, I realized that if someone is going to mock the vision, mission, values, objectives, goals, or strategies of an organization, then it is time to remove that person. While doing so might seem cruel, I've found that such people threaten to take down the entire team with their bitter poison. No matter how talented they are or critical to the organization, these kinds of people destroy athletic teams, dismantle churches, kill nonprofit organizations, and ruin businesses. I think that I'm as evangelistic as they come, meaning I believe that we can communicate the transformational power that is available to anyone who surrenders his life to God. However, a scorner and a mocker who refuses to be taught must be removed. And I had to do this on several occasions within my organization.

After much prayer, wise counsel, and discernment, I gained the courage to remove most of the people in my company that I could not afford to help. The risk of the investment of resources, loss of customers, and decrease in coworkers' productivity outweighed the uncertain return on these people's willingness or ability to change. This removal was never void of God's desire to bring them back to Him. Consequently, I always attempted to part ways on good terms, offering help so that each person could find a new organization where he or she could experience a new opportunity and be a better fit.

The most frequently recorded command in the Bible is "Don't be afraid." Consequently, a recurring theme in the Bible states that we should be strong and courageous because God is with us wherever we go (see Josh. 1:9). God's presence provides us with the strength and courage we need for wise behavior. He moves us from fear to faith. We don't have to be afraid to share with others our experience of applying the Word to our lives. Rather we can trust God, who gives us the courage to be vulnerable toward others.

Be Courageous

Share with someone your experience of applying a selected verse or passage to your life. That person will be honored that you were courageous enough to open up to them about the changes God is working out in your life.

CREDIBLE

Finally, wise behavior is credible. To be credible, we must give credit to God for our experience of getting into the Word, applying it to our lives, and being courageous enough to share that experience with another person. Both *credible* and *credit* come from the same Latin word *credere*, meaning "to believe or to trust." We are only worthy of trust when we trust in the source of our wise behavior. Wisdom comes from the Lord, so we are credible when we give credit to whom it is due.

Solomon observed: "A man is praised according to his wisdom, but men with warped minds are despised" (Prov. 12:8). "Wisdom" is translated from the same Hebrew word for "wise behavior" that Solomon noted as praiseworthy or credible. The opposite of being praised for one's wisdom is being despised due to one's warped mind. The person with such a mind distorts reality and takes credit away from God. As previously mentioned, wise behavior makes us credible both with God and others. Solomon observed that when we speak credibly, we: "will win favor and a good name in the sight of God and man" (Prov. 3:4).

Credibility affects leadership. A leader finds credibility in a person with wise behavior, but he discovers none in a shameful person. Solomon shared this feeling from his own experience: "A king delights in a wise servant, but a shameful servant incurs his wrath" (Prov. 14:35). At the same time, the credibility of the person with wise behavior propels him to leadership. Solomon said: "A wise servant will rule over a disgraceful son, and will share the inheritance as one of the brothers" (Prov. 17:2). Both "shameful" and "disgraceful" are translated from the same Hebrew word, *bosh*.

Solomon equated acting shamefully with straying from wise behavior: "A man who strays from the path of understanding comes to rest in the company of the dead" (Prov. 21:16). "Understanding" is translated from the Hebrew word *sakal*, also translated as "wise behavior." Solomon noted not only the credibility of one with understanding, but also the lack of credibility of a person without it: "Good understanding wins favor, but the way of the unfaithful is hard" (Prov. 13:15). David gave credit to God for his experience with the wise behavior found in His Word when he wrote: "The law of the LORD is perfect, reviving the soul. The statutes of the LORD are trustworthy, making wise the simple" (Ps. 19:7).

I recall a Sunday where our youngest daughter was ill, so my wife stayed home while our three eldest girls, and I went to church and listened to my brother Stuart deliver a sermon about pride. This was a subject that I had studied and dealt with quite a bit. Stuart concluded his sermon by distributing a test that included forty descriptors of pride. He challenged each of us to find a close confidante who would help us check all the patterns that applied to our personal behavior. Due to my earlier study, I saw no need to ask someone else for input. I speedily completed the test, checking ten characteristics of pride that I still battled. Then I collected my daughters and went home.

After I strutted into the house, Susan asked me about what Stuart had taught. I told her the topic and eagerly displayed my transparency as I shared my keen ability to self-diagnose any hint of pride in my life. I read my list of ten pseudo-problem areas and proceeded to leave the room. Before I did, Susan asked, "Were there more than ten characteristics to choose from?"

"Why?"

"Just wondering," she said.

"Oh! You want to take the test?" I inquired as I confidently handed her my completed test. She took the paper from my hand and carefully read all forty characteristics. I was expecting her to tell me that I had been too hard on myself when she looked up and said, "It looks like you missed one."

"Which one?" I challenged.

"Takes criticism well from others," she said. Ouch.

The assignment was to take the test along with someone else. I had proudly declined. Instead, I cruised on autopilot and subsequently missed a good learning opportunity for God to work in my life. In refusing to give God credit for the lesson he had for me, I missed a check mark. When we refuse to give credit where credit is due, we miss a few blind spots and hinder our growth in wise behavior.

Be Credible

We can pray that our friends will be drawn to repentance toward God through our wise behavior consisting of *convincing words*, *common sense*, *courage*, and *credibility*. Jesus Christ, the Wisdom of God, through His life, death, and resurrection, demonstrated God's ultimate design for wise behavior. Jesus was *convincing*: He knew the Word. Jesus was filled with *common sense*: He applied the Word. Jesus was *courageous*: He shared the Word. Jesus was *credible*: He died for the Word, giving all credit to the Father. Jesus Christ was and is still today the Word of God. Thus, it is Christ in us who is *convincing*, filled with *common sense*, *courageous*, and *credible*. When people ask about your experience with memorizing, applying, and sharing the Word of God, give credit to Him.

Chapter 8

Understanding

SPIRIT-LED

Ed Placencia grew up in a large family with six brothers and six sisters. In this family, daily misunderstandings sometimes led to physical altercations among the siblings. When his dad would come home from work, Ed's mom would point out the guilty from that day's battles, and then another fight would break out. One day, Ed heard about a boxing club where he could fight and earn trophies. Looking for an outlet for his aggression and wanting to hone his skills, Ed remembers, "I thought I had gone to heaven."

Ed was made for boxing. He won four Golden Gloves titles and an AAU title. Ed was the favorite to win the 1966 Pan American Games and represent the United States at the 1968 Olympics in Mexico City; however, he chose to sacrifice that opportunity. Upon graduating from high school, Ed decided that he owed a debt to his country and enlisted in the U.S. Army. There he won three U.S. Army boxing titles while he was stationed in Germany prior to being deployed to Vietnam.

Ed was a member of the 173rd Airborne, Gen. William Westmoreland's special project. They became engaged in the Battle of Hill 875, Dak To, which in terms of American lives lost was the third-bloodiest battle during the Vietnam War. In three days, 260 men were killed. Of the eight hundred men in the 173rd Airborne, only eleven left without being killed or wounded in the battle for this small section of jungle. Ed recalls, "No movie has ever accurately depicted how thick a jungle is. We had to navigate the foliage and the terrain carrying seven days of rations on our back that weighed almost one hundred pounds."

As Ed's unit was making its way through the dense jungle terrain, they found themselves in the middle of an ambush. Bullets zipped through the air as Ed bent down to help a fellow soldier who had been shot in the hip. "Don't leave me!" the wounded soldier screamed. At that moment, there was an explosion. Ed thought he had been hit in the eye. Scrambling to regather his faculties, Ed discovered that he'd been hit by shrapnel. Ed was forced to make a quick decision. "There wasn't a square inch on our uniforms without a hole in them. We pulled back and called in an air strike to bomb the area."

Ed ran point on the retreat. The squad returned to the hill, where they dug into the foxholes for the night. Ed recalls, "I was in my foxhole with two fellow soldiers, anticipating the probability of the enemy's late evening or early morning attack. After fulfilling my first two watches, I planned to sleep for two hours. I closed my eyes and heard a voice call my name. I asked my two foxhole partners if they had called me. Both replied, 'No, Sarge.' This occurred two more times. Then I heard the voice say, 'Ed, get out of the foxhole.' I heard it a second time.

The third time, I heard the voice say more emphatically, 'Ed, get out of the foxhole, now!'"

Not understanding who had spoken the words, but recognizing it wasn't a soldier, Ed climbed out, walked about fifteen feet away, and lay on the ground with his helmet under his head. Five minutes later, two Vietnamese soldiers dropped three grenades in the foxhole, killing Ed's two men. "If I had asked them to come with me, they would have thought I was crazy. I think about that every day. This experience made me aware that there was somebody or something with me in that jungle."

The 173rd Airborne chaplain was Father Charles J. Watters, Ed's spiritual mentor. He was in the field that day and offered communion to anyone who wanted it during the calm before the storm. Ed and his men took it. As they started up the hill, they faced heavy enemy fire. "I saw Father Watters shot twenty to thirty times, but I never saw any blood. All he did was help people. I thought that he had to be an angel, a messenger from God.

"While going up Hill 875, we ran into a regiment of two thousand enemy soldiers in front of us. Another regiment of two thousand enemy soldiers approached us in the middle. Behind us were another two thousand men in hot pursuit. We had only eight hundred guys, and we were facing six thousand. We started to form a perimeter, so we could separate our soldiers from the enemy. We were under tremendous fire. I called my platoon sergeant a half-dozen times—no answer. I reasoned that he might dead, so I decided to go get him, even though the soldier with whom I shared my plan thought that I might be trying to save myself.

"I ran to find my platoon sergeant and came upon a

lieutenant, who would not let me return to get my men. 'If you take another step, I'll have you court-martialed,' he ordered. I took off. He shouted that I had ten minutes to return. On my way to get my men, I ran through twenty to thirty Vietnamese soldiers. For some reason, they couldn't see me."

When Ed arrived, his men were facing fire. He ordered a retreat, but his machine gunner demanded to stay; he knew that if he stopped shooting, the whole squad would be overrun by enemy soldiers. Despite Ed's orders and then his pleas, the gunner refused to go with the others; he kept firing. He was determined to help everyone else get out.

Ed led his guys back to his platoon when the machine-gun fire stopped. "We heard six shots from the machine gunner's .38, which he wasn't supposed to carry. When they later retrieved his body, he was credited for more than seventy kills from his position. If it weren't for him, I wouldn't be here today. Later, he was posthumously awarded the Congressional Medal of Honor for saving our lives."

Ed and his men started back toward the platoon, and Ed knew they would have to go through the enemy soldiers Ed had passed earlier. "I had told my guys not to say a word, just keep walking when you see the enemy. This time, there were fifty of them ready to shoot. Not one saw us."

Many of Ed's men had been wounded. Ed wanted to go back a second time and save them. He asked his lieutenant for permission, only to be told, "Our orders were to leave the wounded."

"Sir, we can't leave them down there."

"Sergeant, if you take one more step, I'll have you court-martialed."

"You got me once. If you can get me twice, have at it."

"You have five minutes," the lieutenant replied.

As Ed gathered only the thirty to forty wounded soldiers who could walk, he saw the Vietnamese coming up the hill. He called out, "Guys, we have to go *now*!" Immediately after, Ed made eye contact with a GI on the ground. This soldier had been shot in the neck. He had also been shot in the ribs, as evidenced by his lung protruding from his upper torso like a balloon. He looked up at Ed and pleaded, "Sergeant, don't leave me!" Ed knew if he and his men tried to save this GI, they would lose the wounded who could walk. Ed says, "Each day when I wake up, I see that soldier asking me not to leave him. And every day, I wonder if I made the right decision to not bring him with us."

Ed's platoon made it through the next two nights alive and gathered the wounded around a tree. A U.S. Marine pilot had heard their distress call. He had two five-hundred-pound bombs left. "We might have given him the wrong coordinates because the bombs hit the tree where we were. The guy on my right lost both of his arms. The guy on my left was severed at the waist. Nothing touched me, but that bomb killed the severely wounded Father Charles J. Watters."

As he surveyed the carnage, Ed was cursing God when he heard the same voice he had heard in the foxhole. This time it said, "Ed, I'm going to tell you why I took Father Watters."

Ed shouted, "How could you take somebody who has done nothing but good and leave somebody like me who has done nothing right in his life? Make some sense of that to me!"

The voice replied, "Father Watters has done on this earth what I sent him to do. When you have done what I've sent you to do, I will take you home, too."

Ed said, "In that moment, my life changed. That was my point of salvation. I understood I was in God's hands. I was going to make it out. I was going to be okay." Ed had been shot six times in those three days. His scalp was peeled back from his skull, the skin dangling below his ear. His jaw had been split open, the skin hanging down and exposing his molars. He eventually passed out from the pain, but was finally rescued and brought to a hospital.

Ed returned to the United States, a man with a new understanding of God's call on his life. "Since 1967," Ed said, "I've been searching for what that purpose is."

Today, Ed would tell you that the voice he heard in the Vietnam jungle was that of the Holy Spirit. He has provided Ed with spiritual leaders, including boxing coaches, Father Watters, commanding officers, mentors, and many others to coach him along his journey. He has given Ed a cool head and equipped him to train young men and women to box competitively as the owner of the same club he first frequented as a boy.

Ed takes every conflict to God, remaining silent, patient, and following His straight path to wisdom. As a result, Ed is one of the most insightful people I know. He takes time to understand the heart beneath a person's words. The boy who grew up with daily misunderstandings with his twelve siblings now experiences very few misunderstandings because he is plugged into the Holy Spirit.

The next pearl for wise conflict management is understanding, noted in Solomon's purpose for writing Proverbs, which is "understanding words of insight" (Prov. 1:2). Understanding occurs through an intimate experience with the Holy Spirit who gives us insight into others: "The fear of the LORD is the beginning of wisdom, and knowledge of the Holy One is understanding" (Prov. 9:10). In order to be understanding, we must be *Spirit-led*, *teachable*, *cool*, and *insightful*.

Proverbs tells us that a person with understanding is plugged into and led by the Holy Spirit. Solomon said: "Knowledge of the Holy One is understanding" (Prov. 9:10). Knowledge of another person involves the kind of intimacy that can be defined as one's innermost being experiencing another's. This kind of knowledge comes about only in a relationship where two hearts connect through trust. In order to be understanding, we must first trust in the Spirit of God with all our hearts.

Inspired by the Holy Spirit, Solomon recorded one of the weightiest sayings in Proverbs to explain how we connect our hearts with God's: "Trust in the LORD with all your heart and lean not on your own understanding; in all your ways acknowledge him, and he will make your paths straight" (Prov. 3:5–6). Rather than trusting in our own fallen understanding, we trust wholeheartedly in God. Being plugged into and led by the invisible power of the Holy Spirit brings us understanding that is from God. Solomon continued, describing that when we gain understanding, we are blessed (see Prov. 3:13).

The determining factor in testing whether we are Spirit-led is the "Five-Second Rule": taking five seconds before every telephone call, text, email, encounter, or meeting to ask the Holy Spirit, "What do you want me to do in this situation?" This focuses our hearts on trusting the heart of God, who gives us the power to selflessly listen and understand the hearts of others.

Remember that the heart is comprised of four chambers: the will, intellect, spirit, and emotions. The will is the chamber of our *choices*. The intellect is the chamber of our *thoughts*. The spirit is the lead chamber of our *prayers*. The emotions represent the chamber of our *feelings*. Consequently, insight into the will, mind, spirit, and emotions of God helps us understand our own hearts as well as the hearts of others. Solomon observed: "He who gets wisdom loves his own soul; he who cherishes understanding prospers" (Prov. 19:8). Understanding is a strong life value that carries with it enormous benefits.

I find that the more I am in tune with the Holy Spirit, the more understanding I am. I almost feel a sense of relief, knowing that I don't have to lean on my own understanding, which often falls short. The Five-Second Rule helps me stay plugged into the Holy Spirit for understanding. When I follow it, my experience has been that the kingdom of God breaks through in ways that would never have occurred had I relied on my own understanding.

You might ask, "Do we really have five seconds before we respond when we're in conversation with our spouses, parents, children, siblings, employers, employees, customers, and vendors?" In my experience, we have these five seconds more often than we realize. At the same time, I would ask you, "Wouldn't you like to plug into the most powerful source in the universe during those encounters?"

As a teaching pastor, I received scores of emails each week inquiring about spiritual matters. Many times I caught myself going on autopilot, recalling and sharing verses I had memorized, without stopping to ask for God's input. Then I would remember the Five-Second Rule. Man, did that practice bring more clarity to my answers and subsequently advanced God's heart in others!

Sometimes we feel like we have little or no insight to offer people. Where does our insight break down? When we disconnect just enough from the Holy Spirit to bring static on the line. You see, Christ promised His disciples that in times of trials, His Spirit would give them the right words to say (see Matt. 10:19–20). The same holds true for us. The clearer our connection with the Holy Spirit, the more we grow in understanding. This develops our spiritual instincts, giving us the Spirit-led power to take on even more trials that challenge our faith.

When we experience static on the line, we often blame God. However, the static resides on our end in the form of a hardened heart, one that ignores the Five-Second Rule. The writer of Job made it clear that when we experience calamity and perceive static in our connection with God, we should not sin by blaming Him (see Job 1:22). Rather, we can invest less time than it takes to find fault and soften our hearts to our source of understanding. Job's friend Elihu said: "It is the spirit in a man, the breath of the Almighty, that gives him understanding" (Job 32:8). In our spirits, we must first connect with the Holy Spirit to discover understanding and gain insight into the heart of God, as well as our own hearts, before we connect with the hearts of others.

Jesus provides the ultimate example of a crystal-clear connection with the Holy Spirit. His connection flowed from His fellowship with the Father. As God in the flesh, Jesus was always plugged into His divine power source. When faced with challenges, temptations, tragedies, or triumphs, Jesus faced the same internal turmoil, but He did not sin. He was Spirit-led.

What about you? When your spouse speaks with a discouraging tone, take five seconds to ask God, "What do you want me to do?" When someone cuts you off on the highway, take five seconds to ask God, "What do you want me to do?" When a coworker or teammate lashes out at you, take five seconds to ask God, "What do you want me to do?" When you are in the midst of a presentation and you're asked a tough question, take five seconds to ask God, "What do you want me to do?" When you're in the fray of a sports competition with the game on the line, take five seconds and ask God, "What do you want me to do?" When any temptation lurks before you, take five seconds to ask God, "What do you want me to do?"

Remain Plugged in to the Holy Spirit

Live by the Five-Second Rule. Before every telephone call, text, email, encounter, or meeting, ask the Spirit of God to lead you. Before you speak any words or take any actions, ask Him, "What do you want me to do?"

TEACHABLE

Second, in order to have understanding, we must be *teachable*. Solomon said that a person with understanding opens the door of his heart to a teacher in his life who will coach and correct him: "He who ignores discipline despises himself, but whoever heeds correction gains understanding" (Prov. 15:32). This is true when we pursue discipleship in Christ, grow in our careers, and live out our roles as Christ followers in our families.

A teacher's correction can come in either the form of reproof or rebuke. The word *reproof* stems from the Hebrew word *yakach*, which means "to prove again." Solomon advised: "Strike a scoffer and the naïve may become shrewd, but reprove one who has understanding and he will gain knowledge" (Prov. 19:25 NASB). A reproof demonstrates again the teacher's desired response, allowing a person with understanding to gain a teachable understanding that sticks.

Solomon observed that when the teacher escalates the correction to the form of a rebuke (*gearah* from *gaar* in Hebrew) or a reprimand, the person with understanding responds to the stiffer consequences through the door of his heart: "A rebuke goes deeper into one who has understanding than a hundred blows into a fool" (Prov. 17:10 NASB).

Employing the Times-Two Rule involves recruiting a teacher. Anyone who undertakes a new endeavor enjoys a relationship with someone who is more accomplished in that field of expertise. Musicians have conductors. Athletes have coaches. Artists have masters. Entrepreneurs have mentors. Why wouldn't we enlist a coach to help us become more understanding as we face life's conflicts? The relationship with such a teacher helps us focus on growing in our understanding as parents, spouses, friends, workers, and disciples of Christ.

As a coach, I have experienced the transformation of many student athletes through the Times-Two Rule. One particular girl was playing for me in a sixth-grade basketball game, her first year of organized competition. She was one of my daughter's best friends—a sweetheart off the court, but a terror on it. If you looked in the dictionary, her picture showed up beside the word *competitive*.

We were in the heat of our first game when I called time-out. This girl turned to the bench, distorted her face, and made body gestures that clearly communicated frustration and anger as she stomped off the court to the bench. I decided to make it a teachable moment. When she arrived at the bench, I called her by name and advised, "Listen, we don't just represent the school, we represent God. What you just did communicated to your teammates, your opponents, and those watching in the stands that you're angry and rattled. Right now, you have a choice. You can either take that same energy and turn it into something positive, or you can self-destruct and hurt your team's chances of winning."

Five years later, during her junior year of high school, her coach engaged in a similar reproof—okay, maybe even a rebuke—during practice when the same pattern surfaced. At that moment, I saw a switch flip in her heart. She chose to respond to the correction with understanding.

The results were significant. She became an amazing leader both on and off the court. She communicated as an effective floor general for the team that won the most basketball games in school history, but her teachable spirit didn't stop there. She carried it to softball, where that team was also the most successful in school history. That team's success contributed to her earning a scholarship to play for one of the top colleges in the nation. She even earned the title of valedictorian of her senior class.

Now, I'm taking zero credit for her success. I merely had a

front-row seat during her entire career because I coached her class through their senior year, and I witnessed the power of a teachable spirit surrendered to the Times-Two Rule. Her ability to be transformed inspired change beyond her situation.

During her senior year of high school, as the assistant coach and a mentor to the head coach of the girls' basketball team, I sat down with him to ask a series of questions. My goal was to produce a document containing our vision, mission, values, objectives, goals, and strategies for the program. My thinking was that we would lay a foundation that future coaches and teams could build upon. We titled our vision, "Champions for Life." Our mission was captured in the phrase "Dying to Win." To become a champion for an abundant and eternal life, we must die to our selfishness in order to win what God has in store for us, both on and off the courts. We do so, in part, by applying the Times-Two Rule to our lives. Sometimes we will be the teacher; sometimes we will be the student. In fact, the greatest student often becomes the best teacher.

Remain Teachable

Jesus offered the clearest portrait of the Times-Two Rule. He taught His disciples to grow in understanding. He reproved. He rebuked. All the while, He was connected with the Father and the Holy Spirit.

Live by the Times-Two Rule by asking someone to coach you in an arena of your life where you can grow in *understanding*. Find someone who is wiser than you in that selected discipline. Meet at least once each month to pursue specific areas of improvement.

COOL

Third, Proverbs says that a person with understanding has a cool spirit: "He who restrains his words has knowledge, and he who has a cool spirit is a man of understanding" (Prov. 17:27 NASB). Heat expands a conflict; cool contracts it. When conflict escalates, we often lose our cool, which impedes our understanding. The heated anger disrupts our connection with God, interrupts our teachable spirit, and abruptly ends our effective communication with others. Being cool helps us avoid misunderstandings by helping us to remain silent, patient, and on a straight path.

- *A person with understanding keeps cool in conflict by knowing when to remain silent.* "A man who lacks judgment derides his neighbor, but a man of understanding holds his tongue" (Prov. 11:12). Silence is cool.
- *A person with understanding keeps cool in conflict by remaining patient.* "A patient man has great understanding, but a quick-tempered man displays folly" (Prov. 14:29). Patience is cool.
- A *person with understanding keeps cool in conflict by remaining on a straight path.* "Folly delights a man who lacks judgment, but a man of understanding keeps a straight course" (Prov. 15:21). Notice that Solomon juxtaposed "a man of understanding" with "a man who lacks judgment." When we are angry, we often lack judgment. That's why Paul said that in our anger, we should not sin (see Eph. 4:26). Straight is cool.

Everyone knows that when conversations become heated, we should count to ten. However, mindlessly counting to ten only defers our anger rather than allowing us to process it. The real Ten-Second Rule reminds us that in the heat of the moment we should invest ten full seconds to take our anger to God. He will cool us down, keeping us silent, patient, and on the straight path.

I have experienced the transforming power of silence, patience, and following a straight course. After a pastoral staff breakfast that got a little heated, a fellow teaching pastor approached me. "I watched you today, and I noticed something," he said. "When the discussion gets heated, you get silent. I don't mean hurt silent; I mean wisely silent. When you finally talk, it cools things down. You bring harmony. I just want to know, how do you do that?"

I shared with my good friend what I'm sharing with you. Heat expands conflict. Cool contracts it. Great wisdom can be revealed with a little silence, a little patience, and following a straight course.

I received a text from a high school student who had responded to my challenge to read a chapter in Proverbs each day that corresponded with the date of the month. "What does 'A fool gives full vent to his anger' mean in Proverbs 29:11?" he asked.

I replied, "Venting anger is foolish. It hurts people, heats up the conflict, and damages relationships. Cool is taking our anger to God. The balance of the verse reads, 'But a wise man keeps himself under control.' That's what David did. He kept himself under control by taking his anger to God. If you want evidence of that, just read through some of David's psalms."

Jesus took His anger to God. He was the ultimate picture of cool. Though He overturned the crafty money changers' tables in the temple where they were taking advantage of unsuspecting seekers of God, He still was coolly connected with the Father. Even on the cross, Jesus took His conflict to Him.

Stay Cool

Practice the real Ten-Second Rule. Take your anger to God. As you begin to heat up, ask Him to cool you down, keeping you silent, patient, and following a straight path. Think about the potential impact of silence, patience, and following a straight course when you take a step back, relax your facial expression, make eye contact, demonstrate an engaging body posture, and use appropriate gestures to cool a conflict. This is just one way that you will experience Christ working through you.

INSIGHTFUL

Fourth, Proverbs teaches that a person with understanding is insightful: "The purposes of a man's heart are deep waters, but a man of understanding draws them out" (Prov. 20:5). Understanding allows us to look and reach inside another person's mind and heart, making us insightful. Solomon said: "Wisdom rests in the heart of one who has understanding, but in the hearts of fools it is made known" (Prov. 14:33 NASB).

The King of Israel also noted how understanding transcends socioeconomic realities: "The rich man is wise in his own eyes, but the poor who has understanding sees through him" (Prov. 28:11 NASB). A poor person with understanding has insight into the pretense that often lies in the heart of the rich.

We learn how to be insightful when we employ the Twenty-Second Rule: Take twenty seconds after each conversation to look past a person's words and into his or her heart. During this time you can examine the choices, thoughts, prayers, and feelings that comprise the source of his or her desires or motives.

Language is only symbolic of what is in the heart. Consequently, the words a person speaks often do not accurately reflect his or her heart. After being Spirit-led with the Five-Second Rule, being teachable through the Times-Two Rule, and being cool through the Ten-Second Rule, we can be insightful through the Twenty-Second Rule.

After meeting with a prospective seller to sign an auction agreement, my dad would say, "Don't merely listen to their words, listen to what they're *really* saying." He was communicating that if we did not understand the heart and desires of a seller, then we could not meet his needs. In business, vocational ministry, parenting, and marriage, we must practice the Twenty-Second Rule to reflect on our conversations and understand the hearts and desires of those we encounter.

My wife, Susan, often feels scolded by me when I attempt to teach wisdom in the midst of our conflict. Too often I foster misunderstanding when I try to police her communication style or tone. I get in the way of insight into her heart, and subsequently she can't gain insight into mine. Instead, our conflict management works much better when I practice the Twenty-Second Rule and delve into her heart and desires in order to understand before I'm ever understood.

My dad was my best friend and my business partner. Unfortunately, I learned that when we obey our fathers as adults, we
assimilate not only their assets, but also their liabilities. Consequently, I needed insight into what portions of his advice were
wise and what portions might be less than advisable. Enter my
dad's brother, Uncle Derald, at one of our weekly meetings in
his office. As I talked to him about the situation, he said that
he had noticed my temperature rising when Dad and I sparred
verbally. He suggested "sifting."

"What do you mean?" I asked.

"Sift through his words. Affirm what is wise. Avoid what is
not," Uncle Derald counseled.

I fired back, "You mean when Dad's yelling at me to meet a
business deadline, even though the system I designed took care
of it months prior, you want me to find something positive to
affirm?"

"Yes," he replied.

I continued, "Do you understand how upset I get over these
kinds of encounters? He's constantly reminding me to take
care of details that I've long since finished. It makes me feel like
he thinks I don't know what I'm doing. If I practiced meeting
deadlines as late as he thinks of them, we'd be broke!"

Undeterred, Uncle Derald proceeded, "I noticed how upset
you get, and I want to offer you a tool to help you to sift."

"What's that?"

"I want you to picture Jesus," he said.

"Next time I'm in this kind of situation with Dad, you want
me to picture Jesus?"

"Yes," Uncle Derald confirmed.

"Where, over his shoulder?"

"That would work," he said.

After my meeting with Uncle Derald, I drove to my office while I applied the Twenty-Second Rule and pondered his suggestions, as well as trying to see into Dad's heart and intentions. By the time I walked through the doors, my mind was on my upcoming appointments, calls, and the tasks at hand, but I stopped by Dad's office to grab a Diet Pepsi from his refrigerator.

"Mitchell, you need to make sure you get the Topsfield auction brochures mailed since the sale is the weekend after our Auburn event," Dad fired at me, referring to our largest auction of the year. I was really struggling as I popped open my can to hear that familiar fizz. The bubbling was similar to what was going on with the hydrochloric acid in my gut. If I hadn't already taken care of that deadline months ago, we would indeed be in trouble.

In an auctioneer family, to win an argument you elevate your tone, accentuate the facts supporting your position, and make a strong emotional appeal. This usually turns up the heat as both parties get louder and louder, pulling loosely supported facts from all over the place until they slide into nothing more than opinions. Eventually, someone has to walk away dissatisfied and angry. Today was going to be another one of those situations.

Then I saw something, or should I say someone. It was Jesus. He was standing behind my dad. I thought about Uncle Derald's advice to improve my insight by sifting. *Yeah, that's right, sifting. Affirm the wise. Avoid what's not*, I thought.

"You are brilliant," I uttered to my father, surprised at the words that flew out of my mouth.

"What?" Dad asked, smiling. He always wanted to hear a compliment again.

"You are brilliant. You must have taught me well. I did it three weeks ago, and the response has been fantastic."

Then I was blown away by Dad's words to me: "You're a better man than I am."

There's something inside each of us that desires approval from our earthly fathers, and I had just received it because I had applied wisdom to my everyday life. Solomon captured the power of this insightful behavior when he said: "A gentle answer turns away wrath, but a harsh word stirs up anger" (Prov. 15:1). Jesus was gentle in heart (see Matt. 11:29). He was insightful, able to peer into the hearts of others (see Matt. 22:18). Through picturing His presence and sifting in this situation, I was empowered to answer gently, turning away Dad's wrath rather than harshly rebutting and stirring up anger.

I couldn't have done it without the Spirit's prompting; without Uncle Derald's teaching along with my study of the Bible, which became my filter to sift the wise from the foolish; without keeping cool; and without taking twenty seconds to look inside the heart of my dad. I had become more understanding through being Spirit-led, teachable, cool, and insightful.

Pursue Insight into Other People

Live by the Twenty-Second Rule. Take twenty seconds after each conversation to look past every person's words in order to peer inside his or her heart. Don't merely focus on their vocabulary, but reflect on what resides in their heart that they were attempting to describe. Be a wise person who understands others by intimately experiencing the Holy Spirit. Be Spirit-led through the Five-Second Rule, teachable with the Times-Two Rule, cool while implementing the Ten-Second Rule, and insightful while engaging in the Twenty-Second Rule. Memorize the Bible verse in this chapter that seems most applicable to your life so that you can begin to assimilate understanding into your life through the Holy Spirit. He will equip you to wisely minimize misunderstandings in your conflict management.

Chapter 9

Wise Communication

ASK QUESTIONS

Two thousand years ago, rabbis asked many questions that engaged the heart in the process of their teaching. In fact, when they engaged with each other in systematic debate, they would typically answer a question with another question, as if to say, "I understand what you are communicating, but what about this deeper truth?" Asking questions revealed deeper motives and deeper truths. It was foundational to wise communication. Jesus modeled this behavior when He engaged with Nicodemus (see John 3). Jesus asked questions, and eventually, Nicodemus surrendered to Jesus' wisdom and insight (see John 19:39).

The art of the well-asked question provides a disarming environment. It helps a difficult person feel less threatened, which allows him to engage his heart while attempting to answer the inquiry. Solomon articulated the power of a question to generate answers when he wrote: "The first to present his case seems right, till another comes forward and questions him" (Prov. 18:17).

I have witnessed this pearl in practice. I had a friend who endured a major transition in his life where his wife just wasn't on the same page. He had been a person who tells, and as a result, he shut her down. As we talked over lunch, I wrote on a napkin the four components of being a person who ASKS, which will be shared in sections throughout the chapter:

- **A**sk questions.
- **S**hare stories.
- **K**ey in on the other person's perspective.
- **S**peak Scripture.

My friend humbled his heart to God and then to his wife. In doing so, he connected with her heart. He called me later and said, "You've got to publish this stuff! It really works!"

Linda McCrary, a friend of mine who led worship at outreach events we conducted together, has also leveraged wise communication to become a person who ASKS. Linda grew up in Youngstown, Ohio, where her mom, who was divorced with five sons, met her dad. Linda was the youngest of their ten children—eight boys and two girls. Both of her parents were musically gifted, so her father would teach the children harmonies as they sang while doing the dishes.

Linda's second-oldest brother died in a car accident while returning to his military base when Linda was four years old. Tragically, her mom heard the news first on the radio—she was completely devastated. Out of her pain, Linda's mother began to write music that would engage the heart and tell a story, connecting others with the Word of God. Linda and her siblings sang those songs, honing their gifts as they performed at churches; at their home Bible study; and touring with an evangelist who, during one service, dedicated Linda's family to God. This family received their big break when they finished second on *The Original Amateur Hour* with Ted Mack, which was in many ways the *American Idol* of the day. Consequently, they moved to California when Linda was sixteen, signing with Light Records and singing with Andraé Crouch. They opened for Pat Boone as the McCrary Five. "Our music was the forerunner of Christian contemporary music, singing my mom's songs."

The McCrary Five broke up as a singing group when Linda was twenty-seven, so she signed with Capitol Records where she met the Jacksons. Sharing the same birthday as Michael, Linda would celebrate her special day with the King of Pop whenever they toured together. They became close friends, and Linda was one of Michael's favorite vocalists to sing on his records. "I was a lost person then. I was not equipped to be away from my family. Although I had told people about Jesus, I never fully surrendered to Him. I was successful at a young age. I had the best of life—homes, cars, and liquor—as I was hanging out with Elton John, Diana Ross, Stevie Wonder, and many other music icons."

At that time, Linda started to experiment with cocaine. Over a period of three short years, Linda became an alcoholic and cocaine addict. "I was homeless, a junkie living on the streets. On a few occasions I was even in lockdown at local hospitals. Stevie Wonder and Andraé Crouch were looking for me; Stevie even reached me on the telephone once, but I was in my own fallen world."

On September 8, 1989, God used a Scripture to draw Linda to Himself. She was uncharacteristically sober in a hotel room, when an airline pilot who had been a fellow user and runner knocked on her door. "He told me that he wanted me to deliver him. Even though I was unsaved, I had always talked about Jesus, so he thought I would have the answers to his life's problems. He kept asking me, and I kept saying, 'No.' Finally, he asked me to read him something from the Bible. I grabbed the Gideon Bible in the nightstand and opened the Word to Psalm 40, the psalm of deliverance. I began to read it aloud, and I was delivered.

"I started crying and immediately called my brother, whose wife had just given birth to their daughter Chantel. Over the next year, God spoke to me daily, healing my body and my mind. About a year later, I was impressed with the fact of how much God truly loved me. That changed my life."

Restored anew, Linda sang with Lou Rawls, Ray Charles, Earth, Wind & Fire, and in films such as *The Lion King*. She reconnected with Stevie Wonder and Michael Jackson in the studio, singing on Michael's last three records. "I was with Michael a month before he passed because we were putting together the music for his tour. I was in the Philippines when he passed. I was so sad for him. We were not made to be worshiped. That put enormous pressure on Michael." Linda assembled and participated in the choir that sang at his funeral.

Since September 8, 1989, Linda has never once touched alcohol or an illegal substance. She attended Christian Assembly, a church in greater Los Angeles, where she met worship leader and songwriter Tommy Walker. "I learned that God had gifted me, not merely to sing, but to lead people in worship." Linda has toured with Franklin Graham, leading others to Christ through her gift of music. "God rescued and restored me. I'm not a recovering addict. I was delivered. I'm a result of the power of the Word of God and my mother's prayers."

Today, Linda McCrary is a person who ASKS: She asks questions that engage the heart. She shares stories through music. Empowered by the Holy Spirit, she keys in on her audiences' perspectives as she connects with their hearts by presenting thought-provoking questions. Finally, Linda speaks Scripture, humbly and wisely, both through song and in her everyday conversation.

God transformed Linda McCrary's life. When a fellow junkie came knocking on her door to be delivered, she was the one who found freedom from addiction. She now uses wise communication to bring His restoration to others.

Do you ever struggle with engaging a challenging person during interpersonal conflict? Do you feel like your hard-hearted counterpart does not listen to your statements? In conflict are you training to be a person who ASKS?

Unfortunately, when we encounter difficult people and the heat gets turned up, we often become people who *tell*. We make stern statements that increase resistance in those with whom we engage. We present our view of the truth much like an attorney trying his case in front of a jury. We focus only on our own perspectives without looking to the interests of our counterpart. Finally, often we either pompously use the Bible as a sledgehammer to pound our challengers over their heads, or we ignore the truth of Scripture altogether, further perpetuating pretense in the conflict.

A teenager struggling relationally with one of her divorced parents called me. I sought to find out whether this girl was one who tells in conflict or a person who asks. Through a series of questions, I discovered that the teen was a person who tells, so we talked about implementing the four components of becoming a person who ASKS the next time she talked to this parent.

When we become a person who ASKS in wise conflict management, we experience the power of these four communication components that were evidenced in the life of Christ (see Luke 20:1–47; cf. Matt. 21:23–27; 22:1–40). Proverbs describes an emerging leader who uses wise communication in one of its twelve purposes: "for understanding proverbs and parables, the sayings and riddles of the wise" (Prov. 1:6). A saying is best delivered in the form of a question. A parable shares a story. A riddle keys in on another person's perspective. A proverb is wisdom from Scripture.

When presented with challengers, Jesus asked questions (see Luke 20:1–8; Matt. 21:23–27). The chief priests, teachers of the law, and elders challenged Jesus' authority to teach and preach. Their religious convictions, their positions in society, and their actual livelihoods were threatened by Jesus, who at one time even disrupted the temple as a response to unscrupulous profit mongers (see Luke 21:45–46). When Jesus responded to the challenge of these religious leaders with a question, He turned the focus from the surface of the conflict back to the hearts of His challengers to expose their motives (see Luke 20:1–8).

A question is one of the humble person's most powerful tools to engage a hard heart. Generally, this engagement process travels from the three resources of life at the surface of the conflict (time, talent, and treasure); through the four primary desires, which are typically dissatisfied (significance, contentment, control, and security); to the four chambers of the heart (will, intellect, spirit, and emotions).

When we ask questions rather than make statements, we shift the focus of the difficult person from the conflict at hand (which is usually over some combination of time, talent, or treasure) to the four chambers of his heart, where he chooses, thinks, prays, and feels. This includes a journey through his desires—the heartbeat that connects his heart with his own attitudes about his time, talent, and treasure.

Ask Questions That Engage the Heart

We endure difficult challengers by training to be a person who ASKS. Asking questions leads to surrender. The wisdom of asking questions that engage the heart applies anywhere and everywhere. It can transform conversations in our homes, our offices, our malls, our hospitals, and our churches. Asking a question rather than stopping conversation by making a statement can generate answers that lead to the light of God shining in the hearts of others. Whether they are husbands and wives, parents and children, or employers and employees, people listen to people who listen.

Rather than falling into the temptation to make harsh or stern statements that produce resistance during conflict, ask sincere questions that provide an environment and process for your challenger to peer inward and generate answers.

SHARE A STORY

Nothing connects with the heart like a story. A story softens the listener's heart toward truth by providing him with an experience in which he often participates, seeing himself in the drama as one who is choosing, thinking, praying, or feeling as the scenes unfold. A story also provides images that help him peer inward. These factors help the listener both remember the detail and continue to engage with the story at the heart level as he discovers its meaning for himself.

The second component of our ASKS acronym involves the following concept: When you're locked in conflict, *share a story* that opens the meaning of the truth you're trying to communicate. Allow your hard-hearted counterpart the opportunity to discover the truth you are communicating as you resist the temptation to hard-heartedly present that same truth. It might be a story that explains why you choose, think, pray, or feel a particular way. Jesus shared stories with those who challenged Him in order to help them see His heart, their own hearts, and the hearts of others. Jesus told stories to keep people open to His message, understanding that truth discovered is vastly more powerful for learning than truth merely presented.

An author once asked me to tell him my story. After I shared for about twenty minutes, he reflected, "Your story is the vehicle through which you will communicate everything else." I want you to ponder the truth of that statement for your own life. Your personal story is the vehicle through which you will communicate everything else to the people around you. A story, but particularly *your* story, carries with it tremendous impact for others to understand and learn deep truths. We have to bring people along to experience the story with us.

The power of a story can open hearts and change choices, thoughts, prayers, and feelings. This was my experience at Common Ground, an alternative gathering we offered midweek at Blackhawk Ministries, where I volunteered as a teaching pastor. Whenever God brought someone new through those doors, I asked them to tell me their story. I listened as broken people shared their pain, as addicts confessed their helplessness, as people told me about the unfulfilled longings in their hearts. When any of them surrendered his or her life to Christ, I would ask that person to share their story of faith with the entire group.

One evening I was hosting a dinner for a hundred supporters of those with addiction. One woman stood at the mic and shared her story with the crowd. At the end, she said, "Sharing my story caused something inside me to heal." At the conclusion of the woman's story a hand went up in the audience. It was another addict in need of restoration. She said, "I've struggled with cocaine addiction, and I've just been released from the behavioral clinic at the hospital. This might be my last chance to get it right. I need what she has." That second woman surrendered her life to Christ in front of a hundred supporters that night because another woman was brave enough to share.

A story is disarming. As renowned author Leonard Sweet says, it is EPIC: experiential, participatory, image based, and connective. It allows listeners to place themselves in the situation of the story and discover deeper truths for themselves, so that deeper learning can take place.

Become a Storyteller

Open the truths you're trying to communicate to your listeners in a personal way. When experiencing interpersonal conflict, use stories to communicate how you choose, think, pray, or feel. Allow your hard-hearted counterpart the opportunity to discover the truth you are communicating as you resist the temptation to hard-heartedly present that same truth.

KEY IN ON THE OTHER PERSON'S PERSPECTIVE

A few years ago, I decided to pull weeds that had grown up in a landscape bed outside our basement windows. Mixed in with the ivy ground cover was some poison ivy. Susan saw me making my way to the danger zone in my running clothes and warned, "Watch out! You should have long sleeves, pants, and gloves on to pull poison ivy."

"Look," I said, "I spent an entire summer pulling thistles from our eight-acre lawn when I was nine years old; I bailed hay several summers in high school; and I have invested countless hours in the woods growing up. In forty-three years, I have never had a reaction to poison ivy!" I proceeded to pull it out so it wouldn't be mixed in with the good ivy. When I was finished, I washed up, just in case, and continued confidently with my day.

Later that week, I noticed bumps on my forearms, but I wasn't sure what they could be. They didn't itch. Just to be sure, I called my doctor and talked with a nurse. She explained what to do. The following day, I saw spots all over my arms. I immediately rushed to my doctor's office, where I received a steroid shot and some insight. Apparently, when we are exposed to poison ivy, it breaks out at different times, though it originates from the initial exposure.

I had been hardheaded and hard-hearted in conflict, and just like poison ivy, that one exposure led to multiple breakouts.

The third word in our ASKS acronym involves *keying in on the other person's perspective* with a thought-provoking question that engages his mind and exposes his heart. Many of us engage in conflict without giving thought to the other person's perspective. Instead, we focus only on our own self-centered viewpoints.

Two thousand years ago, Jesus looked at the hearts of His detractors—spies who had been sent by the teachers of the law and the chief priests. These undercover agents had pretended to be honest, using flattery to trap the Son of Man with questions designed to trip Him up so that they could hand Him over to the power and authority of the governor. Nestled in their pockets was a denarius, a coin worth about a day's wages that featured the image of the emperor Tiberius and an inscription boasting his deity, "Tiberius Caesar, Augustus, son of the divine Augustus." Both the image and the statement would have been repulsive to the Jews living under Roman occupation. After gaining their perspective on the question at hand, Jesus not only exposed the coin, but also their hearts, through the shrewd use of a puzzle involving a thought-provoking question.

Gaining the perspective of the difficult person we're engaging allows us to see as he sees, rather than focusing purely on our own perceptions through our pride's clouded vision. We might not be as shrewd as Jesus was in gaining the internal perspective of hard-hearted challengers during interpersonal conflict, but we must remember that as believers we have His Spirit dwelling in us. We can humbly ask Him for insight into our challenger's heart as we seek Christ's wisdom to develop a thought-provoking question or puzzle that will help uncover the heart and desires of that person. His Spirit can produce in us an authenticity that is void of either flattery or sarcasm and connects us with His Spirit in other believers.

If I would have keyed in on Susan's perspective of my encounter with poison ivy before I jumped in the green stuff, I could have avoided a terrible gift that kept on giving. My reaction to the poison ivy was severe, and then I had a reaction to the healing cream that had been prescribed: It became a destruction cream as my bumps swelled into itchy open sores. People on elevators and public transportation systems avoided me at all costs.

My doctor then prescribed oral steroids. I thought I had discovered a miracle drug when my tennis elbow went away after the first dose. It was also an active ingredient in my newly prescribed cream. It seemed to remove all itching and pain on contact. *Steroid* was my new favorite word. But have you ever heard the phrase "All things in moderation"? Well, I wish I'd taken that advice. The combination of oral and topical steroids took its toll on my body. I experienced so many side effects from steroid overload that it took months to diagnose and remedy them all.

Why didn't I just key in on my high school sweetheart's perspective and save myself the pain? That's the same question each of us could ask ourselves in the midst of our conflict. Susan warned me; I just didn't listen. In doing so, I made a foolish choice that revealed more pretense.

Key in on Your Detractor's Perspective

First, ask the Holy Spirit for insight into your challenger's heart and his subsequent desires. Second, ask the Holy Spirit to give you a thought-provoking question that will engage his mind and expose his hardness of heart.

SPEAK SCRIPTURE

The last part of the ASKS acronym is to *speak Scripture*, humbly applying it to your role in the conflict. When the Sadducees, who did not believe in the resurrection, challenged Jesus, He used the authority of Scripture to bring truth to the conflict. The truth of Scripture brings us back to sure footing in our reasoning and helps us avoid pretense in conflict.

The writer of Hebrews said: "For the word of God is living and active. Sharper than any double-edged sword, it penetrates even to dividing soul and spirit, joints and marrow; it judges the thoughts and attitudes of the heart" (Heb. 4:12). In the spirit of training to be a person who ASKS, we must immerse ourselves in Scripture so that we can speak Scripture with humility. It might sound something like this: "You know, I've been reading Proverbs and attempting to apply it to my own life. Proverbs 18:13 says that a fool answers before listening, and I don't want to do that."

Demonstrating our pride and pretense pushes people away, but speaking Scripture in humility and authenticity disarms them and pulls them toward God. Like the wind directs a sailboat, the wind of the Holy Spirit moves us in a certain direction. Rather than pushing from behind the boat, the wind actually draws the vessel toward its direction. Similarly, when we set the sails of our hearts with the drawing of the Holy Spirit, we navigate through conflict to community.

The most persuasive and penetrating words that we can use in a conflict situation are those that are inspired by God's Word. I have experienced heart transformation, both in my life and in countless others, through hearing the wisdom from the Bible. Every single person I have prayed with to surrender his or her life to Christ did so after an encounter with either reading or hearing the truth of Scripture.

Humbly Present Truth

Apply the truth of the Bible to your role in the conflict, rather than using it to pound your challenger. This will help you to avoid perpetuating pretense. Bring wise communication to your wise conflict management and experience the power of four communication components evidenced in the life of Christ. When encountering a challenging person during interpersonal conflict, train to be a person who ASKS, rather than a person who tells.

First, *ask questions* that engage the heart. Remember that questions generate answers and statements produce resistance.

Second, *share a story* that opens up the truths you're trying to communicate.

Third, *key in on the other person's perspective* with a thought-provoking question that engages his mind and exposes his heart. Ask the Holy Spirit for insight into the perspective of your challenger's heart and his subsequent desires. Next, ask the Holy Spirit to give you a thought-provoking question that will help uncover your challenger's hardness of heart.

Fourth, *speak Scripture*, humbly applying its truth to your role in the conflict, rather than using it to pound your challenger and advancing pretense.

Christ in you will provide wise communication in the midst of your conflict.

Chapter 10

Prudence

IGNORE INSULTS

Jody Martinez has traveled a unique journey through his exercise of prudence. I encountered Jody when he was head coach of the women's basketball program at Bethel College, where he won six NCCAA National Championships. Growing up in the inner city of South Bend, Indiana, Jody could have avoided much trouble if he had learned to ignore insults at an early age. "When people see my name in writing, they expect a Mexican girl, not a six-foot-eight-inch Caucasian dude." The irony of this statement comes from an unlikely story.

Due to his involvement in organized crime, Jody's biological father was in prison when Jody was born. When he was a young boy, Jody's mother married a man of Mexican descent named Frank Martinez, who adopted Jody. "I grew up in an abusive alcoholic home. I witnessed Frank verbally and physically abuse my mom and my younger brother and sister. He abused me as well." Frank left the family when Jody was in sixth grade, but the divorce was not final until he was in ninth grade—the same age as his mother had been when she had quit school.

Jody was always ready to make threats or retaliate whenever conflict came his way. Jody reflects, "I was an angry child, ready to lash out at anyone who got in my way. The turning point in my life's conflict came when I got in a fistfight with my dad. I still remember the scene: He came to our house drunk right after the divorce had become final. My mom was in the shower. He broke down the bathroom door and started hitting her. That's when I snapped. I beat him with my fists until he fell, then had him on the ground in a choke hold. His face was actually turning colors as I tightened my grip in my rage. My mom had to hit me to get me off him." Jody's adoptive father fled the scene and never came back.

In school, basketball became the outlet for Jody's anger. Although he didn't make the cut during the first three years of high school basketball, Jody continued to grow in stature and practiced his game, garnering the attention of legendary coach Homer Drew, who recruited Jody to play for him at Bethel College. When Coach Drew accepted another position after Jody's freshman year, Mike Lightfoot, Jody's high school coach, replaced Drew as the Pilots' head coach. The transition was timely.

In 1988, when Jody was twenty, during the summer after his sophomore year in college, Jody's mother finally told him that he was adopted. "My mom told me, and suddenly a light went on. The fact that I was adopted explained all the dreams I'd been having that seemed to communicate that I had been living a lie. My first question to her was, 'Then who's my real father?' She told me that he'd been a preacher. I learned that he'd been married and that the two of them had had an affair. Mom wanted to continue to talk. I didn't. I took off and left home for a couple of days."

Jody decided to quit college, so he drove to his coach's house to tell him about his decision. "Coach brought out a Bible. I refused to listen to him read anything from it, but Coach held on to it the entire time."

Coach Lightfoot shared his profound perspective with Jody. "Basketball is your life," he reminded his towering player. "It got you off the streets." He asked for permission to pray for Jody, who finally relented. He then prayed these powerful words: "'For I know the plans I have for you,' declares the LORD, 'plans to prosper you and not to harm you, plans to give you hope and a future'" (Jer. 29:11).

In that moment, Jody began to realize the danger in his temper and how it affected the foolish steps he'd taken, the pathway of deception he'd been walking, and his destination of suffering. "The key word for me was *hope*. I needed it to move on. I wanted to start over." He knew he was missing something, but his heart was still hardened to seeking what he needed to understand. His heart finally softened when Coach introduced him to a young woman named Sonya, whom Jody eventually married.

After graduating from Bethel as its all-time leader in points, rebounds, blocks, steals, field goal percentage, and games played, Jody signed a contract to play professional basketball. The travel commitment conflicted with his desire to prioritize his new marriage, so Jody started searching for a different path. He attended a church service with his wife, where they heard a message about forgiveness. In January 1992, at age twenty-four, Jody, responding to an altar call, grabbed Sonya's hand and said, "I want to accept Christ as my Savior. I need to learn to forgive people." She went to the altar with him.

On April 8, 1992, Jody Martinez was baptized on his birthday. Through the transforming work of the Word and the Spirit, Jody slowly learned how to become a forgiver. "I forgave my mom in May 1995. That's when I learned that my biological dad had been a significant member of an organized crime syndicate."

Jody remembers the scene where he confronted his mom. "But you said he was a preacher!" he said.

"He is now, but he wasn't then," she told him.

"Why didn't you tell me?"

"I was trying, but you were stubborn and wouldn't listen," she replied.

Jody realized that his mother was right, but his new life required that he would ask questions, listen, learn, and lean on his heavenly Father. Jody's mother gave him the book *The Enforcer*, a chronicle of his father's life. "Happy Jack" Burbridge had been on the FBI's Ten Most Wanted list in 1967. He and Jody's mother were captured near the Indiana-Kentucky border. The authorities offered Jody's mom a plea bargain in lieu of serving prison time if she would testify against his dad. She agreed, and Happy Jack was sentenced to life in prison.

The prison warden led Jody's biological father to Christ. As a new man with a new purpose, he began to share the gospel with his fellow inmates. Many who heard him tell his story surrendered their lives to Christ. When interviewed annually by the parole panel, he would tell them that the system didn't work, but the Bible did. He was granted an early release in the 1970s and became an evangelist to those sentenced on death row.

Jody knew from his new life in Jesus that there was danger in living a life in which he withheld forgiveness. He didn't want to leave his relationships unreconciled. So he decided to ignore the past abuse and the pain that came with it and met with Frank Martinez, his adoptive father, before he reached out to his biological father. Jody let Frank know that he loved him and that he wanted to keep the Martinez name. Then Jody humbly shared Jesus with Frank, who received Him as his Lord and Savior. The man Jody once nearly choked to death was now a new creation in Christ, delivered from the burden of alcoholism and reconciled with his son.

At age twenty-seven, Jody decided to connect with his biological father. "My mom called a friend who called him in Arkansas to ask if the two of us could get together. He traveled to Indiana with his wife, and I saw him for the first time in the parking lot of a restaurant. I reached out my hand, but he wouldn't take it. Instead, he embraced me and said, 'Jody, you were not born in sin. You were born in love. I loved your mom.'" Jody broke down and wept. It was another new beginning of a reconciled relationship.

Twenty years later, Happy Jack lost his battle with colon cancer. A week before hospice nurses arrived, with his eldest daughter beside him, Jody was able to say good-bye to his father, who pulled Jody close and whispered, "I loved your mother, and I am so happy that you and I were able to have a relationship for the last twenty years."

Jody's response to the prudence that God gave him to reconcile with his biological father was, "God is so good!"

An inductee of both the NCCAA and Bethel College halls of fame, Jody Martinez continues to train young women as assistant women's basketball coach at the University of Illinois. "I used to coach as a former athlete. Now I coach as a teacher." Coach Jody Martinez is a man of prudence. In a journey filled with many twists and turns, God has taught him to truly ignore insults, foresee danger, be informed, and not flaunt his knowledge.

Do you ever feel simple or gullible when dealing with a strong personality during interpersonal conflict? Typically, when conflict comes and our will attempts to occupy the same space at the same time as that of a challenging person, we respond in our foolish self-interest. We immediately react to an insult, blindly speeding into the unknown; we stop pursuing the pertinent information we need to respond appropriately; and we flaunt the little knowledge we have.

In order to wisely manage interpersonal conflict, we must learn to master the pearl of *prudence*. Solomon held up prudence as one of the key purposes of his book of Proverbs: "for giving prudence to the simple" (Prov. 1:4). Where we find wisdom, we find prudence.

Prudence can be defined as "being both shrewd and

innocent." When sending His disciples to advance the news of the kingdom of heaven amid what He knew would be challenging interpersonal conflict for those men, Jesus said: "I am sending you out like sheep among wolves. Therefore be as shrewd as snakes and as innocent as doves" (Matt. 10:16).

As we encounter the wolves of interpersonal conflict, we want to humbly advance the kingdom of heaven in the hearts of those who oppose us. We accomplish this through mastering wisdom's shrewd and innocent practice of prudence. *Shrewd* means "sharp, keen, clever, creative, or cunning." In essence, to be shrewd is to be street-smart. *Innocent* can be defined as "harmless, or without sin." Consequently, prudence is shrewd about discovering the innocent sweet spot where God's interests intersect with our unselfish interests and the interests of others. That's where we discover the raw material of the kingdom of heaven.

When we examine its contextual usages in Proverbs, we see four shrewd and innocent patterns of prudence: *ignore insults, foresee danger, be informed*, and *do not flaunt knowledge*.

All of us fit God's definition of a leader; He expects all of us to connect with and influence others. If you're a student, you're going to influence other students. If you're a mom, you're going to influence your family and other moms. If you're an athlete, you're going to connect with and influence other athletes. The point is that we are all people of influence, and we're going to influence our audiences toward either wisdom or foolishness.

Jesus' leadership style can be defined in the acronym ACTS—aware, connected, touched, spoke—which we can see in the story in Matthew 8. At the conclusion of the Sermon on the Mount, Matthew records that a man with leprosy fought through the crowd of some twenty thousand people to earn a face-to-face encounter with Jesus (see Matt. 8:1–4). In spite of the scores of people bumping into Him, Jesus was *aware* of the man with leprosy's presence, including his heart and his need (see Matt. 8:1–2). Second, Jesus *connected* with the heart, communicating that He was willing to grant this man's request for healing (see Matt. 8:2). Third, Jesus *touched* the leper's need with a deed (see Matt. 8:3). He served the leper at his greatest point of need with an actual touch, which no one else would have been willing to do for fear of catching the condition. Finally, Jesus *spoke* vision and direction toward kingdom building (see Matt. 8:4). Jesus' leadership style was shrewd and innocent. He was aware of His audience, connected with the heart, and touched the need with a deed, before He ever spoke vision and direction toward kingdom building. What would our leadership look like if we wisely did the same?

Too many of us desire to be shrewd rather than innocent or innocent rather than shrewd. The former flows from a sand heart, the latter from a stone heart. A sand heart is evidenced in the high school athlete who has all these classmates following him, but lacks moral fiber woven through the fabric of his life. A stone heart is portrayed in the high school student who has no one following, but remains steadfast in his self-righteousness and judgment of others. God's idea is that we would have clay hearts, humble and wise, leading others toward His kingdom priorities. When we are both shrewd and innocent, we benefit others and ourselves.

An example of being street-smart and harmless occurred for me at an auction, formerly my ideal environment for positive conflict. While I was offering a sparkling Jaguar XKE roadster for sale from the auction podium, I noticed a well-known celebrity slowly walking down the aisle to approach our altar of collector car evangelism. Had the room been a ship, it would have tipped over because the audience immediately leaned closer to the easily recognizable personality. As the auction progressed, the celebrity began bidding on his favorite cars, winning the competition for every single rolling sculpture he desired.

Most likely in an effort to be shrewd, for once the actor decided to stop bidding on a car, one whose red paint glistened in the sunlight. The impeccably restored masterpiece fit his now well-established criteria for addition to his stable, but nevertheless, he shook his head no when I asked him to bid again. He was acting. I knew it because I could read it in his eyes, something I learned from auctioning no less than two hundred thousand collector cars to the shrewdest bidders ever to walk auction sod. But I played his game. As the bidding for the sports car waned, I turned my body away from him as if I believed his masquerade. "Anybody else want to bid?" I inquired over the public address system. Without losing sight of the legendary performer, I lifted my gavel, only to see him dive toward me with his hand up in order to garner my attention, something that he had never lost. He made the last bid, satisfied that he had won the car of his dreams.

I like to think that I was shrewd and innocent. I was *aware* of the bidder. I *connected* with his heart. I knew he longed for the car, and his demeanor communicated that he was going to buy it. I *touched* his need with the deed of service by allowing him to bid, paying attention to him even after he indicated he was not going to make any further advances. Finally, I *spoke* to him after he made his last-second gesture. At the same time, I recognized that the seller preferred that every person who desired his car would have the opportunity to bid on it. Yet I would have insulted the actor if I had communicated that I knew he was pretending.

Whether in the marketplace or in ministry, God desires that amid our interpersonal conflict we would be prudent—both shrewd and innocent—as we direct others toward the sweet spot where our unselfish interests intersect with those of others and God.

Solomon taught: "A fool shows his annoyance at once, but a prudent man overlooks an insult" (Prov. 12:16). A difficult person designs and deploys an insult to generate a reaction—one that gives them control. When we do not react, the insult is defused. The first strategy of prudence is to ignore insults as we encounter the wolves of conflict. Ignoring an insult includes maintaining a listening body posture and attentive facial expressions while we deflect the flaming arrows soaring our way. It requires patience. Usually, our first reaction to an offense is to immediately address it. Solomon advised: "A man's wisdom gives him patience; it is to his glory to overlook an offense" (Prov. 19:11).

If our offender is a friend or even a family member, we will most likely address a pattern of insulting behavior at some point. My friend Jody had to address something similar in his life with his adoptive father. However, Jody would tell you, in the interest of not escalating the conflict, it's best not to address the issue in the heat of the insult. This means looking past the demeaning behavior and following the Twenty-Second Rule to look into the heart of that person.

Jesus taught His disciples to ignore insults: "If someone strikes you on the right cheek, turn to him the other also" (Matt. 5:39). A strike on the right cheek was made with the back of one's right hand (considered the dominant hand). The phrase "strikes you on the right cheek" was an idiomatic expression for an insult. Today, we use similar phraseology when we say, "That was a backhanded compliment." An insult is an attack on who we are—the unique person God has created us to be. In turning the other cheek, we are ignoring the insult in a way that is both shrewd and innocent.

Jesus modeled this. His disciple Peter described Jesus' response to the ultimate insult, which He faced before His crucifixion: "When they hurled their insults at him, he did not retaliate; when he suffered, he made no threats. Instead, he entrusted himself to him who judges justly" (1 Pet. 2:23). "Entrusted" is translated from the Greek *paradidomi*, meaning "to hand over." When insulted, we can hand the insult over to God and do the same with our subsequent thoughts, feelings, choices, and prayers. In teaching about this same idea, Paul offered the imagery of a warrior, advising that believers take up the shield of faith that allows us to extinguish all the flaming arrows of the evil one (see Eph. 6:16).

I was leading a group of Christians through a Bible study that began with a quiz I had created. I thought our answers to the few short questions would demonstrate our need for wisdom. One of the multiple-choice questions read, "An acquaintance of yours has insulted you. Should you: (A) Go to him to discuss the matter and attempt to reconcile it, (B) Go get counsel from a mutual friend on how to handle it, (C) Get even with an insult of your own, or (D) Ignore it?" Not one person in the group selected D. It definitely exposed our need for teaching in this area.

I wish I had applied this idea as well as I taught it. One morning Susan and I were running late for a trip to California with our church staff. As we exited our garage with barely enough time to get to the airport, park the car, check the bags, go through security, and board the plane with our friends, insults were fired back and forth, resulting in retaliation and threats. As God would have it, at precisely that moment our pastor called. Susan and I battled over who should answer my cell phone and assume responsibility for our tardiness. I won; she answered. I'll never forget the language she used to describe to our pastor what I thought of her actions that morning. Then she tossed the cell phone to me. "Dude, are you going to make it?" our pastor asked.

"We'll probably arrive at the airport just in time," I replied.

"No, I mean are you going to arrive alive?"

After we got to the airport safely, Pastor Kelly laughed, looked at the two of us, and said, "I found that it works a lot better to ignore those insults with my wife and address anything that still needs to be addressed much later, after everything has cooled down."

"I like that idea!" my wife shouted.

In the heat of the insult, we rarely think about the other person. That person is typically seeking a reaction to gain control of the situation. This was the case with a customer of mine. He liked to use insults as a means to gain information that would profit him. After falling for it a few times, I read this verse and thought to myself, *I'll apply that to this guy.* Less than a week later, I saw him at an auction. When he fired off an insult that I so badly wanted to address, I simply ignored it. I'm not sure that he knew what to do. His mechanism had been defused, and he was befuddled. In fact, I can't recall him ever trying to use that tactic again.

Have you ever had a work associate who listened to your story in an attempt to be your friend, but then later used that information against you? He or she exploited your vulnerability and used it to their advantage. I've experienced that one too many times, so I've analyzed it and decided that the common thread in each person who did this to me was a deep-seated insecurity that strategized, "I'm going to disarm him so I can get him later." Such people carefully build their plan to set us up to insult when the time is right to use it to their advantage.

Hand Over Insults to God

At work in each person who fires insults is a combination of dissatisfied desires. They are out of control, insecure, and discontent from trusting in their perceived giftedness, rather than their actual godliness. The more they pursue satisfaction of their desires apart from God, the more dissatisfied they become. However, we need to be careful because that same pride is at work in us. When insulted, we are tempted to retaliate and make threats. That's why we need to learn that it's wise to ignore an insult. Pride comes at conflict from the top down and results in foolishness, but humility comes from the bottom up and offers wisdom. When the wolves of conflict insult you, ignore them. Don't retaliate. Don't make threats. Instead, hand them over to God, and deflect the demeaning words with your shield of faith.

FORESEE DANGER

The second part of prudence is that, when encountering the wolves of conflict, we must foresee danger. Rather than speed blindly ahead into our own fallen reactions, we are called to exercise foresight into the potential danger lying ahead in our steps, our pathway, and our destination of conflict management.

Prudence foresees the danger of simple steps. Solomon warned of gullibility in interpersonal conflict: "A simple man believes anything, but a prudent man gives thought to his steps" (Prov. 14:15). Our steps include our words and actions, which will be either simple or prudent. This translates into the need to shrewdly and innocently filter the words and actions of our counterpart to understand the deeper meaning behind them before we take our next step.

Prudence foresees the danger of a deceptive pathway. When we foresee danger, we look forward to the pathway where our next steps lead. This includes the consequences of both our words and our actions. Solomon advised: "The wisdom of the prudent is to give thought to their ways, but the folly of fools is deception" (Prov. 14:8). Simple or gullible words and actions are strewn along the pathway of deception. The word *deception* implies "giving only part of the whole," which means that something is hidden in the communication. Prudent words and actions line the pathway of integrity. As we've seen before in earlier chapters, *integrity* means "complete and undivided," implying that communication is whole and not lacking. We must wisely examine the consequences of not only our words and actions, but also the words and actions of others for either deception or integrity as we proceed down the pathway of communication in conflict.

Prudence foresees the danger of a suffering destination. When we foresee danger, we look to the destination of our conflict management—its effect on the relationship. It will be one of either suffering or safety. Solomon observed: "A prudent man sees danger and takes refuge, but the simple keep going and suffer for it" (Prov. 22:3; cf. 27:12). In the heat of conflict, we often blindly keep going with our simple steps along their consequential pathway of deception. This is what leads to suffering, which shows up in the misunderstandings that affect both parties involved in the conflict. Prudence helps us change our steps so that we take those that lead to safety—a mutual understanding between the two parties found when we follow the wisdom of Christ.

Jesus warned His disciples to foresee danger among the wolves of conflict: "Be on your guard against men; they will

hand you over to the local councils and flog you in their syna-
gogues. On my account you will be brought before governors
and kings as witnesses to them and to the Gentiles" (Matt.
10:17–18). Whereas we might not experience physical perse-
cution for advancing the kingdom of heaven in the hearts of
others, we are guaranteed that opposition will come against
our efforts. Christ, our safe refuge, guides us to foresee danger
in our steps, our pathway, and our destination.

To foresee danger is a matter of the heart. This pearl is paramount in both marketplace and ministry. Whether we are in
board meetings, elder meetings, Sunday morning service planning meetings, or working out marriage and family decisions,
when we're left to ourselves, we often don't look ahead to see
the consequences of our actions.

I remember explaining this concept to my eldest daughter,
Megan, when she was four years old. She was having trouble
with the concept. So I created a hypothetical situation that
illustrated the sense of urgency her mom and I thought should
accompany her obedience to our warnings.

I grabbed my daughter's little warm face and said, "Megan,
if it's raining and your mom and I tell you not to touch a cable
lying in the road, and you don't listen and continue to run to it
and touch it, you are going to get hurt badly. So when we tell
you to do something, it is for your safety."

Satisfied that I had made my point at a four-year-old level, I
began to walk away, only to hear, "Daddy, why is that cable in
the road in the rain?" Because Megan perceived my point, she
began to visualize a danger that appeared real. I think that's
how it goes with God. As our loving Father, He warns us of

danger for our own safety. However, until the danger seems real to us, we fail to stop moving toward the hazard that's in our way.

One of the strongest tools that God used to renew my business relationships was His teaching of foresight. Too often, I sped blindly ahead without considering the consequences of my words and actions. Foresight allowed me to speak more wisely and make wise choices. This caused a significant paradigm shift in my behavior. My dad, the politician, was excellent at implementing foresight when it came to booking an auction. In almost every attempt at signing the deal, I can remember him commenting on whether an action would be prudent based on its potential consequences. He was acting with biblical foresight.

The Bible is incredibly effective at helping us transition from blindness to sight. I have a friend whose office peers used to implement a new vocabulary word every day. Each team member would have to use that word in a sentence as much and as cleverly as possible. I think that idea is really cool. Now, what about doing that with a Bible verse to improve our prudent behavior? When I live my entire day through the lens of a particular Bible verse, I see a spike in my shrewd and innocent behavior. My foresight is clearer. My tasks and relationships flow much better when I can see more vividly any danger that lurks ahead.

Discern Your Steps

When you encounter the wolves of conflict, foresee the danger in your steps, your pathway, and your destination. Ask God if your steps are simple or prudent, if your pathway is deception or integrity, and if your destination is suffering or safety. If you discern that His Spirit is prompting you to see your steps as simple, and therefore, inadvisable, then exchange those steps for prudent ones.

BE INFORMED

The third aspect of pursuing prudence when encountering the wolves of conflict is that we must *be informed*. Solomon referred to this information as knowledge, which we saw earlier as an intimate experience—the connection of our innermost being with God. Solomon wrote: "Every prudent man acts out of knowledge, but a fool exposes his folly" (Prov. 13:16). Prudence flows from knowledge, yet the more we act with prudence, the more knowledge we receive.

A sincere quest for knowledge includes a willingness to be corrected when we are wrong: "A fool spurns his father's discipline, but whoever heeds correction shows prudence" (Prov. 15:5). A prudent person yields to correction. A foolish person does not.

In order to be informed, we need to ask prudent questions. Solomon taught that we should use our ears as well as our hearts: "The heart of the discerning acquires knowledge; the ears of the wise seek it out" (Prov. 18:15). Our shrewd and innocent questions must be directed both vertically to God and horizontally to others. After we ask, we must listen, learn, and lean on God.

Jesus trained His disciples to be informed by the Spirit of

God: "But when they arrest you, do not worry about what to say or how to say it. At that time you will be given what to say, for it will not be you speaking, but the Spirit of your Father speaking through you" (Matt. 10:19–20).

Days before speaking to the high school graduating class at Lakewood Park Christian School, I interviewed a student, a survivor of the Columbine tragedy. She told me that on that fateful day she had spilled taco sauce on her blouse at lunch, so she had driven home to change. When she returned, she saw the horror of emergency vehicles surrounding her high school as her classmates rushed from the building. A couple of her best friends were being held hostage by the orchestrators of the crime in a room where she would have been had she not left earlier. Another of her friends told her about Cassie Bernall's fate. The shooters were walking up to students with guns pointed at them, asking if they believed in God. When they made it to Cassie, they pointed their guns and asked, "Do you believe in God *now*?" She folded her hands as if she were praying, looked up toward heaven, and answered, "Yes." They shot and killed her.

"Have you ever thought about what you would have done if you'd been asked the same question with a gun pointed at you?" I asked her.

"Yes, I have, many times," she replied. "You see, Cassie had witnessed to the two shooters before about her faith in Christ with gentleness and respect. That's why they asked her, 'Do you believe in God *now*?' I know that if I had been in the same situation, God would have given me the same strength to answer yes that He had given Cassie."

When we connect vertically toward God with our hearts, then

we are empowered to connect horizontally in the same way with the Spirit speaking through us. I found the same to be true in my counseling sessions. I remember asking my partner in ministry at the church where we were pastors, "Dude, have you ever given advice to someone and wondered, 'Where did that come from?' because you just knew it wasn't from you, it was from God?"

"Yep. All the time," he agreed.

Ask, Listen, Learn, and Lean

What about you? Are you asking, listening to, learning from, and leaning on the Spirit of God so that you can engage the same way in your relationships? When we are informed vertically, God equips us to be informed horizontally. When you encounter the wolves of conflict, ask prudent questions of God and of others. Then listen to, learn from, and lean on your heavenly Father. The intimate connection you'll experience with His Spirit will allow you to act with prudence.

DO NOT FLAUNT KNOWLEDGE

The fourth aspect of following a life of prudence is that, when encountering the wolves of conflict, we do not flaunt knowledge. Only fools tell all they know. Solomon cautioned: "A prudent man keeps his knowledge to himself, but the heart of fools blurts out folly" (Prov. 12:23). Too often in conflict, we desire to come out on top by flaunting information that is usually derogatory toward our detractor or flattering toward our own cause.

In order to be prudent, we must discern what knowledge is appropriate to use in our conflicts. This discretion comes from seeking the Holy Spirit, who provides us with shrewd and innocent words. The filtering process brings prudence to our conflict management. Solomon observed: "A man of knowledge uses words with restraint, and a man of understanding is even-tempered" (Prov. 17:27). Sometimes the Holy Spirit will guide us to not speak at all. Solomon illustrated the wisdom of silence when he wrote: "Even a fool is thought wise if he keeps silent, and discerning if he holds his tongue" (Prov. 17:28).

Jesus did not flaunt His knowledge. When encountering Herod Antipas, a member of the wolves of conflict, Jesus wisely refrained from answering the deceitful ruler's questions. At times during His arrest, He refrained from answering Pilate as well. However, there were occurrences when Jesus did engage Pilate with words. These are examples of prudence, not flaunting knowledge.

Jesus explained to His disciples that while they were advancing the kingdom of heaven, the Spirit of their Father would be speaking through them. Later, He elaborated: "What I tell you in the dark, speak in the daylight; what is whispered in your ear, proclaim from the roofs" (Matt. 10:27). The Spirit of Christ will guide us in what information is prudent to reveal; however, in no case will He lead us to loosely mishandle the truth.

Don't Tell All You Know

When you encounter the wolves of conflict, resist the temptation to tell all you know. Do not use information to criticize others or flatter yourself. Ask the Holy Spirit to guide you in the discernment of which shrewd and innocent words to say.

When we master prudence, it is not merely we who are advancing the kingdom of heaven amid challenging interpersonal conflict. Rather, it is Christ in us.

Chapter 11

Discretion

SEPARATE WISDOM FROM FOOLISHNESS

George Del Canto grew up in Chicago in a Catholic home of Spanish descent. He attended parochial school and mass every Sunday, where he served as an altar boy. George experienced confirmation, communion, and attended a Catholic high school, but he compartmentalized it all as religion.

George studied international finance, earning his master's degree from the renowned Thunderbird School of Global Management. He moved his family all over the world, including stops in South America, Switzerland, Asia, and London. "I wanted to be a prince of the world in finance. It was always about a bigger and better deal for me because I saw myself as being only as good as my last deal." George's role was to develop relationships with foreign banks and assemble financing for international commodities' shipments, including agricultural products and steel. But God had other plans for George.

George's wife, Marichu, surrendered her life to Christ in 1998 while they were living in Singapore. "I treated it as a woman's thing, but it wasn't for me. We moved to London. Life was all about me. Eventually, I alienated my wife, my family, and my kids." When they would push back regarding the time George invested in his career at the expense of his family, he would reply, "Look at our house, the cars, the vacations." George reflects, "I stopped being a father and husband. I didn't even recognize the person who said that. I was lost in London."

George later discovered that his wife was praying frequently. "She surrounded me with Christian businessmen whom I respected. She took me to church, where I heard the gospel for the first time, and she gave me Patrick Morley's book, *Man in the Mirror*. I read the 'Rat Race' chapter, and it made a lot of sense to me." In May 2000, a large American corporation purchased George's company. That buyer was Enron.

God was drawing George to Himself, the first step of discerning wisdom. "I started listening to Dr. Ed Young on the Internet. There's nowhere to hide when you start listening to the Word of God." In September 2001, Enron collapsed. "They took all the money we had in the company. Our lives were in financial ruin overnight."

George, middle-aged with a family of five, was employed by a finance company in the midst of a monumental financial crisis. Up until this point, this Chicago street kid had been tough enough to handle every situation. Now it was time to separate his walk from his talk. In October 2001, alone in his home study in London, George fell to his knees and prayed to God, "I am toast. My life is over. I am road kill. God, I can't deal with this. It's too much to handle. I can't take this anymore. I give this to you. I accept Jesus Christ. Whatever happens, this is your will. I'm worthless. I'm broken. I need you. I turn myself and my family over to you."

George sensed an indescribable peace. "Almost immediately, I was put in a bubble of calm." He began to separate the long-term benefits of a relationship with God from the short-term pleasures of his worldly success. Over the next few months, his fellow employees who had been ruined by Enron's misman-agement were gnashing their teeth at the deception enacted by the company's executives that put them in this situation. Some of George's distraught team members even committed suicide.

George was about to experience the next steps on his walk. Uncharacteristically, his company chose to repatriate him anywhere in the United States. He and his wife prayed about it, and the answer came to both of them: *Houston*. They flew there and visited sixty houses in three days. "We got in the Realtor's car, drove about one mile away, made a left turn, and then stopped in front of a building. A sign read, 'Welcome to Second Baptist Church, Dr. Ed Young, Jr., Pastor.' Houston seemed like the right place for a new start."

George grew as a believer, but his growth was not without mistakes that provided more opportunities to learn discretion. He formed a partnership with some of his former colleagues. "I was still at the stage of making my own plans and asking God to bless them. I was unequally yoked with my partners, so God brought that to an end." Next, George started a small business from his home office. "It was modest, but we were happy."

In 2005, after being a committed Christian for three years, George prayed, "God, you restored my family. You gave me new life and fellow believers surrounding me. God, what can I do for you?" George was about to receive his answer. His men's Bible study group had been reading *Awaken the Leader Within*, a book that challenged readers to dare to dream something they could not accomplish without God. "By next week's session, we each needed to come up with our own blow-your-socks-off vision for God."

George's wife suggested that he pray, which he did, for two nights. He forgot to pray on the third. The evening before the next breakfast, Marichu asked, "What are you going to tell the guys?"

"I'm going to build an Indy car team to deliver God's Word through motorsports."

"You would be perfect for that," she confirmed.

"What did I just say?" a stunned George asked.

Seeking direction, George called his pastor Dr. Wallace Henley. He asked, "How do you know when you have a vision from God?" Dr. Henley invited him to meet, and he offered five answers to George's question: You know that your vision is from God if the vision has a kingdom purpose, you do not have enough resources to accomplish it by yourself, doors open easily, it is a desire God has placed deep in your heart, and your godly spouse approves.

After hearing those five priceless truths, George inquired of his mentor, "What should I do?"

"Go," Dr. Henley said.

George sent emails to several racing organizations, and thinking he had done all God had required of him, he left on a trip. He never thought that someone would actually reply, but someone did. It was Indy Racing League sales director John Stewart, and the two men agreed to meet.

At the agreed-upon meeting place, the two men started talk-ing. John introduced George to IRL chaplain Bob Hills, when George mentioned to Bob that he attended Dr. Ed Young's church. In his peripheral vision, George saw that John was thunderstruck. John explained, "George, before I was in the IRL, I was in the Christian recording business. I produced Ed Young's son's first record. George, God will greatly bless a Christian team in the IRL. I'll do anything I can to help you." Doors for George's vision were beginning to open.

Thinking he had God's plan figured out, George began to call on companies to solicit sponsorships, but he was repeat-edly turned down. "By 2007, God so blessed my business that I was able to come up with the funds in 2008 to start the team." George's business had become of strategic importance to two large companies. Instead of internally duplicating the efforts of George's company at a greater cost, they passed along their business to George. The reason they chose to do so spoke volumes about George's discretion. They said, "We can trust George. He knows right from wrong."

In March 2008, George met racing legend Davey Hamil-ton, who was making a comeback from a crash that had nearly taken his life. That's when Kingdom Racing was launched. "In 2008, we had a great year of triumph. Kingdom Racing quali-fied in the starting field of the Indianapolis 500. However, in August of the same year my wife began to have issues with her balance. She had her first seizure in September. We hospi-talized her in October when she was diagnosed with terminal brain cancer."

George offered to give up the Kingdom Racing vision. Marichu replied, "No. No. Kingdom Racing will bring many to Jesus." She passed away four weeks later. George was devastated.

"I didn't know if I could get out of bed in the morning. I didn't let go of God, but more importantly, God didn't let go of me. When you lose hope, you find faith. I found faith in my deepest grief."

God prompted George to "get up," and George started walking with God and trying to cope with this loss. Over time, he began to ask if God wanted him to remain alone. "If not, God, you'll have to bring a wife to me," George prayed. George frequented a sushi restaurant where he often talked with a waitress he knew. She introduced him to her mom, who was named Maricarmen. The two started talking, and a few weeks later, George invited her to join him at Second Baptist Church at 11:00 a.m. for their first date. Eventually, they married. Discretion won again in George Del Canto's life, and today he continues to connect the racing world with the Word of God.

Have you ever heard the saying "The cream rises to the top"? The adage stems from how cream is divided from milk—à la a cream separator. A cream separator introduces air and uses centrifugal force to separate the heavier skim milk particles from the lighter butterfat (cream) particles. The separator's motion results in the cream rising to the top. Originally, this was done so that dairy farmers could maximize the revenue from their milk by producing a commodity that would last longer. Without a cream separator, their entire product could spoil. Consequently, they separated the *valuable* from the *vulnerable*.

The word *discretion* means "to separate." Proverbs tells us that during interpersonal conflict, we need to introduce the air of the Holy Spirit's wisdom so that we can separate what is valuable from what is vulnerable. This Spirit of Christ allows what is valuable, the cream, to rise to the top. Without discretion, our lives, our relationships, and our efforts to manage conflict will spoil: Foolishness will spoil wisdom; actions will spoil words; short-term pleasure will spoil long-term benefits; what's wrong will spoil what's right. Consequently, we must ask ourselves this question: "When two objects attempt to occupy the same space at the same time in our lives, how will we separate the valuable from the vulnerable?" In essence, how will we allow the cream to rise to the top so that we do not let it all spoil? Wisdom's answer is discretion (see Prov. 1:4). From Proverbs, we learn that discretion separates *wisdom from foolishness*, *walk from talk*, *long-term benefits from short-term pleasure*, and *right from wrong*.

First, discretion separates wisdom from foolishness. As he set the course for his collection of wise sayings, Solomon emphasized how the search for wisdom must be paramount in our lives in order for us to choose it. We cannot discern wisdom from foolishness if we cannot distinguish authentic wisdom from counterfeit wisdom when we see it.

> My son, if you accept my words and store up my commands within you, turning your ear to wisdom and applying your heart to understanding, and if you call out for insight and cry aloud for understanding, and if you look for it as for silver and search for it as for hidden

treasure, then you will understand the fear of the LORD and find the knowledge of God. For the LORD gives wisdom, and from his mouth come knowledge and understanding. He holds victory in store for the upright; he is a shield to those whose walk is blameless, for he guards the course of the just and protects the way of his faithful ones. Then you will understand what is right and just and fair—every good path. For wisdom will enter your heart, and knowledge will be pleasant to your soul. Discretion will protect you, and understanding will guard you. (Prov. 2:1–11)

In order to discover wisdom, we must value it greatly. We must be willing to accept it, store it up, listen for it, apply our hearts to it, call for it, cry aloud for it, and pursue it as if we're searching for hidden treasure, understanding that it comes from God. His Spirit gives us discernment between wisdom and foolishness so that the cream of wisdom can rise to the top in our interpersonal conflict.

Of course, the most valuable of the two is God's wisdom. Left to ourselves, apart from the activity of the Holy Spirit, foolishness rises to the top during our conflict with others, leaving us vulnerable.

Solomon noted how foolish a beautiful woman looks when she lacks discretion: "Like a gold ring in a pig's snout is a beautiful woman who shows no discretion" (Prov. 11:22). I often refer to this verse with our four girls. In fact, the eldest two can finish the line before it finishes coming out of my mouth. Frequently, I say it this way: "Don't ever be more beautiful on the outside than you are on the inside." Lasting beauty flows from the fear of the Lord that is the beginning of wisdom. Remember that the fear of the Lord is humility directed toward God. The ability to separate wisdom from foolishness comes to us when we humbly submit to our Creator and pursue wisdom from His Spirit, who in turn protects us from foolish behavior and its consequences. God's discretion guides us to separate the valuable from the vulnerable. In order to separate the two, we must gain an intimate knowledge of what is truly valuable.

I am told that federal agents who fight currency counterfeiters do not spend a great deal of time studying the fake bills. Instead, they become intimate with the authentic money, studying every intricate detail, including the weight and texture of the paper along with every unique marking where the ink soaks into the material. In order to separate the valuable from the vulnerable, these agents become intimate with what's truly valuable, using it as their standard to judge what has no value.

Too often, we miss this when it comes to God. We become so familiar with the vulnerable that we miss the valuable, namely, His wisdom. We find God's wisdom when we accept it as valuable, store it up in our hearts like a priceless gem, listen for it in every encounter of life, take time to apply it to our hearts, call for it regardless of where we are, cry aloud for it to satisfy our desires, and look and search for it as for hidden treasure that will reveal the meaning of life, all the while understanding that we can find it only in the person of God. That's when we understand the fear of the Lord. This isn't the kind of fear that an employee has toward an intimidating boss. Rather, this is a fear like that of a son's confidence in the strength of his loving father. The former is fear that God will stay; the latter is fear that God will go away.

I am not talking about rule keeping or self-righteous morality. I tried that when I was a good rule keeper, attending church three times a week only to learn that those of us with hardened religious hearts tend to preach principles that are void of a personal relationship with the Creator of the universe. In essence, legalistic people with hearts of stone are afraid of God as if He were a taskmaster. That's not the kind of relationship God desires.

Begin a Journey of Discretion

Think of a beautiful girl from your high school years who lacked discretion—the ability to separate life's most valuable from its most vulnerable. Now think of someone who had less beauty on the outside, but lasting beauty on the inside. Who is more beautiful today? The ability to separate wisdom from foolishness begins with humility toward the Spirit of God, accompanied by an all-out pursuit of His heart intersecting with street smarts. Begin your journey of discretion, separating wisdom from foolishness, by storing up Scripture in your heart. Memorize one verse from the Bible, and let it sink into your heart as you apply it to your life.

SEPARATE WALK FROM TALK

Discretion also separates walk from talk. Solomon noted the wisdom behind discerning the difference between a person's walk and their talk, even when we may be the one demonstrating the inconsistency.

Wisdom will save you from the ways of wicked men,
from men whose words are perverse, who leave the
straight paths to walk in dark ways, who delight in doing
wrong and rejoice in the perverseness of evil, whose
paths are crooked and who are devious in their ways.
(Prov. 2:12–15)

In the book of Proverbs, the idea of walking in "dark ways"
is often combined with perverse talk, or with speech that alters
truth. Those vulnerable paths are crooked and dark as opposed
to valuable paths that are straight and full of light. Dark is evil.
Light is good. Consequently, the person who walks those dark
paths often disguises his speech with false light. Discretion
from the Spirit of God guides us to separate the two so that
when we're motivated to accept those words because they're
the ones we want to hear, we do not act naïvely upon those
words.

Solomon warned that we must not lose our focus on discretion because it will give us a safe walk, one that is straight and
full of light. That walk is commensurate with our talk when
we pursue the Holy Spirit.

My son, preserve sound judgment and discernment, do
not let them out of your sight; they will be life for you, an
ornament to grace your neck. Then you will go on your
way in safety, and your foot will not stumble; when you
lie down, you will not be afraid; when you lie down, your
sleep will be sweet. Have no fear of sudden disaster or
of the ruin that overtakes the wicked, for the LORD will

be your confidence and will keep your foot from being
snared. (Prov. 3:21–26)

"An ornament to grace your neck" in this context refers to
the heart beating through the arteries. Discretion gives us life
that flows from the heart. A heart that beats for God perpetu-
ates life. Walking with Him allows us to discern the words of
false light and recognize a walk that is apart from His design,
even when our own walk does not match our talk.

I noticed the need to separate walk from talk when I stood
in a church foyer with a godly woman who was separated from
her husband. For several months he had lived with another
woman in a different state while refusing to support his children. Yet he told this woman what she wanted to hear: "I still
love you; I don't love her. There's nothing between us; I really
want to be with you." Her emotions were torn because of the
contradiction between her husband's words and actions. I
encouraged her to apply discretion to this situation and separate his walk from his talk. If his words were true, they would
match his actions. I believe that call for discernment brought
wisdom to her situation.

This situation is repeated in all kinds of situations in our
experience. A politician tells us what we want to hear, while
his actions oppose his promising words. A salesman over-
promises and underdelivers. A preacher says one thing from
the pulpit and does another in his personal life. An organizational leader casts a vision and implements a strategy that
contradicts the vision. A bank writes a peacemaking letter to
a borrower who is a month late on his mortgage payment, but
employs an attorney to begin foreclosure. A coach commits

playing time to a recruit, but it never materializes. A friend says, "I'll be there for you," but he can't be found when crisis comes. Through his actions, a parent communicates to his child, "Do as I say, not as I do."

Weigh Words against Behavior

When you engage with another person and experience negative conflict—tension that includes at least one sinful option—begin to use discretion to separate that person's walk from his talk. Look past his words into his behavior and weigh the two. Ask the Holy Spirit to guide you in this process and help you to act accordingly. Let the cream rise to the top as you separate the valuable from the vulnerable.

SEPARATE LONG-TERM BENEFITS FROM SHORT-TERM PLEASURE

The third aspect in our look into discretion involves separating long-term benefits from short-term pleasure.

> My son, pay attention to my wisdom, listen well to my words of insight, that you may maintain discretion and your lips may preserve knowledge. For the lips of an adulteress drip honey, and her speech is smoother than oil; but in the end she is bitter as gall, sharp as a double-edged sword. Her feet go down to death; her steps lead straight to the grave. She gives no thought to the way of life; her paths are crooked, but she knows it not. (Prov. 5:1–6)

The consequences of short-term pleasure include long-term detriments. When we learn to discern the difference, we become adept at equating selfish short-term gain with long-term pain.

Too often when a married man is tempted to pursue another woman sexually, he rarely thinks of the long-term consequences of his short-term pleasure. However, he needs to think beyond the act to include long-term detriments. Pursuing adultery risks his standing in the community, his marriage, his relationship with his children, his career, and even his ability to effectively minister to others until he is proven repentant. The result of his infidelity is devastating to all parties concerned. If only he would learn to ask the Holy Spirit for discretion, listen to that prompting, and obey, then he would be following the pathway to wisdom's long-term benefits.

If you find yourself in this kind of a situation, I want to remind you that it's not too late to apply discretion. You might think that you're going to be happier without your spouse, but I want to share with you what I have learned from reading many divorce documents. If you have children, you will have a judge tell you when you can and can't see them. You will be yoked tightly with your divorced spouse, and that relationship will rarely be a good one. A court will dictate vacations, visitations, and holidays. This relentless bondage will wear down your future mate, becoming a major contributor to that relationship's complexity because you overpromised and underdelivered.

Before you consider divorce for whatever reason, I plead with you to apply discretion to your situation and carefully weigh the long-term benefits of staying together against your short-term pleasure.

Separate Valuable from Vulnerable

Compare the potential devastation that will come to your life with the long-term benefits that discretion offers: gained credibility in your community, deepened family relationships, trusted friendships, the ability to respond to ministry opportunities, strengthened marketplace productivity, whole assets, increased autonomy, and decreased economic burden. Ask a loving God to make clear what is best for you. Listen to His prompting to separate the valuable from the vulnerable.

SEPARATE RIGHT FROM WRONG

Fourth, discretion knows how to separate right from wrong. In the three thousand years since Solomon's writings, little about human nature has changed. Too often our culture finds it increasingly difficult to separate right from wrong. Read how Solomon described the benefits of discretion's protection as he juxtaposed right and wrong:

> Then you will walk in the ways of good men and keep to the paths of the righteous. For the upright will live in the land, and the blameless will remain in it; but the wicked will be cut off from the land, and the unfaithful will be torn from it. (Prov. 2:20–22)

Righteous refers to "someone who is right in God's sight." The antonym of righteous is *wicked*, which means "someone who is wrong in God's sight." The Spirit of God guides us to make the distinction between the two. Unfortunately, left to ourselves, we choose to determine what is right and what is wrong based on our own fallen, inconsistent, inequitable standards. Given this reality, it only seems natural that the believer would want to connect with the Spirit of God in order to discern what is right or wrong in His sight. That's all well and good outside of a conflict situation, but it becomes tough to do in the heat of the moment. Solomon reiterated that we need wisdom in order to do so.

I, wisdom, dwell together with prudence; I possess knowledge and discretion. To fear the LORD is to hate evil; I hate pride and arrogance, evil behavior and perverse speech. (Prov. 8:12–13)

Once again, discretion flows from an all-out pursuit of wisdom that begins with humility directed toward God. When we bend the knee to and surrender our ways to Him, we learn to hate what is wrong because God hates what is wrong along with its source, which is often pride. The humbled heart is open to the influence of the Spirit of Christ, and thus is open to wisdom that leads to discretion when it comes to discerning right from wrong. Unfortunately, since the first sin in the Garden of Eden, humans have determined for themselves what is right and what is wrong. This is how some scholars define "the knowledge of good and evil" (Gen. 3).

After a church service one night, I gave a guy a ride home. On the way, he shared some of his struggles, including his persistent use of marijuana. He told me that it confused him how something that could legitimately be used for medicinal purposes could also land a person who buys or sells it in jail. His next statement revealed a lot: "It's as though someone has decided for himself what is right and what is wrong." This opened the door for me to explain that, since that first sin, someone has made that decision. It is fallen humanity. I emphasized that people will never be satisfied until we have a better understanding of God's perspective of right and wrong that's developed from reading the Bible in its context. This discussion sparked a desire in him to pursue God—a desire that eventually led him to fully surrender his life to Christ as his Savior and Lord.

I pray at night before I go to sleep. During that time, I often have ideas that relate to the things I'm praying for. I have learned over the years that those insights are the still, small voice of the Holy Spirit. After discerning these promptings were of the Spirit, I began to take a risk and implement what He prompted me to do. Consequently, I have tried to become a rapid Holy Spirit responder. Those of us who are in a restorative relationship with Christ must learn to become rapid Holy Spirit responders in order to apply His discretion to our lives. He answers us in our spirits when we seek Him, so it is imperative that when we get these messages, we do what He tells us to do.

An example of these messages occurred when I was memorizing the Sermon on the Mount. I would recite it at night, after I would pray and just before I would fall asleep. One night, when I came to the "love and pray for your enemies" part, a competitor came to mind. I sensed God wanted me to pray for him and maybe demonstrate love to him in some way. However, I realized something unbecoming about myself. I could not pray for him to be blessed in the same way I had just asked God to bless me and my business. I wanted to discern for myself what was right and what was wrong. In this case, I thought my business practices were right, and his were wrong. Consequently, I prayed something like, "God, I hope he knows you."

As only God could design, I encountered my competitor the morning of an evening auction I was going to conduct. He was sitting on a bench in the courtyard of the California hotel where we were staying. I had just finished working out, and I was carrying my toasted bagel and fresh-squeezed orange juice when I saw him. I attempted to hide my face with my bagel and cup, but my bald head gave me away. I sat down beside him, when he ran his fingers through his long hair and said, "God is with me again today." As envy pulsated throughout my body over his long hair, I uttered the most spiritual response I could muster, "No way!" I was shocked he had expressed a deep, heartfelt spirituality. When I inquired more about his statement, I discovered he had surrendered his life to God at an Alcoholics Anonymous meeting.

I learned two things that day. First, God had enough resources to go around. I could actually pray for my competitor to be blessed in the same way I wanted to be blessed financially. I did not have to discern what was right or wrong. Rather, I could trust God to do so. Second, my competitor and I were to become good friends, collaborating together, until his untimely death from a rare disease that took his life much too early. I'm thankful God prompted me, orchestrated our connection, and gave us the quality time we shared together on this side.

Desire Deeper Perception

Fear the Lord. Humble your heart; your desires; and your time, talent, and treasure to God in order to wisely implement discretion between right and wrong. Operate by yielding to the judgment of His Spirit in you, rather than defaulting to your own fallen, inconsistent, and inequitable determination of what is right and wrong. Pray to God specifically to lead you to know the difference, whether you're in a conflict situation or not. On your own, you cannot reliably separate the valuable from the vulnerable; rather, the Spirit of Christ in you leads you to do this through His power and His wisdom.

Chapter 12

Wise Counsel

GUIDANCE FROM THE WISE

Curtis Smith grew up in Memphis, Tennessee. At age nine, his family moved to a suburb that featured a local cable television station operated by the district high school. When he was a freshman in high school, the fifteen-year-old Smith responded to a public address announcement asking for sports commentators. He landed a spot in the schedule and started to call play by play for different athletic events, including wrestling. As he got better, he knew he had discovered his calling to be in broadcasting. Curtis, already a believer, continued to follow the Lord's leading through Campus Crusade for Christ at Southern Illinois University. After completing his bachelor's degree in communications at college, where he met his wife, Jessie, Curtis furthered his education at Mississippi State University. There he studied to become a meteorologist.

Curtis and Jessie moved to Louisiana, where Curtis was

working in television. During that time, a former coworker from his college days in Illinois contacted Curtis about her Fort Wayne station's weekend weather opening. Curtis was reluctant to consider the job, but after discussing it with Jessie, he decided to send a tape to the station. A few days later, the station's news director offered to fly Curtis to Fort Wayne for a tryout.

After Curtis completed his trial run by delivering the weather forecast on camera, the station manager called Curtis into his office. After a short discussion, Curtis decided to get straight to the point. "My wife is pregnant," he said, "and I don't have a ton of time. If you think you're going to offer me the job, I need to know sometime soon."

"Okay," said the news director. "We want to offer you the job."

Curtis called Jessie, who agreed that he should take the position, and they should move to Fort Wayne. After a year with this ABC affiliate, Curtis moved up to the number one position. I met Curtis at Blackhawk Ministries, and we soon became friends. One day Curtis and I were talking. "Have you ever thought about writing a devotional from a meteorologist's perspective?" I asked. "You could call it, 'Confessions of a Weatherman.'" Curtis filed this idea away in his mind.

A few years later, Ken and Nora Stewart, co-owners of HearCare Audiology and friends of Curtis, asked him if he could get his station to broadcast a trip to the Holy Land. Curtis laughed, scoffing at the idea that he could do anything overtly religious on his network. But Curtis took a step of faith and met with his station manager, who agreed to send Curtis on the trip and broadcast his reports daily.

Curtis took the trip of a lifetime, traveling with the team to Tel Aviv, Bethlehem, Jerusalem, and other parts of Israel, while fitting children for hearing devices. Many of the children the experts at HearCare treated heard sounds for the very first time. Curtis's experiences were broadcast live on his station on location from the Church of the Annunciation, the Church of the Nativity in Bethlehem, the Church of the Holy Sepulchre, and the Garden Tomb. Twice, Curtis even read the Bible on the air. He told me, "Never did I think that would happen. I read the Bible at the Church of the Annunciation and the Gates of Jerusalem."

Curtis reflected on how wise counsel led to God transforming his career: "Jessie and I didn't go looking for the job in Fort Wayne. We didn't pursue the mission trips. I would never have seen myself as a television preacher, but God has brought that to me through leading others to bring me wise counsel. I feel like there has been a shift in my career toward greater meaning and purpose. Now I know God will use us wherever we are."

Since that time, Curtis has traveled to Africa, Haiti, and Guatemala, preaching in area churches and delivering the gospel message—all because he continues to follow wise counsel, which has led him to his latest role outside network television as an ambassador to churches for a large health-care provider.

Where do you go for wise advice? When experiencing interpersonal conflict, we either use or refuse wise counsel. Some of us are so bent on going solo in our decisions that we rarely seek input from others, even overlooking God's Word and His wisdom in others. Still others of us carelessly pursue advice from foolish sources, placing our faith in advice that doesn't have God's interests at heart.

Our next pearl of wisdom is wise counsel. Solomon noted its importance for us as we seek to make wise decisions: "A wise man will hear and increase in learning, and a man of understanding will acquire wise counsel" (Prov. 1:5 NASB). The New International Version translates *wise counsel* as "guidance." In essence, it is sound advice.

After King Solomon died, his son Rehoboam succeeded him as king. Rehoboam had watched his father write three thousand proverbs, rule over God's people, and offer wise advice to many while building an immense and powerful kingdom. He also had witnessed his dad take on seven hundred wives and three hundred concubines, who led him astray (see 1 Kings 11:3). He gazed in wonder as his dad pursued earthly knowledge for the sake of contentment, pleasure for the sake of gratification, money for the sake of security, military might for the sake of control, and possessions for the sake of significance.

On his first day as king, Rehoboam was presented with conflict: The people of Israel had asked him to lighten their load (see 1 Kings 12:1–5). Rehoboam's first order of business was to address that conflict, as his kingdom dangled in the balance (see 1 Kings 12:1–5). Solomon's proverbs offered Rehoboam insight into the heart condition of those who seek wise counsel compared with those who don't: "The way of a fool seems right to him, but a wise man listens to advice" (Prov. 12:15).

The entire assembly of Israel had approached young King Rehoboam and presented him with this conflict: "Your father put a heavy yoke on us, but now lighten the harsh labor and the heavy yoke he put on us, and we will serve you" (1 Kings 12:4). Rehoboam immediately sought wise counsel from the elders who had served his father, asking them specifically how they would answer the group (see 1 Kings 12:6). They responded with their wise guidance: "If today, you will be a servant to these people and serve them and give them a favorable answer, they will always be your servants" (1 Kings 12:7).

I think it is worth noting that Rehoboam sought more than one counselor. Why? Solomon said that wisdom is discovered when we seek many advisors (see Prov. 11:14; 15:22; 24:6).

Solomon pointed to four pillars that undergird the pursuit of shrewd advice. Each one focuses on recognizing the heart of the person providing the information. Wise counsel is *guidance from the wise, absent from the wicked, success from the Lord,* and *sweet from a friend.*

To find wise counsel, we must seek it. Women are typically very comfortable with this idea; unfortunately, men often feel that seeking wise counsel is admitting failure, rather than building on an available strength (cue the jokes about asking for directions). But once we decide we're willing to pursue sound advice, how do we find it? Wisdom is predicated on having a relationship with God. Consequently, when we look to find wisdom, we must find someone who is characterized and known by healthy relationships.

In the battle of interpersonal conflict, we need the counsel of more than one confidante in order to experience success.

Solomon advised: "For waging war you need guidance, and for victory many advisers" (Prov. 24:6). If we do not seek wise counsel, we lose. King Solomon warned: "For lack of guidance a nation falls, but many advisors make victory sure" (Prov. 11:14). Our best efforts to plan our way through conflict will fall short without the input of others. Solomon taught: "Plans fail for lack of counsel, but with many advisors they succeed" (Prov. 15:22). He also communicated the wise way to plan for conflict management: "Make plans by seeking advice; if you wage war, obtain guidance" (Prov. 20:18). The wise in heart seek wise counsel even when planning their approach to navigating conflict.

I have discovered this in my own life as well. Sometimes I seek wise counsel, but the advice does not rest well in my spirit. This unrest can stem from a combination of me not clearly explaining my circumstances, or the person I had asked for wisdom not knowing enough about my situation. We also have to be careful not to just seek out advice from people who will tell us what we want to hear.

Sometimes we find wise counsel; sometimes it finds us. Three people in my life have contacted me with unsolicited wise counsel because each of them was following up on a prompting of the Spirit. The first person is Lonnie Rex of David Livingston Ministries. He has called me on the cusp of several different crises in my life—situations he knew nothing about except for the fact that he had received a nudge from the Holy Spirit. One of those times was when the IRS raided our business (before the raid became public knowledge). The second person is Gregg Bettis, former president of Kids Across

America. He has been known to call me out of the blue and ask, "What in the world is going on with you? The Holy Spirit has prompted me to pray for you so much lately." One of those times was when I was deciding whether to walk away from my company to become a carrier of God's message of restoration. The third person is Tim O'Brien, an entrepreneur and car collector who has called me on many occasions to ask, "Is everything okay? You have been brought to mind during my prayer time on many occasions the last couple of days." Would you believe that every single time he has called and inquired, I've been wrestling with a heavy issue? The common thread in each of these three people is the humility that brings encouraging wisdom.

Seek Guidance from the Wise

In the midst of your conflict, seek wise counsel from more than one credible source—perhaps from a friend, family member, coworker, pastor, small group leader, business owner, or teacher. Resist the temptation to go it alone on autopilot as you maintain control of your own life. Then ask the Holy Spirit if the counsel you receive is consistent with the wisdom in the Scriptures. Finally, use the wise counsel to help you plan your approach to wise conflict management.

ABSENT FROM THE WICKED

Second, wise counsel is absent from the wicked. Their deceit can mask foolish counsel to look like wisdom. Solomon cautioned: "The plans of the righteous are just, but the advice of the wicked is deceitful" (Prov. 12:5). The advice of the wicked is not wise counsel at all, but a trap. The bait lures us to follow and to bite, but hidden inside is a hook. A wicked counselor deceitfully hides the hook of the consequences of his selfish motives inside the bait of gratifying our own selfish desires.

Rehoboam refused the good advice of the elders and turned to the young men who had grown up with him (see 1 Kings 12:8). He asked them for counsel as to how to answer the assembly (see 1 Kings 12:9). These wicked, opportunistic parasites had a vested interest in Rehoboam's decision because their quality of life had depended on the king's economic flow and political power. The young men offered their deceitful advice:

Tell these people who have said to you, "Your father put a heavy yoke on us, but make our yoke lighter"— tell them, "My little finger is thicker than my father's waist. My father laid on you a heavy yoke; I will make it even heavier. My father scourged you with whips; I will scourge you with scorpions." (1 Kings 12:10–11)

Their self-serving attitudes should have provided Rehoboam with a clue that he was being deceived. Instead, he trusted in his own selfish interests and fallen wisdom. Following the deceitful advice of his peers, he increased his burden on the people (see 1 Kings 12:14). Rehoboam's choice to use the foolish counsel led to his loss of power.

I have witnessed this Rehoboam scene time and again

at collector car auctions. Typically, when a wealthy person attends his first sale to start his car collection, he attracts many new advisors. They tell him what he wants to hear in order to gratify their selfish interests; every bit of advice they give is predicated on what benefits their financial security. The result is that often the new collector makes foolish purchases and pays too much for the wrong cars. At times I was able to step in and offer wise counsel, while at other times I was perceived as being one of the people with only selfish interests in mind. Because of deceit, or the presence of a hidden agenda, deciding whether to follow wise counsel can resemble the first steps of walking a tightrope.

Rehoboam's motley crew of contemporaries was supposed to help him become a better leader; their wits would sharpen his. However, their brand of fallen wisdom—street smarts without God's heart—didn't help sharpen anything. Rehoboam needed discretion to separate wise guidance from wicked deceit. Unfortunately, he made the wrong choice.

Recognize and Refuse Deceit from the Wicked

When you are seeking advice, listen for self-serving clues embedded in the words of your chosen advisor. Next, filter the advice through wisdom's biblical grid to discern whether the counsel is deceit from the wicked. Then ask yourself if you are motivated solely by a selfish benefit to follow the tainted advice. If self-serving cues exist, refuse the deceitful counsel. Finally, seek the wise counsel of another trusted mentor. Remember, it never hurts to get a second opinion.

SUCCESS FROM THE LORD

Third, wise counsel offers success from the Lord. Solomon preached: "There is no wisdom, no insight, no plan that can succeed against the LORD" (Prov. 21:30). In seeking wise counsel, we must remember the information we receive is merely advice. By definition, we are still accountable for our own decisions regarding conflict. At the same time, the Father has given us access to the Holy Spirit, whom Jesus called our Counselor. Consequently, if the advice we obtain from another person conflicts with an unmistakable Holy Spirit prompting, then we must follow the wise counsel from God because it will lead to the success He has in store for us.

His vision will be followed by His provision.

Any challenge we experience in interpreting God's prompting is not due to the Sender; rather, the static is typically on our end. Therefore, God's leading can be confirmed through wise counsel from a Spirit-led person who clearly understands our circumstances. Occasionally, this confirmation will require asking two or more people. By no means does this mean we keep asking until we hear only what we want to hear. As a check against the desire to become lord of our own lives, we are wise to remember that a genuine Holy Spirit prompting is consistent with the Bible, wise counsel, and the life and teachings of Christ. If the advice you're getting conflicts with any of these three, keep looking.

As a consequence of following the deceitful advice of Rehoboam's peers, the nation of Israel split. Rehoboam ruled only over Judah, which included the tribe of Benjamin (see

1 Kings 12:20). Jeroboam, Solomon's former labor secretary, presided over the nation of Israel. Rehoboam prepared for war with Jeroboam in order to reunify the country. He had gathered all 180,000 of the fighting men in Judah and Benjamin when God spoke through Shemaiah, who was known to be a wise man of God (see 1 Kings 12:21–22). Yahweh warned Rehoboam not to fight (see 1 Kings 12:23–24). This time, Rehoboam followed God's wise counsel and experienced success.

In order to receive wise counsel from the Lord, we must become rapid Holy Spirit responders. Timing can be critical, so we must not wait when His prompting is clear. When my business was struggling, God prompted me to pray each night on my knees beside my bed, as I had seen my dad do while I was growing up. While I prayed, I pictured myself walking through my office, and I prayed specifically for each employee. Then I prayed for some of our customers, especially those who were selling their entire collections at auction with us, as well as some vendors and a few competitors.

While I was praying, something unique happened. Many ideas came to my mind that could potentially improve our business. I asked Uncle Derald if he thought this was wise counsel from God. He said, "Try it and see." I did, and it was. The positive relational results of implementing ideas that came to me while I was praying specifically for others convinced me that God's vision is indeed followed by His provision.

I have many people come to me asking for advice, and when I do, I share with them that my role is to help them discern their own Holy Spirit promptings—those that are consistent with the Bible, wise counsel, and the life and teachings of

Christ. This is how they will find out for themselves that God's vision is followed by His provision. I also tell these people how critical it is for them to make sure they provide me with all the necessary information for me to advise them wisely. If they hold back something vital, then they know that my counsel might be flawed because I don't have the entire story.

Succeed with Wise Counsel from the Lord

Become a rapid Holy Spirit responder. When the Spirit tells you to do something, don't delay! Take every conflict to God in prayer and listen for His prompting. Verify whether the counsel you're receiving is from Him by determining its consistency with the Bible, wise counsel, and the life and teachings of Christ. When all three are in agreement with your discernment of the Holy Spirit's prompting, then follow the wise counsel from the Lord. When you humble your heart to His agenda for your life, He will work in all things for your good through the advancement of Christ in you (see Rom. 8:28–29).

SWEET FROM A FRIEND

Fourth, wise counsel is sweet from a friend. Solomon illustrated: "Oil and perfume make the heart glad, so a man's counsel is sweet to his friend" (Prov. 27:9 NASB). When we are experiencing interpersonal conflict, it is wise to seek the sweet wise counsel of a true friend who has our best interests at heart. As opposed to wicked deceivers acting from their selfish interests—like those who had grown up with Solomon's son

Rehoboam—a credible friend can guide us to the sweet spot where God's interests intersect with our unselfish interests and the interests of others. Our hearts will rejoice when we define the target of profitable conflict management in these terms, and we use the sweet wise counsel from a friend.

Rehoboam's grandfather David had realized that wise counsel from his friend, Jonathan, was sweet. In fact, that wise counsel spared David's life. Later, David married Bathsheba, who gave birth to Solomon, Rehoboam's father. While Solomon was young, David taught him wisdom that Solomon passed on to his son Rehoboam.

I can't think of anyone whose wise counsel was sweeter to me than that of Chris Schenkel, the hall of fame ABC sportscaster. Chris used to check in on me every couple of weeks. Consequently, he was close enough to my situation to offer me wise counsel because he had my best interest at heart. Two times in my life, I had considered selling Kruse International. The first time, Chris counseled me not to do so. The second time, he agreed with my prompting from God, and my decision was proven to be right and good.

Not only did I receive wise counsel from a friend, but God has used me to offer wise counsel to friends as well. As I grew in wisdom, my influence increased among my customers, vendors, and employees. I remember one such customer who had a heart of gold; however, he was struggling in his relationship with his adult son. This entrepreneur had wanted his namesake to take over the family business, but the two of them had fought one too many arguments; they were living in separate states and not speaking at all.

On my way home, I dictated a letter to my friend, whom I respected greatly. I offered him my perspective—that of a son in a family business. I noted that sons often see their fathers as being in a stronger position to initiate the reconciliation, especially since the son typically perceives the father as initiating the conflict. I shared a story about my dad and me that illustrated my point. The letter flowed because I was communicating with my friend's best interest at heart.

A couple of days later I remembered the letter and thought, *What have I done? I can't send that letter, or my friend will be so angry with me for giving unsolicited advice that I will not only lose his multimillion-dollar auction, but also his friendship!* I quickly called out to my assistant, "Hey, you didn't send that letter to _____ yet, did you?"

"Yes," she replied.

I was heartsick. I was certain I had ruined a treasured relationship. I wrestled with the conflict I perceived I had created for about two weeks. Then I received a handwritten note from my friend. I hesitated to open it, afraid of what was inside. But when I did, I realized that rather than being angry with me, he was overjoyed. He had taken my advice and reconciled with his son, who had since agreed to assume responsibility to lead the family business. Once again, wise counsel was sweet from a friend.

Taste the Sweet Wise Counsel from a Friend

Read the story of David and Jonathan recorded in 1 Samuel 20. During your next interpersonal conflict, seek the wise counsel of a friend like Jonathan who has your best interest at heart. Experience the benefit of sound advice from a person who not only knows you well, but who is also familiar with the Bible's wisdom as well as the heart of God. Use your friend's wise counsel, and taste the sweet success intended by your Creator. This insight comes from our wise Counselor, the Spirit of Christ, dwelling in us (see John 14:26).

Chapter 13

Discipline

TEACH

Cam Tribolet lived a life void of discipline at a young age. His mother and father were rarely home, devoting much of their time to their two taverns in Fort Wayne. At age eight, Cam started sneaking a beer from the cooler or sipping liquor as he walked by the inventory. His drinking escalated in junior high school, where it became normal for him to drink during the day. By the time he entered high school, Cam was drunk almost every day, frequently sneaking alcohol into the school building. He remembers, "I was always in trouble, but always found a way to get out of trouble."

At eighteen, Cam was living on his own, partying every night, when he started a daily cocaine habit. In addition to being a tavern owner, Cam's dad was also a contractor who had taught Cam how to work hard, which Cam had to do in order to maintain his expensive cocaine habit. Then tragedy struck.

"August 31, 1986, was the worst night of my life and the best night of my life. I had been out drinking all night at strip clubs, places where I shouldn't have been. I got home and decided to pack up some beer to make the last call at a bar. I was drunk and high when I stopped at the light at Coliseum Boulevard and Lima Road. A car pulled up next to me. I remember three guys in a four-door blue car, two in front, one in back. I rolled down my window, thinking they wanted to talk. The guy in the backseat of the vehicle got out and walked up to my window. He hauled off and punched me in the face. I'm getting punched, while the others were beating on my truck. That's when everything went black."

One of the three men had shot Cam three times in the stomach. To this day, Cam does not know who pulled the trigger or why. "I made it across the street, crossed the center line, crashed into a building, and passed out, since I had lost so much blood." The time was 3:30 a.m. An EMS vehicle arrived, and the EMTs assumed Cam was merely a crash victim. They transported him to the hospital, where emergency room doctors undressed him, discovering Cam's three bullet holes. They rushed him to surgery.

One bullet had traveled through Cam's aorta, one through his bowel, and one through his intestines, lodging in his spine. Cam's punctured bowel resulted in an infection that permeated his body. Doctors were able to repair Cam's aorta, but the repair failed, so they gave him a new aorta in his neck, down through both legs. Within two weeks of being admitted to the hospital, gangrene set in. The doctors were forced to remove both of Cam's legs due to the infection.

Cam was in a coma the entire time. He received a tracheotomy so they could regulate his breathing. During this time, he experienced kidney failure and liver failure. His heart stopped multiple times, leading surgeons to install a pacemaker. Physicians told his parents that no one could survive this much trauma, so his mother and father made funeral arrangements, even selecting Cam's casket. "The grace of God unfolded. I could hear people in my room. They were talking, crying, yelling at me, as if I couldn't hear. The doctors brought me back to life thirteen times."

Cam can recall six visions during that period. "I saw the light of Christ. I was in a building, cutting through a window-sill, and inside the wall cavity was a bright light. I felt someone behind me shove me into the wall cavity, forcing me toward the light. I pushed myself out, and everything went black again.

"In another, I was a movie star, exiting my trailer. The director asked me to go into the light for the next scene. I wouldn't go. He told me that the book he held said that I should. He screamed for me to go to the light. I refused and went back into my trailer."

In a separate vision, Cam noted, "I was rising up from my bed. I turned around. Everything went black. The doctor later told me that was the team shocking me back."

A battle for Cam's soul took place in one of his most vivid visions. "I was lying in the ICU. I was looking at an image of Christ on the cross, hanging above the glass doors in front of me, when he came down off the cross and became a full-sized man. I couldn't see his face, but I could tell who it was. He walked to my bed. I saw the light. All the other times, I had rejected it. This time, the light felt different to me. I welcomed it. He came next to me, and he turned into a hideous creature with rust-colored skin and wrinkly yellow eyes. He started walking backwards and climbed back on the cross. That was a fight between good and evil that night. Someone was coming to get me. Based on the life I had led up to that point, the devil was coming to get me, but Christ won."

Thanks to the medical attention he received, Cam's infections subsided, and the doctors brought him out of the coma. "I mouthed to the nurse that my legs hurt. She couldn't understand me, so she had me write down what I was saying. She replied that my legs couldn't hurt because they were gone. That's when I completely lost it. They had to restrain and sedate me." The nurse thought Cam had already been told about the double amputation.

Devastated, Cam lost his will to live. "I lost my house, my job, my insurance, my fiancée, and my self-esteem. I was declared indigent. I wanted to kill myself. There was no way I was going to live like that." Cam had been weaned off cocaine, but his new drug of choice was morphine, as he hit the pump every seven minutes. Cam remained in the hospital for eight months, surviving dozens of surgeries. Discipline would be his only pathway to rehabilitation, a pathway that only God could design.

About six months into his hospital stay, Cam started physical therapy. He weighed a mere 130 pounds and was jaundiced. He did not look or feel well. Cam remembers, "They slid me on a tilt table. When they flipped it, the blood rushed to my head, and I started to get sick. I looked up at the person holding the thing for me to vomit in and thought, *You are beautiful!* At that moment, I began to think that life wasn't so bad. I wanted

to live." The woman who inspired him was named Sue. Cam
confessed, "I repeatedly asked for her to help me." Cam learned
that her physical therapy expertise, myofascial release (MFR),
brought scar tissue to the surface in order to increase circula-
tion and healing and reduce pain. He thought to himself, *I've
got a lot of scar tissue*, so he eagerly asked the doctor for a pre-
scription requiring Sue's MFR. The doctor obliged.

Over time, Sue fell in love with this man. She saw beyond
all the negative aspects of his past life. Her therapy and rehab
made him stronger. Cam was fitted with prosthetic legs and
learned how to stand and walk again. He eventually made his
way out of the hospital and received outpatient therapy from
Sue. Cam trained hard to develop the core muscle strength
that would become invaluable to his mobility. He tested those
muscles, often falling, only to rise up again and continue
on his track of discipline. In six months, Sue and Cam were
engaged. Within a year, they were married. They have now
been together for nearly three decades.

Cam had to go back to school to learn a new skill set. He
chose to train as a fire sprinkler engineer; however, the retrain-
ing did not stop there. After the accident, Cam had stopped
hunting, selling his guns and bow. His brother-in-law witnessed Cam's progress, so he encouraged him to hunt again
and talked him into buying a bow. During his first year back in
the fields, Cam hunted from the ground until he learned how
to shimmy up a tree and get into a tree stand. From there, he
shot his first buck since before the shooting.

Cam thought, *If I can climb a tree, what else can I do?* He
mastered downhill skiing, kayaking, swimming, basketball,

and other sports. The transformed Cam contacted Buckmasters about hunting in Canada. Eventually, they asked him to help disabled hunters learn how to push past their disabilities and start to hunt again. Cam learned how to take what he had learned and use it to inspire others. He taught, trained, tested, and transformed many who had experienced tragedies.

As a hunting consultant, he traveled the country, meeting and helping hundreds of people, including Roger Davenport, a man from Wisconsin. The two of them worked together for five years, inviting kids to Roger's ranch and helping them learn how to hunt. Roger retired, but he contacted Cam again after reading *Purpose Driven Life* by Rick Warren. He told Cam, "I know my purpose: to work with disabled kids and teach them how to hunt." Cam joined him in the endeavor.

Cam filmed thirteen episodes of *Way Outfitters*, a television show that filmed him fishing with disabled, disadvantaged, and terminally ill children in Key West; he also hunted with disabled and terminally ill American veterans in Texas and Canada. Helping to bring discipline to others in need led Cam to yearn for personal spiritual discipleship.

"I was in Kansas where I was invited to church. Just picture a Norman Rockwell painting of a white church with a tall steeple, nestled at the end of a dirt road—that was the church I went to that day." Cam walked in the sanctuary using his cane, where the church members kindly greeted him. Since his pants covered his prosthetic legs, he knew his disability wasn't the reason for the congregants' warmth. There was something else about them, some quality he couldn't quite put his finger on. Cam remembers, "I never felt so welcomed." At the same time, unbeknownst to Cam, Sue was checking out churches in Indiana, seeking answers to her faith questions and desiring a relationship with God.

"We talked and decided to attend Grabill Missionary Church, which she had visited. We slipped in the back row to hear the message. It was as if Pastor Bill was speaking directly to me. At forty years old, I broke down right there in my seat. That was the day I changed. I fully surrendered my life to Christ."

Cam Tribolet was taught, trained, tested, and transformed into a new creation in Christ—one who would spend his entire career continually working to bring discipline to others in need.

The next pearl of wise conflict management is *discipline*. *Discipline* and *disciple* share the same root word, meaning "learner." In order to be wise disciples, we must surrender ourselves—including our conflict—to God, in a way similar to an athlete surrendering his will to a coach. For example, Jesus Christ's disciples were seen with Christ, worked with Christ, and shared life with Christ. When people saw them, they called them "Christians." Their discipline of being with Jesus made them act as He did, just as an athlete would while under the direction of a coach. Similarly, God's design is that we, as disciples of Christ, would reveal who He is to all onlookers.

To that end, God's wisdom empowers us to experience discipline. Proverbs is written "for attaining wisdom and discipline" (Prov. 1:2), and "for acquiring a disciplined and prudent life" (Prov. 1:3). Solomon taught that we should actually *love* discipline: "Whoever loves discipline loves knowledge, but he who hates correction is stupid" (Prov. 12:1). In his theme verse of Proverbs, Solomon warned that only a fool would despise discipline.

Whether we are leading our children, our teams, or our employees in the marketplace, discipline is paramount. Discipline means that our job is to work ourselves out of a job. That's the role of a parent. When we make disciples, we know we have achieved success when those being coached are making disciples who are making disciples. The key to this multiplication is discipline. Without it, we remain unteachable, untrained, untested, and untransformed.

Race car drivers are among the most disciplined athletes in all of sports. Using an oval racecourse illustration, we see that Solomon's track of discipline has four turns: *teach, train, test,* and *transform.* Each turn must be navigated, or discipline does not make a full lap of wise conflict management, and the result is relational wreckage (see Prov. 5:23). Let's look at all four aspects of this in turn.

Turn one, as we've seen through Cam's story, is teach. This is defined as "I do. You watch." During this process, something is inspired, modeled, and explained, and that something is retained. King Solomon believed that humility toward God was the first step of being teachable: "The fear of the LORD teaches a man wisdom, and humility comes before honor" (Prov. 15:33). "Teaches" is translated from the same Hebrew root word for "discipline." Solomon revealed: "Instruct a wise man and he will be wiser still; teach a righteous man and he will add to his learning" (Prov. 9:9).

Solomon communicated both the value and transferability of teaching: "Listen, my son, to your father's instruction, and do not forsake your mother's teaching" (Prov. 1:8). "Instruction" is also translated from the same Hebrew root word for "discipline." Solomon taught that we prosper from instruction, especially when we learn to trust God in the process: "Whoever gives heed to instruction prospers, and blessed is he who trusts in the LORD" (Prov. 16:20).

Solomon described how the right word spoken at the right time with the right tone advances the teaching process: "The wise in heart are called discerning, and pleasant words promote instruction" (Prov. 16:21). The key blessing of instruction is that it makes us wise: "Listen to advice and accept instruction, and in the end you will be wise" (Prov. 19:20). If we cease being teachable, then we will be less likely to experience the kind of intimacy with God that is only discovered through being His disciple: "Stop listening to instruction, my son, and you will stray from the words of knowledge" (Prov. 19:27).

Jesus navigated turn one of discipline by teaching His disciples. He inspired, modeled, and explained His disciplines to His band of original followers by living out wisdom in their midst. We should do the same with our children, employees, and teams.

When I was five years old, my dad told me that I was not going to be hanging around the house and watching cartoons on Saturdays. Rather, I would go to auctions and work with him, carrying clerk sheets from the auction ring to the cashier's office through rain, sleet, snow, and hail. I was like the Pony Express. A clerk sheet was a record of the most recent items sold, including the price and buyer of each lot. Each sheet was in triplicate so that the auctioneer, the seller, and the buyer would each have a copy of the clerk ticket.

I remember one rainy Saturday I got stuck in the mud with clerk sheets in hand. I stepped into the ooze, and soon found that I simply couldn't move. Just when I was ready to give up, a couple of Amish men grabbed me under my arms and pulled me out of the mire. I looked down and saw that my boots were still stuck in the thick, wet clay. I remember thinking that it looked like a chocolate shake. My Amish saviors set me on a trailer, pulled my boots from the mud, placed them back on my feet, and sent me on my way to continue my work.

Well, what I didn't realize from my early auction experience was that Dad was modeling the concept of "I do. You watch." All through my growing-up years I watched him auctioneer as I stood mesmerized by his clarity, charisma, and ability to convince, knowing that one day I would become that kind of auctioneer.

Teach First by Being Teachable

Navigate turn one in Solomon's track of discipline by implementing "I do. You watch." Inspire, model, and explain the discipline you would like to instill in your disciples. Select the right words at the right time with the right tone of voice. Like a coach, encourage the people whom you teach, but also instill the discipline that comes from knowing Jesus Christ and His wisdom.

TRAIN

Turn two of discipline's oval track is train. This can be stated as, "I do. You help." Training equips disciples with the tools to be successful. It assimilates what is inspired, modeled, and explained into transferrable skills, one step at a time. In essence, training represents an apprentice program. Solomon wrote about the lasting benefit of establishing training early in the discipline process: "Train a child in the way he should go, and when he is old he will not turn from it" (Prov. 22:6). He described a 24-7 training process in terms of discipline (see Prov. 6:20–23). Contrastingly, Israel's king painted a bleak picture of the future potential of those who lack training (see Prov. 24:30–34).

Jesus trained His disciples by allowing them to help Him live out His disciplines (see, for example, Luke 10:1–17). They assimilated His training into a transferrable message that changed the world. We must provide opportunities for our children, employees, and teams to help us.

In a family business, there was an unlimited supply of those opportunities for me to be trained. I made my first business deal when I was five years old. I was negotiating a raise with Grandpa Russell, who had paid me one dollar a day to transport those clerk sheets from the auction to the cashier. I explained to him how some auctions resulted in one hundred clerk sheets, while others had only totaled a few. He replied, "Oh, don't worry. You'll still get the dollar for those auctions with a few clerk sheets."

"No, I think that I should have an incentive," I offered. That was a pretty big word for a five-year-old, but I understood it.

"How about ten cents a clerk sheet?" Russell asked. My heart almost exploded out of my chest when I realized that I could earn ten dollars a day at the big auctions. Then another thought came racing to my mind—I would earn only thirty cents a day at some auctions, which would result in a dramatic cut in pay.

"Deal," I said as I stuck out my hand to shake on it, "with a minimum of a dollar a day." I wouldn't go backward from this deal. As any auctioneer delights in the confirmation of a deal, Grandpa Russell shook my hand in agreement. Apparently, I had learned a little more than just how to carry clerk sheets from helping at the auctions.

Tony Hulman, known for resurrecting the Indianapolis Motor Speedway after purchasing it at the conclusion of World War II, used to frequent the Auburn Cord Duesenberg festival and auction each Labor Day weekend. I remember when I was in elementary school riding with Dad and Tony in a golf cart through Eckhart Park in Auburn, where the great classics were on display, before the famous parade. Tony was quite charismatic, and everyone would want to hear Tony repeat his legendary phrase, "Gentlemen, start your engines!"

Tony had noticed how Grandpa Russell worked with three of his sons and now a grandson in the family business. Tony had also earned the business from his father, so Tony asked Russell, "How have you been able to successfully assemble and maintain your team of family members in the business?" His unspoken desire was to provide incentive for his grandson, Tony George, to thrive in the Hulman family enterprise. Russell's answer was, "Give them the opportunity to work, and allow them to earn as much money as possible." In other words, "Teach, train, test, and transform."

Equip Yourself and Others

Navigate turn two of Solomon's track of discipline: "I do. You help." Initiate an apprentice program with your children, your teams, and your employees. Allow them to help you in your chosen discipline so that they can assimilate what is inspired, modeled, and explained into transferrable skills, one step at a time. My drills started as a five-year-old. As you are training, develop drills to train your learners in the desired skill set.

TEST

Turn three in our oval of discipline is test. Translated, this is "You do. I help." Solomon instructed that discipline is a precious choice: "Choose my instruction instead of silver, knowledge rather than choice gold" (Prov. 8:10). Continuing with the precious metal imagery, Solomon observed: "The crucible for silver and the furnace for gold, but the LORD tests the heart" (Prov. 17:3; 27:21). God tests us in order to refine us.

A refiner introduces heat to metal intending to draw the impurities to the surface of the crucible or furnace. The deepest impurities rise last, only after the most intense heat. Conflict is the heat that reveals our impurities. Through the heat of conflict, God gives us opportunities to fail in conflict management. This testing makes us stronger and wiser by bringing our impurities, or mixed motivations, to the surface. Discipline is the tool that God uses to fashion us into His disciples, revealing His character in us as He brings wisdom into our lives.

An indicator of our level of discipline is evidenced in how

we respond to praise. Building on the refinement illustration, Solomon taught: "The crucible for silver and the furnace for gold, but man is tested by the praise he receives" (Prov. 27:21). We must be careful to give credit to God and others when we are praised, resisting the temptation to advance our selfish desires.

Jesus tested His disciples for the discipline that He had taught and trained by giving them a controlled environment in which they could apply what they had learned. The intensity of experience paired with the opportunity to fail brought the impurities of His disciples to the surface, much like heat that refines precious metals draws imperfections to the top.

Peter, one of Jesus' disciples, described the value of this process: "In this you greatly rejoice, though now for a little while you may have had to suffer grief in all kinds of trials. These have come so that your faith—of greater worth than gold, which perishes even though refined by fire—may be proved genuine and may result in praise, glory and honor when Jesus Christ is revealed" (1 Pet. 1:6–7). Testing our children, employees, and teams by giving them opportunities to fail helps us discover the areas that need to be either augmented with additional instruction or flat-out corrected.

The summer before my freshman year of high school, my teammates and I attended a basketball camp in Wisconsin where we were blessed with the presence of Al McGuire, recently retired head coach of the national champion Marquette Golden Eagles. He shared with us his struggle since retirement with these words: "I need an opportunity to fail." At the time, the phrase didn't register with me, but it never left my mind. I realized later that he was expressing his need for a challenge. He wanted to continue to be tested.

I can't write about the concept of "You do. I help." without reflecting on how my dad lived out this pattern with me. When I was still five, I was holding the portable public address system for my dad when he handed me the microphone and said, "Now it's your turn. Sell these jars." I was scared to death. I looked at my dad to see if he was serious. I longed for the safety of watching Saturday morning cartoons on television. I scanned the bidders who had followed us down the cellar steps to bid on a few old canning jars. I told him I would do it under one condition: I would hide around the corner so the bidders couldn't see me while Dad held the speaker in view of the potential buyers. All I would have to do is call bids like I had pretended to do many times before in the comfort of my own home.

Before I started to auction the jars, Dad leaned down to say, "Don't worry. I'll be right beside you to help you while you do it." I started the bid at seventy-five cents, which was difficult to pronounce in an auctioneer's chant. We quickly made our way to the market price and sold the jars. That was the first time I can remember auctioning something for real money to live bidders. Dad was training me to be an auctioneer at an early age.

Fast-forward to my first collector car auction after I had earned my auctioneer's license. Dad looked at me and said, "Now it's your turn. Sell the next car." It was a beautiful red 1959 Cadillac Eldorado Biarritz convertible restored by its owner, Bud Ward, who was famous for his stunning paint jobs. I remember several bidders who sympathized with my rookie status jumping in to bid, partially to help me because they wanted me to be successful and partially because Bud's Caddy was so nice. I sold the car for a strong price that reflected the beginning of the 1959 Cadillacs' rise in market value.

I learned later that when Bud saw Dad speak these words to me, he turned to the person next to him and said, "Oh no. What is Dean doing?" I know this because Bud told me that story. However, he followed up his story with this statement: "Mitchell, since that day, I've always requested that you sell my cars. You're batting a thousand with me."

I share that story of Dad living out the concept of "You do. I help." to demonstrate the risk he took, but also to show you the return that both he and the customers received. Notice how customers were willing to help me, a young auctioneer, become successful. I recognize today just how priceless good-will is to someone's business. Think about how that one seller, Bud Ward, needed to provide the first car for me to experi-ence testing. But also reflect on the fact that I had been taught and trained before I was ever tested. Sure, my impurities rose to the top, but my dad was there to remove them and cor-rect them. He was giving me what Al McGuire coveted: the opportunity to fail. After all, my dad knew that his job was to build into me so that eventually he could work himself out of a job.

Just like my dad tested me, so also God tests our hearts. I've been told that the man given the most ink in the Old Testa-ment is David. The shepherd, poet, songwriter, musician, war-rior, prophet, and king wrote one of the Bible's most powerful prayers requesting God's testing of the heart. It is David's refin-ing prayer of search and surrender: "Search me, O God, and know my heart; test me and know my anxious thoughts. See if there is any offensive way in me, and lead me in the way ever-lasting" (Ps. 139:23–24). God answers this prayer by continually refining our hearts through removing our impurities and restoring our lives.

Embrace the Refining Process

Ask God to test your heart for impurities, or mixed motivations. When they arise, ask Him to remove them. In the same way, navigate your children, employees, and teams through turn three of Solomon's track of discipline, "You do. I help." Just as in sports the best test is a scrimmage, so we must hand the wheel to those who will eventually need to stand on their own and take our place. Provide them with opportunities to fail. Do not panic when the impurities rise to the surface. Rather, rejoice that the refining process will continue the learning experience, and use it as an opportunity to work your way out of a job by instilling discipline.

TRANSFORM

Turn four in discipline's oval is transform, or correct, the impurities that rise to the top during the testing process. This can be summarized as "You do. I watch." In fashioning metal, the refiner removes the impurities that float to the surface and continues the process in order to make the metal pure. The refiner knows that he has achieved purity when he sees his reflection in the metal. Christ knows that we are His pure disciples when

He sees His reflection in us. This is most notable when we are making disciples who make disciples through Solomon's four-turn oval track of discipline. Navigating through turn four reveals Christ the Refiner in us.

Solomon noted that correction is ineffective by using words alone: "A servant cannot be corrected by mere words; though he understands, he will not respond" (Prov. 29:19). At least three general approaches to correction exist: positive reinforcement, negative reinforcement, and punishment.

Positive reinforcement offers a reward for the desired behavior. Solomon said that discipline offers hope.

Negative reinforcement removes an existing benefit as a result of behavior that's contrary to what is desired. Although this kind of reinforcement brings resistance and pain, this discipline eventually brings peace in the relationship as right behavior brings delight to our souls.

Punishment is the consequence for repeated undesirable behavior. Solomon upheld punishment when disciplining children in order to save them from greater peril. In essence, the king of Israel advocated the axiom, "Short-term consequences are better than a long-term crisis." Punishment drives out the folly that is resident in the heart of a child. Solomon advocated that punishment for children flowed from love, whereas withholding punishment is actually hate. This love originates from the heart of God: "My son, do not despise the LORD's discipline and do not resent his rebuke, because the LORD disciplines those he loves, as a father the son he delights in" (Prov. 3:11–12). These loving disciplinary actions benefit the yielding person who is corrected: "He who ignores discipline comes to poverty and shame, but whoever heeds correction is honored" (Prov. 13:18).

Remember Solomon said that we should love discipline; however, he also communicated clearly regarding the opposite: "Whoever loves discipline loves knowledge, but he who hates correction is stupid" (Prov. 12:1). He went on to say that the stupid person who ignores correction actually despises himself, while the person who heeds correction gains understanding. He said that only a fool spurns his father's discipline, whereas one who responds affirmatively to correction shows prudence. Solomon explained that a person's response to transforming discipline even affects others: "He who heeds discipline shows the way to life, but whoever ignores correction leads others astray" (Prov. 10:17). How we respond to correction shapes our families, our companies, and our teams.

Jesus corrected His disciples when they were missing the mark. He removed the impurities that floated to the surface after they had been given the opportunity to fail. Discipline is 3-to-1 formative to reformative. According to Jesus' disciple Peter, transforming correction is positively received when it is preceded by teaching, training, and testing (1 Pet. 1:6–7). Too often we omit one or more of the four turns. Correcting misbehavior after first teaching, training, and testing is priceless for children, employees, and teams to instill discipline.

My close friend's eldest son received a full-ride scholarship to play basketball for Coach Tom Izzo at Michigan State University, one of the nation's most successful programs over the last two decades. Knowing that Izzo can get pretty fiery, I asked my friend Kelly Byrd how his son Russell would respond to Coach Izzo getting in his grille. Kelly's response was telling: "He will be fine, because Russell knows that Coach loves him." Did you hear that? A Division I NCAA athlete can willingly receive correction from a feisty Italian disciplinarian when he knows that it flows from a loving heart that wants what is best for him. Love is expressed in all four turns of Solomon's track of discipline: teaching, training, testing, and transforming.

Contrast Coach Izzo's pattern of discipline with that of lesser coaches. Both you and I have witnessed an incomplete attempt at discipline that focuses only on turns one and four. They merely teach then expect transformation. They talk, then correct in anger. All the while they miss training and testing, an omission that comes at the expense of their players, the team, and themselves.

My dad finished Solomon's track of discipline with me by living out the concept of, "You do. I watch." During our last eight years in business together, Dad basically watched me flourish in the role he had taught, trained, tested, and transformed me to undertake. However, I realized that true success would never occur for me until my heavenly Father had refined my heart.

I remember in the late 1990s I had completed a really good run at the auction block during a prestigious private car collection auction. This was one that I had signed, marketed, executed, and now auctioned myself. At one point toward the end of the auction my dad leaned over and said, "Mitchell, you are the best in the world."

Ever since I'd been a five-year-old boy, all I ever wanted was to hear my dad speak those words to me. Finally, from his perspective, I was the best.

Now, you're probably wondering if I implement Solomon's

track of discipline with my four daughters. Well, I try. One example unfolded with my daughter Lilly. When she was about three years old, my friends at our local Christian bookstore gave me *The Young Learner's Bible Storybook* by Mary Manz Simon. It is a unique work that teaches the young reader different skills such as prepositions, numbers, machines, and opposites that are woven into the fabric of each story.

Our pattern of reading through the Bible followed Solomon's track of discipline. Our first time through the book, I read and Lilly watched. Our second time through it, she was a little older. Consequently, I read out loud, but Lilly would finish my sentences. I read; she helped. Our third time through the book, Lilly read, and I helped her with the words that she struggled to pronounce. Lilly read; I helped. Finally, our last time through the book when she was about six years old, Lilly read while I watched.

Another gut-wrenching example of Solomon's track of discipline was revealed the day we dropped off our eldest daughter, Megan, for her first year of college. I had thought this would be a day of celebration because we had anticipated it for so long. Man, was I wrong. Everything seemed to be fine until we came to that final moment of saying good-bye. I watched Megan hug her mother for the last time as a dependent daughter living in our home. They squeezed tightly for what seemed like an hour. Susan began to cry. Megan reciprocated. I couldn't take it anymore. My emotions began to well up inside me so much that I started to cry. Realizing that this moment could linger for hours and that it could hinder Megan more than help her, we quickly got in the car. Her mom and I cried all the way home.

The finality of having your baby leave your house is devastating at first. When we returned home, I felt like I was Chevy Chase in the scene in *Christmas Vacation* where he's locked in the cold attic, crying as he watches old home movies. Megan had written notes to both of us and each of her sisters, hiding them in our bedrooms. If our college campus tears had represented a hard rain, this next set was a typhoon. Susan and I had done the same for Megan. Following are our letters to each other.

Megan,

During the past several weeks I have been blessed with many images and dreams of you as a little girl. I want you to know that God's greatest gift to me has been the opportunity to share life with you. Thank you so much for how you have approached life joyfully and wisely as a beautiful young woman who is a leader with a compassionate heart. You have taught me so much about life. You are a much better person than I am. I love you so much, and I am so proud of you. Every time I see your picture or hear one of our songs, I will smile even though I'm hurting on the inside. Now, pursue your dreams as you encourage others with the attractive, unique expression of Christ in you. I'll pray for you all the time.

Love,
Daddy

Daddy,

Thank you for "walking across the room" to me when I was four and teaching me about God and his son. Thank you also for not stopping there. I am thankful that I have a dad who cares and wants me to grow. I will miss being coached by you, not just in basketball, but in life. Well, you'll still be my coach in life, I just wanted to use that phrase. I'm really glad you were home instead of gone working while I was growing up. I am so thankful that I had two parents who are so involved in my life and love me so much. Thank you for teaching me so many wise things. I know if I ever have a question, I can ask you and you'll know the answer or have a way to find it. Thank you for loving me through the good and the bad. I hope to be able to prove my responsibility even more while at college. You'll always be my best, good-looking dad! I love you and I'll miss you.

Love,

Megan

My job was to work myself out of a job, and although on the trip home from college that day I had reflected on my many regrets, I realized that, by God's grace, Megan had caught from her mom and from me how to navigate Solomon's track of discipline.

Correct with a Heart of Love

Work yourself out of a job by implementing "You do. I watch." Review your correcting process. Do you transform only after you teach, train, and test? Ask God if you have been harsh or lenient. Examine how you can best transform your children, employees, or teams through a wise combination of positive reinforcement, negative reinforcement, or punishment, all preceded by teaching, training, and testing. All the while, transform with a heart of love in order to provide and protect those involved so that Christ the Refiner is seen in them.

As we navigate the race of life, we must fix our eyes on Christ (see Heb. 12:1–2). At the same time, we must inhale and exhale the Word of God, our divinely inspired instrument for all four turns (see 2 Tim. 3:16). When we teach, train, test, and transform disciples, we will not be the ones nestled in the drivers' seats; rather it will be Christ in us navigating the four turns of discipline.

Chapter 14

Knowledge

SURRENDER CONFLICT TO GOD

My good friend and mentor Duane DuCharme grew up in a small Midwestern town, population 1,800. Everyone knew everybody, which made the sting of conflict even greater when Duane's father left his family when Duane was just four years old. Duane's godly mother responded by working hard to make ends meet without accepting government welfare.

At school, Duane was shy and passive, often mocked by other students for being so poor, as evidenced by his ragged clothes and bent eyeglasses. He was shoved, tripped, spat upon, and even had his face rubbed in the dirt. Duane's problems were aggravated when his father returned home, supposedly to reconnect their family. Duane's overwhelming joy at the thought of having a whole family again turned to bitter grief when his father returned as the town alcoholic, spending his nights at local bars getting drunk and searching for a nocturnal companion. This gave the kids at school more fodder for their explosive, relentless bullying.

In high school, things changed for Duane. He was the starting quarterback, lettering three times in varsity football, as well as the starting pitcher in his baseball team's state championship run, culminating in two undefeated seasons: a big accomplishment in a very small community. Everyone attended the games except Duane's dad, who without a word permanently walked out of his life late in Duane's high school career. Feeling unloved and unwanted, Duane learned that he couldn't trust anyone, and his insecurity deepened.

At the beginning of Duane's senior year of high school, despite his success on the field, his classmates voted him "least likely to succeed." Consequently, he quit school immediately following his football season and joined the U.S. military. The discipline Duane learned in the Service helped, but it lacked transformation since Duane was trying to handle his life on his own, without God.

After his stint in the military, he married in his early twenties, and he and his wife had two children. Then Duane bought a motorcycle, joined a rock band, and turned to alcohol to numb his pain. When Duane's son came home from elementary school and told him he was confused about how to describe his dad's job at show and tell, Duane sought out a legitimate career with the township assessor's office. While there, he noticed how unsuspecting real estate owners were overpaying on their property taxes. He saw a business opportunity where he could teach them how to lower the assessment of their property tax values, while earning a percentage of their savings.

Five years into his business, Duane was working around the clock and building an empire. He convinced himself that hardening his heart to everything and everyone and pursuing wealth would protect him from being let down by anyone. His wife ended up divorcing him because of his hard heart, but his business thrived, with 325 employees in twenty-five offices strategically planted in major U.S. cities plus Toronto. Duane sold his company for $35 million and retired at an early age— for a few weeks, that is. His entrepreneurial spirit led him to Naples, Florida, where a real estate boom was unfolding.

Through wise investments and strategic market opportunities, Duane eventually parlayed his wealth to $125 million. He sold his beachfront home for $13 million, and, within a few weeks, transferred the title to a $56 million marina. Eventually Duane met a woman who was instrumental in helping him to accept Christ as his Savior at a Good Friday service. The two of them traveled to thirty countries together and lived well, but because Duane was a slave to the almighty dollar, he leveraged his investments through borrowing money. Then the world financial crisis hit in 2008.

Duane attempted to salvage his net worth over the next few years of free fall in the financial and Florida real estate markets. He sought cash anywhere he could raise it, including repayment of $500,000 in loans that he had extended to a business partner. The loan repayment was two years overdue, so Duane pressed for repayment. His partner told him that he could only repay it with laundered drug money. "I don't care where you get it," Duane said, "even if it's from your mother. I need it now."

As a conflicted believer, Duane read Proverbs and was

prompted by the Holy Spirit not to follow through with accepting illegally laundered monies as repayment for the loan. But
Duane justified the action because he needed to remain sol-
vent. Besides, he thought he would never get caught. Again,
in his hotel room, the Spirit called Duane not to proceed, but
his heart was too hard to respond to that call. An hour later,
Duane picked up the cash from his partner. Within ten minutes, he found himself surrounded by five squad cars out of
which came eight federal agents who placed him under arrest.

Duane's business partner had been previously busted for
drug conspiracy and turned State's evidence against Duane for
a reduced sentence. Duane had fallen for the sting operation
levied against him; he was booked, fingerprinted, and jailed.
Although incarcerated about a thousand miles from his home,
news of Duane's arrest flooded his hometown's news media.
The social embarrassment was too much for Duane's wife, and
she filed for divorce.

On the fifteenth day of living in a jail cell, the man who had
once been one of the wealthiest people in the country broke
down and lay on the cold concrete floor, sobbing and crying
out to God in utter desperation. The man who had always
protected his heart was now willing to surrender his conflict
to God and began begging for intimacy with Him. "That day,
God shattered me into a thousand pieces," Duane says. "I surrendered and gave my life over to Jesus. After I did, for the first
time I felt the love of Jesus in me."

Duane even surrendered the outcome. "On my knees, I
promised Jesus that from that day forward, He would be the
center of my life regardless of the outcome of my legal situation." Duane saw the foolishness in his past behavior and

sought to understand the motives of the government's case against him. The process opened Duane's heart to wisdom. Two days later, a criminal attorney who had been hired by Duane's best friend arrived. Although Duane had known nothing of his business partner's illegal drug-dealing activities within the companies he owned, Duane had been charged with a Class A felony for money laundering, an offense that carried an eight- to twenty-year sentence in a federal penitentiary with no chance of parole. This was basically a life sentence for someone Duane's age.

Duane began to humbly and wisely spell out his motives to his legal counsel. On the twenty-second day of Duane's incarceration, bail was posted, and he was released from prison with pending criminal charges. Duane traveled back to his hometown, where he faced desertion by some of his friends, and yet forgiveness from others. Still Duane continued to surrender his conflict to God. He looked objectively at the motives of the people who rejected him, and humbly and wisely examined his own motives, all the while hoping to solve his conflict by discovering some sort of common ground with the United States government. Several months later, God offered a miracle that Duane believes flowed from his intimacy with the Almighty. His likely life sentence was reduced by plea bargain to thirty-six months' probation beginning with six months of home detention.

About a week after his sentencing before a federal district court judge, Duane received a call from a pastor asking to meet with him. He invited Duane to join him at the church's Celebrate Recovery meeting. After attending three weeks of meetings, it became apparent that Duane needed knowledge that only God could provide, and Celebrate Recovery was the tool He would use. Duane immersed himself in the ministry.

Today, Duane is ministry leader of a Celebrate Recovery group of more than one hundred fellow addicts. He is also Indiana's state representative for Celebrate Recovery and has been used by God to draw countless alcohol and drug addicts toward intimacy with Christ. Because Duane learned to surrender his conflict to God, today he lives a life of encouraging others toward following Jesus as a way to manage their hurts, hang-ups, and habits.

In order to resolve interpersonal conflict, we must ask the Spirit of God to help us connect with the innermost part of the person involved. This involves seeking out knowledge, our next pearl of wise conflict management. One of the twelve stated purposes of Proverbs was for giving knowledge to the young (see Prov. 1:4). The Hebrew word for knowledge (*daath*) comes from the same root word used when the writer of Genesis said that Adam "knew" his wife and she conceived. While we're not talking about that kind of knowledge here, the word does imply a deep and intimate understanding of another person.

Without deep knowledge of another person's thoughts and motives, negative conflict runs amok. The prophet Hosea, who at the call of God had married unfaithful Gomer, charged the wayward Israelites with God's perspective on the cause of negative conflict among them: "My people are destroyed from lack of knowledge" (Hosea 4:6).

In nearly three millennia, little has changed. Today, marriages, families, ministries, and marketplace relationships fail from a lack of intimacy, or knowledge. Our problem is at least fourfold. First, we hold on to conflict, mulling over our selfish perspective on the two objects that are attempting to occupy the same space at the same time. Second, we foolishly seek the satisfaction of our selfish motives, neglecting to discover the thoughts and motives of others involved in the conflict. Third, we fail to effectively communicate our own motives to the people with whom we're in conflict. If we attempt to do so, we often speak with pride and foolishness, usually describing only our own selfish desires. Finally, we leave the conflict unresolved.

Proverbs tells us that seeking out this kind of knowledge of another person deepens our relationships and increases our strength to resolve conflict. Our relationships are deepened through intimacy, or the experiential connection of our innermost beings with the hearts of others through the Spirit of God. Solomon reflected: "By wisdom a house is built, and through understanding it is established; through knowledge its rooms are filled with rare and beautiful treasures" (Prov. 24:3-4). The "rooms" refer to the *inside* of a house, which gives us an image that represents any collection of relationships assembled to achieve a common goal—whether the association be in marriage, family, ministry, or the marketplace. Those relationships comprise rare and beautiful treasures in our hearts.

Knowledge strengthens our capacity to wisely manage conflict in those relationships. Solomon continued: "A man of knowledge increases strength" (Prov. 24:5b). Therefore, this kind of knowledge helps us to intimately navigate through conflict to community in our relationships. Solomon gave us four steps to wisely connect with the innermost part of the person with whom we are having conflict: *surrender our conflict to God, seek the motives of the person involved, spell out our motives humbly and wisely,* and *solve the conflict by discovering common ground.*

"The fear of the LORD is the beginning of knowledge" (Prov. 1:7). The "fear of the LORD" involves surrendering our motives, the person involved, the problem, and the outcome to God. Surrender removes whatever pressure we may feel to force the success of our selfish outcomes and frees us from labeling the other person as "the problem." Surrender is possible through prayer—the intimate connection of our hearts with God's heart. In this context, God shapes our hearts and desires so that they come to resemble His will, mind, spirit, and emotions along with His subsequent desires regarding the conflict (see Ps. 37:4).

Solomon described the benefits of an all-out pursuit of the source of knowledge, which is God's heart and His desires: "Then you will understand the fear of the LORD and find the knowledge of God. For the LORD gives wisdom, and from his mouth come knowledge and understanding" (Prov. 2:5–6). Proverbs records this divine trio of God's attributes (wisdom, understanding, and knowledge) as the power by which He created the heavens and the earth: "By wisdom the LORD laid the earth's foundations, by understanding he set the heavens in place; by his knowledge the deeps were divided, and the clouds let drop the dew" (Prov. 3:19–20). Knowledge is a key element in our creation of wise conflict management because it flows from our surrender to God.

Solomon's father David described a surrendered relationship with God as paramount to knowledge, picturing his Shepherd as the wellspring of that intimate connection. David wrote: "O LORD, you have searched me and you know me" (Ps. 139:1). He noted that we do not obtain knowledge on our own, for we are too finite: "Such knowledge is too wonderful for me, too lofty for me to attain" (Ps. 139:6). Then David offered his refining prayer that God would first search his heart, and second, help him surrender any part of his inner being that he had held back from the Almighty: "Search me, O God, and know my heart; test me and know my anxious thoughts. See if there is any offensive way in me, and lead me in the way everlasting" (Ps. 139:23–24). Both Solomon and David saw surrender to God as the key that unlocks knowledge for wise conflict management.

Solomon noted: "The eyes of the LORD keep watch over knowledge, but he frustrates the words of the unfaithful" (Prov. 22:12). When we hold on to our conflict through the white-knuckling of our selfish desires, we experience God's opposition. God's perspective focuses on knowledge. As a result, those who surrender to Him and possess that knowledge will discover His views regarding their conflict. However, the unfaithful are those who lack the intimate connection with God that knowledge brings, and they experience His opposition in their conflict.

I'm still quite capable of white-knuckling my selfish desires in conflict, especially with my wife, whom I've known for a very long time. She was my middle school friend and my high school sweetheart. In the heat of conflict, I have to make a conscious effort to surrender my motives, the person, the problem, and the outcome to God. I'm sure she does the same with me. Surrender says to God, "I can't. You can." "Left to myself, I can't satisfy my desires. I can't change the other person in this conflict. I can't fix this problem. I can't control the outcome. You can."

Surrender Your Conflict to God Through Prayer

Surrender your motives, the person involved, the problem, and the outcome. Ask God to shape your heart and desires to reflect His, giving you the knowledge for wise conflict management. Stop white-knuckling any selfish desires.

SEEK THE MOTIVES OF THE PERSON INVOLVED

Step two is to seek the motives of the person involved. Solomon wrote: "The heart of the discerning acquires knowledge; the ears of the wise seek it out" (Prov. 18:15). Most poor interpersonal conflict management focuses on the arguments—not the underlying interests or motives—of those involved. Solomon saw this as foolish, saying: "The discerning heart seeks knowledge, but the mouth of a fool feeds on folly" (Prov. 15:14).

We seek the motives of the person involved by asking and listening. Solomon taught: "Apply your heart to instruction and your ears to the words of knowledge" (Prov. 23:12). First, ask questions that search the innermost part of the person in order to open the door to the motives behind their words. For example, we might ask, "What do you desire? Why?" The answer to the question "Why?" typically reveals their motives. Second, listen to the answers to your questions, which helps you reach in and connect with the innermost part of the person, namely their motives. Seeking to understand those motives shifts you from focusing on the outward person to exploring the inward thoughts and feelings of that person.

All the while, we must beware of the fool who might be resident in us. Solomon cautioned: "The mocker seeks wisdom and finds none, but knowledge comes easily to the discerning" (Prov. 14:6). He concluded: "Stay away from a foolish man, for you will not find knowledge on his lips" (Prov. 14:7). In our frailty, we tend to interpret and apply these verses exclusively toward the behavior of others involved in our conflict. However, it is crucial that we examine our own motives to see if they are foolish or wise.

I was reading a passage in Scripture to my wise uncle David, applying it to a difficult person in my life. Uncle David smiled and said, "We read the Bible and want to apply it to the other guy in our conflict, but we need to first apply it to ourselves." I got the message: "Beware of a fool; it might be you."

Too often in conflict, we foolishly focus on the surface at the expense of the core motives underneath the argument. The potent combination of asking revealing questions and listening intently clears the pathway to the heart that beats with each person's desires, or motives. I have discovered this to be true through my experience of managing conflict both in the marketplace and ministry.

In conflict management, Uncle Derald always attempted to move from the surface to the core motives. I drive by his gravesite several times a week. His headstone reads, "Trust in the LORD with all your heart and lean not on your own understanding; in all your ways acknowledge him, and he will make your paths straight" (Prov. 3:5–6). This powerful Bible passage is going to have to be true in our lives for us to find the pathway from a person's outward nature to their core motives. Rather than leaning on our own giftedness, we must trust in God with all four chambers of our hearts and the heartbeat of our desires as we acknowledge Him with all three resources of our lives in order to travel the pathway to another's heart.

Our pathway into a person's heart starts with the surface issues they are most obviously concerned about: their time, talent, and treasure. The next step in our journey inward examines what that person's heart desires: significance, contentment, control, and security. In conflict, every person is seeking satisfaction of these four primary, God-given desires. Every choice, every thought, every prayer, and every feeling is made through this pursuit inside the four chambers of the heart: the will, intellect, spirit, and emotions. Our journey from the surface to the heart is necessary for wise conflict management, and the combination of asking and listening clears its pathway.

Ask and Listen

First, ask questions that reveal motives of the heart: "What do you desire? Why?" Second, listen to what motives the person is attempting to describe. Move from focusing on the outward nature to exploring the inward thoughts and emotions of your counterpart. Finally, beware of the fool; it might be you.

SPELL OUT MOTIVES HUMBLY AND WISELY

Step three is to spell out our motives humbly and wisely to the other person involved in our conflict. Solomon wrote: "The lips of the wise spread knowledge; not so the hearts of fools" (Prov. 15:7). By first surrendering our conflict to God and seeking our counterpart's motives, we are then able to communicate our own pure motives to the other person with a humble heart and wise words that connect with their heart.

Solomon cautioned us to choose our words humbly and wisely, using restraint: "A man of knowledge uses words with restraint, and a man of understanding is even-tempered" (Prov. 17:27). *Restraint* in Hebrew is *chasak*, meaning "to darken." We will experience knowledge if we humbly and wisely keep proud and foolish words in the dark. For example, when discussing a parenting strategy with our spouses, we might humbly and wisely say, "My desire is to protect our children from making a mistake that might have severe consequences for them and for those around them." When we are not even-tempered and fail to use our words with restraint, we might proudly and foolishly say, "Our children learned their foolish behavior from you!"

Speak Knowledge

Use restraint by keeping proud and foolish words in the dark so that you can experience knowledge. Solomon said that one who can spell out his motives humbly and wisely is rare and valuable: "Gold there is, and rubies in abundance, but lips that speak knowledge are a rare jewel" (Prov. 20:15).

DISCOVER COMMON GROUND

Step four is to solve the conflict by discovering common ground. Solomon warned: "With his mouth the godless destroys his neighbor, but through knowledge the righteous escape" (Prov. 11:9). To paraphrase, our words either build bridges or walls. Knowledge seeks and discovers common ground in both persons' motives in the interest of building bridges. Intimacy with the Holy Spirit provides us with insight into understanding others so that we are equipped to discover common ground where we can build bridges that solve conflict. Solomon restated the theme of Proverbs with this secret to conflict resolution in mind: "The fear of the LORD is the beginning of wisdom, and knowledge of the Holy One is understanding" (Prov. 9:10), and "Every prudent man acts out of knowledge, but a fool exposes his folly" (Prov. 13:16). In other words, a prudent person builds bridges; a foolish person builds walls. Building bridges that connect motives provides the opportunity to explore many options to solve conflict.

Most spouses share exactly the same motives: love, joy, peace, faithfulness, and fulfillment; but they often spend too much time focusing on the outward person at the expense of exploring the inner person. They focus on divided ground rather than common ground. As a result, they often build walls rather than bridges. Men often want to fix their wives, focusing on the surface of the conflict, thereby constructing a wall. But when men take the time to listen to their wives and feel what they're feeling, they begin to connect with the inner workings of their spouse, building a bridge. For instance, after a woman shares feelings of sorrow with her husband, rather than fix her with words, he might try to feel what she's feeling by holding her hand and repeating what her nonverbal cues were expressing, "I know you feel hurt. I hurt too."

Building bridges on common ground will begin to solve most marital conflict. The same holds true for the balance of family, ministry, and marketplace relationships. Solomon offered insight into the benefits of discovering common ground: "For wisdom will enter your heart, and knowledge will be pleasant to your soul" (Prov. 2:10). Bridging a common ground connection of the innermost workings of two or more people satisfies their heartfelt desires, or motives.

Just as a bridge isn't built overnight—and if it were, we wouldn't want to cross it—so we must not try to speed up the process of discovering common ground in our motives. Solomon wrote: "It is not good to have zeal without knowledge, nor to be hasty and miss the way" (Prov. 19:2). The New American Standard Bible says, "hasteth with his feet." Too often, we are hasty to presume what another person's motives might be, and we manufacture common ground without first connecting with the heart and genuine desires of the person involved in our conflict. At that point, it is impossible to walk across a bridge because it has not been carefully built. Consequently, we miss the way.

I once saw an amazing picture of a bridge that spanned a mile-wide river. There was just one problem; it didn't connect in the middle. You see, the construction crews started on each side of the river, focused only on their side, and evidently did not communicate effectively about where they were going to meet in the middle of the river. The result was that the two halves of the one bridge never connected because they ended up about two bridge widths apart. Unfortunately, this is how most of us approach conflict management: Left to ourselves, we focus only on our selfish positions, rather than the interests of all involved, including God. And as a result, just like that failed bridge, we can never meet in the middle.

In the collector car auction business, I had to build a bridge every two minutes so that a buyer and a seller could cross it. However, that didn't mean I was in a hurry. In fact, I began constructing those bridges long before I auctioned the car. I built those bridges through trust by communicating wisely with both consignors and bidders during the marketing phase prior to the auction. In some cases, the people on my team had walked across a communication bridge hundreds of times with the same customer. We knew his motives and were able to communicate in a manner that connected his interests with others, including God's.

Bridges are not built merely with words; rather, they are constructed a brick at a time through nonverbal cues: our facial expressions, body posture, hand gestures, and tone. My wife, Susan, recently told me that she was originally attracted to me in high school because I had such a great sense of humor. She went on to share this insight with me: "Humor defuses me. Your perfectionism infuses me with anger." Wow, that really got my attention. When conflict occurs, I have a choice. Do I smile, using nonverbal cues that communicate a soft heart, or do I hurriedly correct, fix, and perfect with a hard heart? The choice is up to me. One is wise; the other is foolish.

What about you? Do you build bridges or walls with your words and your nonverbal cues? How would your life change if you would focus on building bridges?

Use Words That Build Bridges

Explore the inner workings of the other person instead of focusing on their outward demeanor in the conflict. Don't be in a hurry to force someone into a manufactured quick fix. Proceed with caution using Solomon's four caveats: beware of white-knuckling your selfish desires regarding the conflict; beware of a fool, it might be you; demonstrate a concern for the poor; and do not be in a hurry. When we experience an intimate connection with our counterpart in conflict, we won't be doing so alone; rather, we will be connecting through Christ in us.

Chapter 15

Learning

MOTIVATE WITH HONEY

When he was just ten years old, Rob Staley's mother received a call from the Kosciusko County Police Department that his father had been killed in a tragic accident. From that moment, Rob's life began to spiral out of control. Bitter at God for taking his best friend, the man with whom he played catch and rode together on his Harley-Davidson after a hard day's work in his dad's tree-service business, Rob blamed God and lost all his motivation to learn. Therefore, school was always a struggle for this young man.

At seventeen, Rob, who had been raised Methodist, along with two other friends, was invited by an elderly Pentecostal woman to a church service. They agreed to go with the intent of making fun of those who attended. Rob, his friend, and his girlfriend ended up at the altar, faces on the ground, surrendering their lives to Christ. Rob remembers the exact date and time of their transformational experience. "It was a restoration on the spot at 11:30 a.m., February 17, 1974. At that moment, I decided to turn my feet and walk directly toward God."

Involved in athletics and socially connected at his high school, Rob arrived on his campus the following Monday with a Bible in his hand and a mission in his heart. He shared his experience and invited his classmates to attend a Bible study. A revival broke out. More than one hundred students showed up at a weekly prayer meeting in his public school auditorium. Rob says, "I learned the real solution to a jacked-up kid was not another educational program, athletics, or the band, but a change of the heart." The student who at one time had no interest in learning was now motivated to attend college because he had a vision to teach others. Rob received a scholarship to play basketball and earned his education degree.

Applying his passion for learning, Rob began teaching after he graduated college. After the first year in the classroom, he was motivated to work toward his administrator's license. He dug into the information, soaked it up, and warehoused it so that he could recall it to reach struggling students. Two years later, Rob's vision led him outside the classroom; he completed his master's in education administration. He was hired as an assistant principal at Fairfield Junior-Senior High School and Concord High School, and he quickly moved up the ranks to serve ten years as principal of Concord High. That's where God began to shape Rob's heart for struggling students, teaching them how to be motivated, to dig, soak, and recall.

To create a safe environment for learning, Rob was a strict administrator, often suspending disruptive students who had legal problems. That's when a friend who was also a deputy sheriff challenged Rob. "By creating a safe school through expelling problem students," this deputy said, "you are putting them on the streets. When kids go on the streets, they have an eight times greater chance of ending up incarcerated in a detention facility than if they stay in school."

Rob was challenged by this statement to do something about these kids in jail, and his deputy friend gave Rob a badge: He made Rob the assistant chaplain of the Elkhart County Jail. "You can go wherever you want to go, give them books, distribute Bibles, and talk with them about anything you want."

Rob learned that 75 percent of crime is committed by high school dropouts. From the time he started his prison ministry in 1995 to the present, Rob has met with hundreds of the kids he dismissed from school who found themselves in the county lockup. "God has used my mistakes and my restoration to help me connect with students who are struggling. When I let them know that my dad died when I was ten, it becomes one of the most powerful connections I can make with a student who has experienced the death of a parent. Not many principals were in trouble with the law and suspended from high school with a 1.9 GPA. I was in the lowest twenty percent of my class. So I can relate to these young people."

When Rob encountered each troubled student, he saw a reflection of himself as a young man. He knew that he had to do something more; he had to put what he was learning into practice. Rob sought the biggest addict and drug dealer in his school and asked him to come to a Bible study. This young man's mom forced him to go, and Rob and he sat in a pastor's basement for the study. On the way home, this young man told Rob, "I've never heard anything like what I heard tonight." When Rob asked him to come back the next week, he agreed.

The second week, as Rob drove him back to his house, a train stopped them at the tracks.

"At that moment, during our discussion about that night's Bible study, the Holy Spirit convicted this troubled young man. He started crying; he grabbed me and said, 'I need this Jesus!' " When they returned to his house, they prayed in his driveway, and he surrendered his life to Christ. In six months, the motivated and newly reformed drug dealer invited all his drug-dealing friends to the Bible study so they could learn about a God who loved them. The gathering outgrew the house and moved to a church. As attendance swelled, they decided to revamp a local theater to house the demand. More than one hundred fifty students attended each week. In 1994, after helping hundreds of young people, they sold the theater, and Rob began a journey to learn more about his target audience: "I went in the jail to seek to understand—If I could do something different as a high school principal, what would it be?"

The incarcerated students explained, "We are bored. Could we learn at our own ability level and move at our own pace? Could we sit on couches in a living room environment, acting like we are a family talking about life and, by the way, talk about God?"

In 2004, Rob founded the Crossing, an accredited, alternative Christian school with multiple campuses. The first school met at a warehouse with six computers and six of the students that Rob had expelled. By the end of the year they had hired two teachers who tutored twenty-five students. Enrollment doubled the next year. Today, at all twenty-nine campuses, 2,500 students sit on couches in adult-led small groups for thirty minutes each day to talk about life. Rob calls it "scattering seed." "We intertwine biblical concepts as to what absolute truth is, rather than what your opinion might be. When we're all done teaching at the end of the day, the teachers and students play basketball, soccer, or engage in some other activity, such as vocational training in our tree service, the same business that my dad taught me." This environment motivates the students to dig, soak, and recall.

Rob's twenty-year relationship with statewide school administrators connects him with opportunities to restore the most challenging students, including one young man who pointed a .45 caliber automatic pistol at fellow students, threatening to kill everyone on his school bus. His principal called to enroll him in the Crossing after he was released from jail. Another restoration story features a fourteen-year-old boy who argued with a security officer at the local mall, left the campus, and then returned with a rifle, shooting twenty-three times at the retail outlet. This of course made the local news, as a SWAT team was called to the scene; the dramatic takedown was broadcast on the local television stations. Seeing the incident, Rob prayed, "God, please bring him to my school." And God did, with amazing results. Rob says, "School is an avenue for us to bring troubled students to Christ." Each troubled student that he helps takes Rob back to his own restoration event.

The Crossing's business model includes sharing state tuition dollars that would otherwise go unused with a local school corporation. Rob often asks public school administrators, "Would you allow me to take your most radical kids with the biggest behavioral problems to my school? If you transfer a portion of the tuition back to us to fund our school, we'll take them." Rob does this work with amazing results. In the communities where the Crossing operates, crime and violence in their communities decrease as the students become positive contributors to society.

The Crossing's model works for more than 85 percent of the students the first time they enroll. "If they don't make it, they usually die or go to jail. We are their last chance before those consequences appear on their horizon. To this date, we have buried seventeen students; we've lost eleven to suicide."

That's why Rob takes the "prodigal son" approach, allowing any expelled student to return, if they desire. One student left for jail three times and still kept coming back to school. Finally, he was transformed. Another of the students, expelled several consecutive years, piled up ten felony charges. He even carried a tommy gun in the backseat of his car. The young man finally accepted Christ in the county jail, and at twenty years old, having been released on bond, he came back to the Crossing to get his life together. That student graduated, attended Bethel College, earned his associate's degree, and was hired at the Crossing as a teacher who motivated the most challenging of students to dig, soak, and recall.

Rob makes a promise to every student who graduates from the Crossing: "If you complete post-secondary schooling, we will hire you." Nearly twenty graduates have been hired at the accredited alternative Christian center for learning that is bursting at the seams. The Crossing looks to double its enrollment in the next year.

In dealing with these difficult students, Rob has tapped into the truth that we have two options for dealing with interpersonal conflict: We either protect our pride or learn in our humility. The final pearl for wise conflict management is

learning. Solomon taught learning as one of the twelve purposes of Proverbs: "Let the wise listen and add to their learning" (Prov. 1:5). Proverbs offers four insights to learning both
for and from conflict. The "Thirty Sayings of the Wise" begin
with four insights to learning: "Pay attention and listen to the
sayings of the wise; apply your heart to what I teach, for it is
pleasing when you keep them in your heart and have all of
them ready on your lips. So that your trust may be in the LORD,
I teach you today, even you" (Prov. 22:17–19).

When it comes to learning, we must pay attention, listen,
apply our hearts to learning wisdom, and keep the wisdom in
our hearts ready on our lips. The purpose of learning wisdom
is to lean on God. We can remember these insights in four
images: *motivate with honey, dig like miners, soak up like sponges,*
and *store up His commands.*

First, we must learn to pay attention (see Prov. 22:17). "Pay
attention" is translated from the original Hebrew for "bend the
ear." Rabbis motivated their young students to pay attention by
giving them a spoonful of honey before learning. The "Thirty
Sayings of the Wise" records this motivation: "Eat honey, my
son, for it is good; honey from the comb is sweet to your taste.
Know also that wisdom is sweet to your soul; if you find it,
there is a future hope for you, and your hope will not be cut
off" (Prov. 24:13–14).

In order to learn wisdom for conflict, we must motivate
with honey, with our ears bent to our earthly sources of heavenly wisdom. This motivation should occur in all four chambers of the heart: will, intellect, spirit, and emotions. When we

are humbly motivated to learn wisdom with all four chambers of our hearts, we choose it, meditate on it, pray for it, and want it. Consequently, it helps us to discover how we are motivated to pay attention.

Harvard Professor Dr. Howard Gardner has researched this topic, discovering seven intelligences that exist in each person in varying degrees. Each of these acts as an internal motivation to learn. They include:

- *Interpersonal*—the gift to connect with others; (biblical examples are Lazarus's sister Mary, Peter, David, and Barnabas)
- *Intrapersonal*—the gift to connect with our own emotions (Joseph, David, Samuel, Daniel, John)
- *Math/logical*—the ability to work with numbers and systematize thought (Noah, Paul)
- *Musical*—the mastering of instruments and vocals (David, Moses, Solomon)
- *Bodily kinesthetic*—disciplining one's body like an athlete (Samson, David and his mighty men)
- *Linguistic*—being good with words (Aaron, David, Solomon, Paul)
- *Spatial*—the ability to see how pieces fit within space (Noah, Nehemiah)

Dr. Gardner has added to his original list an eighth intelligence: *naturalistic*—the ability to interact effectively with the environment (Adam and Solomon). Careful review of this list can help us to understand how we, or the people around us in either the home or the marketplace, learn most effectively.

★   ★   ★

In the midst of conflict, we either protect our pride and fail, or learn in our humility that begins with God as our object and succeed. Solomon observed vertical humility as the source of wisdom: "The fear of the LORD teaches a man wisdom, and humility comes before honor" (Prov. 15:33). In order to humbly learn from our conflict, we must motivate like honey as we humbly pay attention to our counterparts in conflict. The more we protect our pride, the less we pay attention vertically to the interests of God and horizontally to the interests of others.

Solomon noted how the humble pay attention and learn from conflict management: "Flog a mocker, and the simple will learn prudence; rebuke a discerning man, and he will gain knowledge" (Prov. 19:25). While in our conflict, we should pay attention to our motives, examining our hearts for the kind of pride that selfishly protects only our interests. We accomplish this by asking ourselves, "What is motivating me in this conflict?" Next, we must ask ourselves if our answer is consistent with God's wisdom. Our motives during the conflict might seem innocent to us, but God examines our hearts to weigh our desires for pride or humility.

When we pay attention to others, they pay attention to us. One of the greatest examples of this truth for me was a man named Burl Keener. Burl traveled with me for at least a year, attending each one of our fifty annual auctions. Burl enjoyed buying and selling cars, though his ability to do this was enhanced by his incomparable skill at selling annuities and insurance. Burl was one of the most outstanding salespersons

I have ever met. His warmth connected with people almost immediately and his undivided attention made the people he encountered feel as though they were the only people in the world who mattered.

One of the most significant traits that I learned from Burl was how he progressively repeated nearly every line that was spoken to him. It was his signature form of active listening. For example, if I would say, "Hey Burl, I went to the store," Burl would reply, "You went to the store?" Then I would say, "Yes, I bought some chocolate." Burl would then add the previous two components to my story and repeat them back to me in the form of a question as if he were extremely interested: "Wait. Wait. Wait. You went to the store, and you bought some chocolate?" "Yes. It was the best chocolate I have ever tasted." "What? You went to the store, bought some chocolate, and it was the best you ever tasted?" Burl would inquire with bated breath.

Well, you get the picture. One day, I asked my salesman/politician father if he had observed Burl's notable character trait. It surprised me when Dad answered, "Oh yeah!"

"What, you noticed that Burl Keener repeats everything you say?" I asked, needing confirmation.

"Sure. That's what all great salesmen do," Dad replied as if to communicate that he had done so for years. "You should try it sometime."

So I did. My wife and I were driving 126 miles from my office to Indianapolis for a function. As we pulled out of our Auburn parking lot, I began to implement Burl's active-listening technique. Every line Susan spoke to me, I repeated back in the form of a question. After the first few miles, I realized that she was in a pretty good mood. As the mile markers clicked off, so did my progressive repetition of her words; this seemed to spark her attention. We had started at mile marker 126, and our destination was mile marker one. By mile marker fifty-five, she was turned toward me, smiling, completely engaged.

By this time, I was feeling a little guilty. *Do I tell her now or never tell her and just continue to reap the benefits?* I wondered. I chose the former, and I was shocked at her response: She didn't care. She loved it. It reaffirmed my belief in this technique, and I'm sure would have reaffirmed Burl's as well. When we pay attention to others, they pay attention to us. People listen to people who listen.

Pursue Development of Your Motivations

In order to learn wisdom *for* conflict, write down the two intelligences from the list above that best describe you, and pursue the development of these motivations. To learn *from* conflict, ask yourself, "What motivates me in this conflict?" Next ask, "Are my motives consistent with God's wisdom?"

DIG LIKE A MINER

Second, we must dig like miners. This means that we get into our Bibles and read a chapter each day in Proverbs. As we dig into the pages of the Scriptures, we mine for the wisdom that

God offers through Solomon's writings. In order to dig like miners, we need to determine where and how we dig.

Do we dig best in light or dark settings? Eating and drinking, or abstaining from both? Where are we most comfortable: in hot or cool settings? Where will we do our best learning: with background noise, through TV or music, or do we need quiet?

Next, how do we dig: with *what* (concrete) or *why* (abstract)? Concrete diggers search for facts, while abstract diggers seek ideas and theories. Some of us need to know *why* before we care to know *what*.

We flesh out our desire to dig like miners in our conflict by listening to the other person involved. Solomon taught that we listen best when we are wise in heart. This wisdom helps us separate wise conflict management from foolish and shapes our words to be peaceful, which enhances learning. Solomon reflected: "The wise in heart are called discerning, and pleasant words promote instruction" (Prov. 16:21).

An educator friend of mine attended a conference that focused on the learning environments of students living in this high-tech age. He shared with me that the big topic was how teens were doing their homework: while they texted, chatted online, watched television, and listened to their iPhones. The incredible discovery was that despite all the distraction, they continued to learn. That's impressive. However, do you think that these mass texting social media fanatics are learning from conflict in the same manner? The answer remains to be seen.

You might learn the same way, but the important thing is for you to learn both where and how you dig best. When you think about the environment where you might enjoy reading the Bible each day, try to understand where and how you best learn: Do you learn best in a quiet room in the morning or in a restaurant with friends? When you read, do you flourish by asking "What?" or "Why?" Would you learn more effectively if you listened to the Bible on CD in your car rather than reading in print or an online Bible?

If you are a creative type, you might learn best by journaling as you read. At the outset of each new year, my brother Stuart, pastor at our church, distributes notebooks to each of the church's attendees. He invites them to write their notes about the sermons in these books, rather than on bulletins that often get misplaced or thrown into the trash. I have found that this little trick has a big impact. I have outlined entire passages of Scripture and created teaching tools that I can easily reference by using the notebooks he's given me.

Over seventeen years my former assistant watched my spiritual metamorphosis positively affect how I managed conflict. That change stemmed from my digging for wisdom in order to learn *for* conflict so that I could learn *from* conflict. My hope is that the same will happen for you.

Mine for Wisdom

To learn *for* conflict, get out your Bible and read a chapter each day in Proverbs. Dig for the wisdom God offers through Solomon's writings. Determine where you dig best and whether you are a concrete or abstract digger. Knowing whether you dig for *what* or *why* enhances the probability that you will find the richness for which you are mining. In order to learn *from* conflict, listen to the other person involved.

SOAK UP LIKE A SPONGE

Third, we need to develop a system to retain the information we mine when reading the Bible so that wisdom soaks into the fabric of our lives. This soaking system enhances our retention by helping us hang the information we need to learn on something we already know. I put this into practice as I learned to retain the days of creation in order. First, I borrowed a list of images that related to numbers. For example, one was a tree, two a light switch, three a three-legged stool, four a car, five a glove, and six a six-shooter revolver. Next, I connected God creating light on the first day with a tree to remember it was first. The tree became an imaginary light bulb. My light switch was floating like a cloud to indicate God created the sky on day two. Stools were sprouting from the ground like vegetables from a garden to remember land and vegetation were created on day three. Cars flying through the night sky reminded me the sun, moon, and stars were created on day four. A glove shaped like a fish and another shaped like a bird helped me remember God created fish and fowl on day five. Finally, cattle shooting six-shooters became imagery for me remembering God created animals and man on the sixth day. Solomon advised: "Instruct a wise man and he will be wiser still; teach a righteous man and he will add to his learning" (Prov. 9:9). To be effective, a soaking system should be visual, imaginative, and active.

We must determine how we best retain, or soak up like a sponge, as we apply our hearts to wisdom. We soak in either sequential or random order. Sequential soakers develop a memory system with a prioritized order. An example is outlining information in a systematic (often chronological) order, creating bigger buckets into which the smaller, more detailed information will fit. An example could be taking notes in a college class or during a sermon in a church service. This is often the style used when writing a book. The author divides the bigger ideas into chapters, and then the supporting explanations, illustrations, and applications are strategically placed in their related sections. Random soakers don't prioritize order; rather, they can take in information however it best relates to them. I knew an attorney who was a random soaker. He would rapidly sift through his clients' explanations of the facts surrounding their cases, only to pull out what was pertinent to their defense. Order did not matter.

When we use visual images, imagination, and action, as well as determining how we soak best, in sequential or random order, we are equipped to recall, not merely recognize, what we have learned. For example, many of us can remember praying in school that our teachers would give us multiple-choice tests over essays so that we could merely recognize the answers.

One effective method for soaking for recall is "mind mapping," which features three functions: centering the big idea, chunking the parts into no more than four components placed in circular order with each connected to the central idea by drawing a line, and linking each component with the next as well as the big idea in the center. This is accomplished by sketching images for each component. The placement of the images on different quadrants of the page allows for *recall* rather than mere *recognition*.

Applying these principles helped me learn to prepare for

conflict. I became so impassioned by the potency of mind mapping that I even mind mapped the Bible. I traveled almost every week to one of our auctions and always stayed in a hotel. Whenever I had downtime, I watched TV in my room. Over time I began to realize how much time I was spending watching TV. Consequently, I went on a fast from television for nine months because I saw how valuable that quiet downtime was. During that period, I read through the entire *Life Recovery Bible*, centering, chunking, and linking the Scriptures' major themes in every book of the Bible in an effort to remember the information. I began in July and finished my outline during March Madness.

In order to learn from conflict, we must observe our behavior as well as that of others in order to soak up wisdom. Proverbs notes that when our hearts soak up what we observe during conflict, we can say: "I applied my heart to what I observed and learned a lesson from what I saw" (Prov. 24:32). This soaking satisfies our thirst for wisdom, which is an endless wellspring of life for conflict management: "The teaching of the wise is a fountain of life, turning a man from the snares of death" (Prov. 13:14).

During that same nine-month period, I worked on learning from conflict. I applied what I learned from the Bible to my life as an auctioneer and business owner. I experienced a softening in my heart that could only be credited to the divine. Consequently, I found myself less concerned about protecting my pride during conflict. The more I got into the Word, the more it got into me. The result was deepened relationships that led to a more profitable business—not merely for the bottom line, but also for a higher level of customer service and impact. I indeed learned that the teaching of the wise is a fountain of life that turned me from the snares of death.

Develop a System

To learn *for* conflict, develop a system to remember a key verse or concept in Proverbs. Hang the new information on something you already know. Make the system visual, imaginative, and active. Perhaps learn to create a mind map. If you are a sequential soaker, develop your system with order. Outline the order of what you are trying to remember before going deeper and adding to it. If you are a random soaker, then you can identify big ideas and proceed with adding the concepts that apply best to your situation.

STORE UP HIS COMMANDS

Fourth, we must store up the wise sayings we have learned and organize them for efficient recall. "Keep them in your heart and have all of them ready on your lips" (Prov. 22:18). Solomon wrote that wisdom would come to us if we would function as storehouses: "My son, if you accept my words and store up my commands within you . . . then you will understand the fear of the LORD" (Prov. 2:1–5). Solomon went on to clarify that recalling flowed from storing up wisdom in our hearts: "My son, do not forget my teaching, but keep my commands in your heart" (Prov. 3:1). This occurs when we *soak* with the same method that we *recall*.

Consequently, we must determine how we recall what we

learn. We recall by seeing, hearing, or doing. Soaking in the same manner that we recall enhances the learning process. For example, if we use images to soak, then we see the same images when we recall. If we use sounds to soak, then we hear those sounds when we recall. If we use action to soak, then we perform an action when we recall.

Next, we must determine whether we recall big or small concepts. If we recall big concepts, we are global thinkers. We remember the book title, maybe a few chapter titles, as well as the major concept. If we recall small concepts, we are analytical. We remember the parts better than the whole, details more than broad concepts. Recognizing what we recall equips us to develop a system to soak in the same style in which we recall. This compensates for our weaknesses in learning. For example, if we are analytical, we should outline the big ideas of a book by first scanning it so that we do not miss the main message, overlooking the forest for the trees.

In order to learn *from* interpersonal conflict, we need to store up information that is shared during our conflicts. Too often we fail to create a system to retain and recall this information. The result is a wrong word spoken at the wrong time, when God intended the opposite for the benefit of all involved. Solomon offered the following wisdom for our words: "A wise man's heart guides his mouth, and his lips promote instruction" (Prov. 16:23). When we function as storehouses for wisdom, we promote learning for ourselves as well as for others.

Understanding how I soaked and recalled helped me retain knowledge from the books I devoured. Uncle Derald taught me to pick up a book and first scan it. Some books are so well outlined that I could absorb the big idea by scanning and highlighting the major points. Then I would dive in and read the book through the lens of the big idea, highlighting more pertinent information. Finally, I would outline the major themes in my personal form of mind mapping. This equipped me to recall and apply what I had learned to my business, and often to the lives of those who had sought me out for wise counsel.

For example, I worked with one high school freshman who had a learning disability. After quizzing her for a few minutes, I realized that she absorbed little of what I said. However, when we came to a diagram where she had learned the parts of a plant, she rattled off each component almost faster than I could take it in. She was a visual learner. She was also quite athletic, thus kinesthetic. I explained to her that from that point on in her education, the responsibility would fall on her, not her teachers, to develop visual devices to soak in the information in the same way that she recalled it (through diagrammed images).

I want you to realize that all these methods are learned skills that can bring wisdom to your life. You can learn both *for* and *from* conflict. These skills helped me better connect with customers, vendors, employees, and even competitors. I learned more about each individual; better yet, I retained the information about those people, as well as car auction sale prices, telephone numbers, and even some relatively useless facts. Uncle Derald used to say, "If you can't recall it, you probably never learned it."

After learning these four key components of learning, I began to pray each day as I dropped off my girls at their school:

"Dear God, help us to be motivated, miners, sponges, and warehouses, and actively seek those who are being left out."

A few years after reciting that prayer every day on the way to school, our eldest daughter, Megan, earned her driver's license, so she began driving two of her sisters to school. I really missed that time with them. Though it lasted less than ten minutes, it was a treasured moment where we connected with God and with one another.

Megan graduated and was moving to college a few weeks into her sisters' school year, so I was reassigned to school drop-off duty. It was a bittersweet morning after Megan had said her good-byes to her sisters, but pulling into the school driveway that day, I learned something. Megan had prayed that same prayer with her sisters every day for the previous two years.

She had leaned to learn and learned to lean.

My prayer is that you would do the same.

Lean In

To learn *for* conflict, recall your memory verse or concept and apply it to your life. Whether you recall either big or small concepts by seeing, hearing, or doing, construct a system to help you soak and recall in the same way. In order to learn *from* conflict, store up the valuable information shared during times of interpersonal tension, retaining and recalling it in a fashion that allows you to communicate wisely.

We were designed to learn wisdom so that we would lean on God, rather than lean on ourselves, protecting our pride. Solomon summarized the purpose of learning wisdom: "So that your trust may be in the LORD" (Prov. 22:19). Humility toward God is the beginning and the end of wisdom. Consequently, we lean to learn, and we learn to lean.

Jesus Christ is the wisdom of God. He invites us to learn from Him because He is humble in heart. When we humbly accept His invitation, we begin new life as His disciples with His Spirit dwelling in us. Consequently, when we learn both *for* and *from* conflict, it is not merely we, but Christ in us, doing so.

Conclusion

Now that you have made the journey through *Street Smarts from Proverbs*, I encourage you to develop a system to memorize these twelve amazing pearls of wisdom: righteousness, equity, justice, wise behavior, understanding, wise communication, prudence, discretion, wise counsel, discipline, knowledge, and learning. In doing so, you will dramatically increase the likelihood that you will apply them to your life, especially as you navigate through conflict to community.

I remember mind mapping the twelve words of wisdom from Proverbs for the first time and then reciting each trait to myself every night before I fell asleep, so that they could guide me to the wisdom discovered only in Christ. Over time, these truths were assimilated into my life to the point where I experienced the restoration of my relationships in my career, with my friends, and with my family.

My prayer is for you to not only memorize and apply these twelve words of wisdom and their traits, but also to mentor someone else who will then do the same. If we all respond to this call to pursue God's wisdom, then we will be ready to be used by God to restore our world together, as we navigate through conflict to community.

Acknowledgments

Susan, thank you for modeling Solomon's twelve words to the wise to me. I love you.

Megan and Daniel, thank you for being such a wise daughter and son-in-law. You minister to so many through your careers.

Kelsey and Zach, thank you for inspiring, modeling, and teaching God's wisdom. Your life ahead together will bless others because of your joy in Christ.

Lilly, your determination filtered through the Holy Spirit is contagious. Thank you for teaching me how to live in the present and enjoy every moment.

Haley, thank you for bringing such joy to our lives through your enthusiastic heart for God. I'm blessed with a front-row seat to see how He shapes your life.

Mom, thank you for modeling Christ to me and making the church a priority in our lives.

Dad, thank you for teaching, training, testing, and transforming me in the auction business.

Stu, thank you for your teaching and leadership every Sunday. I'm proud to call you my brother. My family adores yours.

Derek, thank you for sharing your literary gifts with me and countless others. I look forward to one of your books being depicted on the big screen.

Mike Vander Klipp, thank you for copyediting our first draft and for saying that this is the best book on Proverbs you ever read. You offered just the right words at just the right time.

Les Stobbe, thank you for being an agent who believed in me and this work.

Keren Baltzer, Grace Tweedy, and the entire team at Faith-Words, thank you for your priceless contribution to bringing this book to the reader who will be blessed by Keren's final edits.

Garrett Cooper, thank you for reviewing the book through the lens of someone who lives Solomon's twelve words and for being my second Uncle Derald.

Bill Hybels, thank you for responding to God's vision for your life. I will be forever grateful for your messages and your investment in me.

Alyssa Welch, Shirley Woods, Will Robbins, Larry Lance, Ed Placencia, Linda McCrary, Jody Martinez, George Del Canto, Curtis Smith, Cam Tribolet, Duane DuCharme, and Rob Staley, thank you for portraying Solomon's twelve words to the world.

About the Authors

MITCH KRUSE is host of the television program *The Restoration Road with Mitch Kruse*, which airs on sixty networks throughout the world, where he teaches the Bible through stories of restoration. Mitch's first book, *Restoration Road*, chronicles his story paralleled with Jesus' Parable of the Prodigal Son. Mitch also appears monthly on radio.

Mitch was the youngest licensed Realtor in the nation and the first person to sell a vehicle for a documented $1 million cash while he earned his bachelor of science degree in business administration from Indiana University. For seventeen years, Mitch Kruse was owner, CEO, and auctioneer of Kruse International, the world's largest collector car sales organization. After selling his company to eBay, Mitch earned his master of arts and doctor of religious studies degrees with high distinction from Trinity Theological Seminary. Mitch and his wife, Susan, live in Auburn and have four daughters. You can visit his website at www.mitchkruse.com.

D.J. WILLIAMS has been in the entertainment industry for twenty years. His writing credits include *Restoration Road* with Mitch Kruse, *The Disillusioned*, *Waking Lazarus*, and contributing writer for *Holy Bible: Mosaic*. Based in Los Angeles, D.J. continues to develop, produce, direct, and write for television, film, and print.